DATE DUE

APR 2 1 1998			
MAY 1 1 1998			

𝔖𝔱𝔞𝔫𝔡𝔞𝔯𝔡 𝔏𝔦𝔟𝔯𝔞𝔯𝔶 𝔈𝔡𝔦𝔱𝔦𝔬𝔫

THE HISTORICAL WRITINGS

OF

JOHN FISKE

ILLUSTRATED WITH MANY PHOTOGRAVURES,

MAPS, CHARTS, FACSIMILES, ETC.

IN TWELVE VOLUMES

VOLUME VIII

CONTENTS

X

THE ENGLISH AUTOCRATS

CONTENTS

CONTENTS

CONTENTS

CONTENTS

XII

ix

CONTENTS

x

CONTENTS

CONTENTS

XV

KNICKERBOCKER SOCIETY

xvi

CONTENTS

CONTENTS

XVI

CONTENTS

XVII

THE MIGRATIONS OF SECTS

CONTENTS

LIST OF ILLUSTRATIONS

LIST OF ILLUSTRATIONS

xxiii

CONTENTS

CONTENTS

THE DUTCH AND QUAKER
COLONIES IN AMERICA

X

THE ENGLISH AUTOCRATS

WHEN baffled Peter Stuyvesant with an aching heart turned over to Colonel Richard Nicolls the fair province of New Netherland, and the old local names — not yet old in years but destined to be forever venerable in memory — gave place to the name and titles of the new master ; when the little town on the tip end of Manhattan Island became New York, and Fort Amsterdam, its quaint citadel, became Fort James, and far up in the northern wilderness Dutch Orange received Scotch baptism as Albany ; the revolution was more quiet and peaceable than A peaceful almost any other that is recorded in revolution history. Few political changes have been greater in their consequences. By transferring from Dutch into English hands the strategic centre of antagonism to New France, it brought about an approach toward unity of political development in the English colonies and made it possible for them at length to come together in a great Federal Union. Such remote results were not within the ken of James, Duke of York. Thoughts of commerce rather than of empire filled his mind, and none could deny that the trade in peltries and the possession of a superb seaport were fit objects of princely care. A bigot and despot by natural temper, he had nothing to gain and everything to lose by exhibiting such qualities as lord-proprietor of this Dutch domain. But for tact and moderation this bloodless conquest could hardly have been made ; without continued moderation and tact it might prove hard to keep. Conciliation was the watchword, and no better person could have been found to carry out such a policy than Richard Nicolls, one of the most genial and attractive figures in early American history. He was honest and sensible, frank but courteous in speech, open-hearted and liberal-minded, a man of refined tastes and an excellent scholar withal, fond of his Greek and Latin books, and speaking Dutch and French like a native. Wherever he went he won all hearts, and so it was in New Amsterdam. The citizens were undisturbed in person or property, and it was soon felt that their rights were better protected than ever before. The old Dutch local government of burgo-

Richard Nicolls

2

masters, schepens, and schout was retained for a year, and then those officers were replaced by mayor, aldermen, and sheriff. A code of laws was promulgated, known as " The Duke's Laws," and none could complain of it as wanting in liberality. The patroons were confirmed in their estates, henceforth called manors, jury trial was introduced and the criminal code amended, and it was provided that no Christian should be in any wise molested for his religious opinions. The arrival of Englishmen upon the scene brought the Church of England and its services; but everything was amicably arranged, and for a time the Dutch Reformed service was held in the morning and the English in the afternoon at one and the same meeting-house.

While in these respects the Duke's laws were so liberal, they provided nothing like constitutional government for the people of New York. There was no legal check upon Nicolls's arbitrary will; and if the four years of his governorship were long remembered as a kind of golden age in the history of the colony, it was purely because of his admirable character. As Samuel Maverick wrote to Lord Arlington, it was wonderful how this man could harmonize things in a world so full of strife; even the Indians felt the effects, and were " brought into such peaceful posture " as never before.

A good autocrat

New Haven tended to simplify matters. By
the Duke's charter New York would have
swallowed that colony. So between two un-
palatable cups New Haven chose the less
bitter. The "Christless rule" of democratic
Connecticut was not so bad as the equally
Christless rule of despotically governed New
York. New Haven preferred to submit to the
Winthrop charter. Everything now depended
upon the justice and wisdom of Nicolls; his
representations would have great weight with
the Duke of York and the king. Had he insisted upon the Connecticut River boundary
he would probably have got it. But such a
disregard for the Winthrop charter seemed to
him both dishonourable and contrary to public
policy, and he soon accepted a boundary line
which seemed fair to all parties. Connecticut
was to have Stamford, but Westchester County
was to belong to New York. The dividing line
was to start at Mamaroneck Creek and
run north-northwest until it should
intersect the southern boundary of
Massachusetts, keeping always as much as
twenty miles distant from the Hudson River.
This sounded reasonable enough, but people's
knowledge of American geography was still
very slender. New York historians have accused
the Connecticut commissioners of playing a

6

trick upon Governor Nicolls.[1] Such charges are easy to make, but difficult to prove. It does not seem likely that the Connecticut men, had they correctly conceived the geography of the case, would have proposed a line so ridiculous as to invite speedy exposure. A line starting at Mamaroneck Creek and running north-northwest would have crossed the Hudson River at Peekskill and would have intersected the prolonged boundary of Massachusetts near the northwestern corner of Ulster County, five and thirty miles west of the river! The error was soon discovered, and was rectified in 1683, when the boundary was placed very nearly in its present position, though it was long before all questions connected with it were settled. This decision furnished a basis for determining afterwards the western boundary of Massachusetts and still later that of Vermont.

On the other hand, the whole of Long Island, having been expressly mentioned and given a central place in the grant to the Duke of York, was declared to be his. Nicolls named it Yorkshire and divided it into three ridings. Nantucket and Martha's Vineyard were likewise annexed to New York, and so remained until 1692, when

Yorkshire, Dukes County, and Cornwall

[1] See, e. g., Brodhead's *History of the State of New York,* ii. 56.

7

they were handed over to Massachusetts. The name of Dukes County still commemorates the brief season when Martha's Vineyard was the property of James Stuart, Duke of York. The island of Pemaquid also, with a district of mainland between the Kennebec and St. Croix rivers, called the County of Cornwall, was included in James Stuart's proprietary domain ; but this, with all the rest of Maine, was added to Massachusetts after the accession of William and Mary.

While Nicolls was busy settling boundaries and making the change from Dutch to English rule as pleasant as possible for all parties concerned, his colleagues Cartwright and Maverick were wasting breath and losing their tempers in the effort to outwit or browbeat the magistrates and parsons at Boston, — such men as Bellingham and Norton, Leverett and Simon Willard. In the summer of 1665 Cartwright

Cartwright sails for England, but lands in Spain

sailed for England, carrying with him papers tending to convict the Massachusetts people of disloyalty. With this evidence he hoped to persuade the king to rescind their charter ; but in mid-ocean he was captured by a Dutch cruiser, who seized all his papers and set him ashore in Spain, jocosely remarking that the climate would cure the gout under which he was groaning. By the time Cartwright arrived in London the

king was too busy with the Dutch war to mo-
lest Massachusetts. Thus the English capture
of New Amsterdam, with the resulting compli-
cations, would seem to have given a fresh lease
of life for twenty years to the charter of the
stiff-necked Puritan republic.

After Cartwright's departure, Maverick stayed
some time in Boston, ready to welcome the
news of a *quo warranto* ; but none such came.
In January, 1667, Sir Robert Carr came to
Boston from Delaware, intending to embark for
England. One cold Saturday evening Carr and
Maverick, with half a dozen boon companions,
had grown somewhat noisy over a Pleasant
steaming bowl of grog at the Ship Saturday
evenings in
Tavern, when a constable stepped in Boston
and told them to break up and go home. They
were desecrating the Sabbath, which it was then
the fashion to regard as beginning at sundown
of Saturday. But the company defied the constable and drove him away with blows. On the
next Saturday evening the party again assembled at the tavern, but prudently adjourned
across the street to the house of a merchant
named Kellond, where another constable, Arthur
Mason, found them in a hilarious mood. He
told them it was well for them that they were
in a private house, for had he found them across
the way he would have haled them off to prison.
Angry words ensued, in the course of which

9

Carr said that it was he who beat the constable, and he would do it again. Mason retorted that it was lucky for the party that he was not the constable who found them at the tavern. "Sir Robert asked if he dare meddle with the king's commissioners. 'Yes,' says Mason, 'and if the king himself had been there I would have carried him away;' upon which Maverick cried out, 'Treason! Mason, thou shalt be hanged within a twelvemonth.' Sir Robert Carr spake to Sir Thomas Temple and some others of the company, to take notice of what passed, and the next day Maverick sent a note to Mr. Bellingham the governor, charging Mason with high treason for the words spoken."[1] The governor behaved with tact and bound Mason over with sureties to answer at the next court. Presently Maverick, whose wrath had had time to cool, asked permission to withdraw his charge, inasmuch as he felt satisfied that Mason's words, though "rash and inconsiderate," were not malicious and indicated no "premeditated design" against his Majesty's government. Bellingham astutely replied that "the affair was of too high a nature for him to interpose in." The sagacious grand jury found simply "that the words charged were spoken," and the verdict of the court was that Mason should be

[1] Hutchinson, *History of Massachusetts Bay*, Boston, 1764, i. 254.

"admonished in solemn manner" by the governor. Thus were the skirts of Massachusetts cleared of any insinuations of complicity with treason in which gossip-mongers might indulge. Hutchinson is right in saying that though the anecdote may seem trivial, it is full of instruction. As for the pot-valiant Sir Robert Carr, he sailed for England and died suddenly the day after landing. Maverick found the social atmosphere of Boston too austere, and was glad to remove to New York and accept from the duke the present of a house on Broadway, where he seems to have spent the remainder of his days.

The feeling of Nicolls toward Boston may be inferred from his remark, "Our time is lost upon men who are puffed up with the spirit of independency." He seems to have had no more sympathy than Stuyvesant with popular government; and like his predecessor he found more or less trouble with the towns upon Long Island, which preferred the methods in vogue upon the Connecticut River to those of Manhattan. But his unfailing tact and good sense overcame all obstacles and made him a pattern for beneficent despots.

His attention was soon called in an unexpected way to the mainland west of the North River's mouth. Except for the settlements at Hoboken and Pavonia, and more recently at

Bergen, in what is now Jersey City, little had been done in that direction. The Passaic and Raritan rivers flowed through a wilderness as yet untrodden by white men. Nicolls named this fair country Albania and felt a lively interest in its development. In 1664 he granted the region west of the Achter Koll, or Back Bay — which we now call Newark Bay — to several families from Jamaica on Long Island. From this place an Indian trail furnished easy overland access to the hamlets on the Delaware. The patentees — John Ogden, Luke Watson, and their associates — numbered in all some eighty persons. They had scarcely begun to take possession when Nicolls learned that the Duke of York had already given away the whole territory between the North and South rivers. It was so easy for a prince to show his gratitude for favours received by making wholesale gifts of unknown land in America ! The grantees were Sir George Carteret and Lord Berkeley of Stratton. The latter was brother of Sir William Berkeley, the famous governor of Virginia, and figures occasionally in the history of that commonwealth and of Carolina. Carteret belonged to a family which had for several generations been prominent in the island of Jersey. He defended his island stoutly against the Roundhead soldiers, and he was the last com-

Settlements west of the Hudson

The grant to Berkeley and Carteret

mander on British soil to lower the king's flag. Both Carteret and Berkeley seemed worthy of a reward for their conspicuous and devoted loyalty, and one can easily fancy James's comfortable sense of generosity tempered with thrift as he looked over the map of New Netherland and marked off this spacious unknown wilderness to bestow upon his friends. But when the affair came to Nicolls's ears, he made such representations to the duke as to weaken his belief in the thriftiness of the transaction and cause him to repent of his haste. He persuaded Berkeley and Carteret to give back the land between the North and South rivers, in exchange for an extensive tract to the west of the latter. But this was encroaching upon Maryland, and gave rise to an altercation between the Duke of York and Lord Baltimore. The net result was that nothing further was done, and accordingly Carteret and Berkeley took possession of their proprietary domain.[1]

In August, 1665, Philip Carteret, a cousin of Sir George, arrived with several families and established himself just behind the Achter Koll, in the very region which Nicolls had granted to Ogden and his associates. The settlement was called Elizabethtown, after Elizabeth, wife

[1] Mellick, *The Story of an Old Farm, or Life in New Jersey in the Eighteenth Century*, Somerville, N. J., 1889, p. 105; a monograph of remarkable merit.

of Sir George Carteret, a lady of somewhat Puritan proclivities, concerning whom Pepys testifies that " she cries out against the vices of the court, and how they are going to set up plays already. She do much cry out upon these things, and that which she believes will undo the whole nation." [1] Philip Carteret undertook to satisfy Nicolls's patentees by making compensation for the lands to which they laid claim, but Berkeley and Sir George refused to sanction this, on the ground that the Duke of York no longer owned the territory when his agent Nicolls made a grant of it ; so that the grant was simply void. Out of these circumstances grew various legal disputes which were not all disposed of until more than a century had elapsed.

Founding of Elizabeth-town

The province thus carved out of New Netherland was named Nova Cæsarea, after the Latin name of the island of Jersey, the home of the Carterets. People, however, preferred the vernacular form of the name, and called it New Jersey. The form of government established by the proprietors, in their instrument known as the " Concessions," was a striking contrast to Nicolls's amiable despotism in New York. The sway of the governor, Philip Carteret, was limited not only by a council but also by an assembly elected by the people.

The name New Jersey

[1] Pepys' *Diary*, October 15, 1666.

14

Most liberal terms for purchasing lands were offered to settlers, and entire religious liberty was promised. The result of this was an immediate influx of settlers from New England. A party from the Piscataqua country founded Piscataway by the river Raritan; others from Haverhill and Newbury made the beginnings of Woodbridge; but the most important accession, in some respects, came from the lately extinguished republic of New Haven. There were many persons in that colony who could not endure the thought of annexation to Connecticut. The two communities stood for widely different ideas. Among all the New England colonies the Puritan theocracy was most dominant in New Haven, whereas in Connecticut it was weaker than anywhere else except Rhode Island. In New Haven none but church members qualified for communion could vote or hold office; in Connecticut there was no such restriction. The tendencies of Connecticut, under the impress of the genius of Thomas Hooker, were democratic; those of New Haven, under the guidance of John Davenport, were toward an aristocracy of " the saints." The civil magistrates there were " pillars of the church." Annexation to Connecticut meant giving votes and offices to men of unregenerate hearts; it meant administering justice by codes of secular law

Unwillingness of New Haven leaders to be annexed to Connecticut

instead of the inspired law of Moses; it meant letting in a flood of democracy and ending forever the rule of the saints. Accordingly, when Davenport heard of the decision of the royal commissioners, he sadly exclaimed, " The cause of Christ in New Haven is miserably lost ! "

At this crisis the offer of complete civil and religious liberty in New Jersey produced a notable effect upon the New Haven towns. Those persons who were willing to be citizens of Connecticut (and these were a majority of the population, including probably most of the unenfranchised) might stay at home and be contented. The minority who could not abide the change might go to New Jersey and there live according to their theocratic notions. The removal of Exodus from these irreconcilables tended to make New Haven the change easier for Connecticut. In to New Jersey; 1665–67 several parties from Guilford, Branford, and Milford settled Robert Treat and Abraham Pierson on the Passaic River and made the beginnings of a flourishing town there, which was at first called Milford, from the home of one of its founders, Robert Treat. But the name was soon changed to Newark, after the English home of its pastor, the venerable Abraham Pierson, a true spiritual brother of Davenport. As for Robert Treat, he returned in 1672 to Milford, played a distinguished part in King Philip's War, and afterward became governor

of Connecticut. It is Pierson who must be regarded as the continuator of the New Haven colony's existence in that of its daughter, Newark. The larger part of his Branford congregation followed him thither, and their town constitution provided that none but communing church members should vote or be eligible to office. Sixty-four men signed this constitution, of whom twenty-three were from Branford, and forty-one from New Haven, Milford, and Guilford. Six out of this number made their marks, — a small proportion of illiteracy for the seventeenth century. It has been well said that, "after 1666 the New Haven of Davenport and Eaton must be looked for upon the banks, not of the Quinnipiac, but of the Passaic. The men, the methods, the laws, the officers, that made New Haven town what it was in 1640, disappeared from the Connecticut colony, but came to full life again immediately in New Jersey." [1] As for the aged Davenport, he moved to Boston and became pastor of the First Church there.

The government of New Jersey was similar in form to the earlier governments founded in Virginia, Maryland, and the New England colonies; all alike were developments from the ancient English county court. The New Jersey legislature consisted of governor, council, and

[1] Levermore, *The Republic of New Haven*, Baltimore, 1886, p. 120.

representative assembly, and it was as well understood as in New England or Virginia that

there could be no taxation save through
the assembly. But important constitutional questions came up at once for
discussion, as in the first years of Massachusetts.
The representatives of the people were annoyed
at the veto power exercised over them by the
governor and council, and accordingly they insisted on meeting in joint session, where their
own numbers were sure to prevail. This attempt
was successfully resisted by the proprietors, but
the immediate result was that Governor Carteret's first assembly, which met in 1668, broke
up in some disorder, and it was seven years
before there was another legal assembly. There
was also the quarrel over quit-rents, which broke
out in New Jersey as in so many other colonies.
Quit-rents were always extremely unpopular.
Carteret's colonists refused to pay them, and
their opposition, organized as it was in town
meetings, was too strong to be overcome. In
1671 the towns chose an illegal assembly, with
James Carteret, a weak and debauched creature,
a younger son of the lord-proprietor, for its president. For the moment constitutional government, according to the " Concessions," seemed
overthrown, and Philip Carteret returned to
England. The persistent energy of Sir George
Carteret, backed by the Duke of York, very

soon restored order, but meanwhile
ley lost his faith in the success
prise and sold out for £1000 all
interest to a Quaker, John Fenwick, his
in trust for another Quaker, Edward a party
Byllinge. This panic sale from Lord Quakers
Berkeley to Quakers was one of the pivotal
events in American history, for it soon resulted
in bringing William Penn to the New World.
But before we can enter upon this eventful
story we must return for a while to the island
of Manhattan and see what was going on there.

The peace of Breda, signed on St. Bartholo-
mew's day, 1667, formally ceded New Netherland to the English, in exchange for Surinam
in South America and the island of Poleron, one
of the Banda group near the Moluccas. On
New Year's, 1668, the peace was proclaimed in
New York, and Governor Nicolls was able to
add the welcome announcement that, for the
next seven years at least, that province was to
enjoy free trade with the Netherlands. Private
affairs demanded Nicolls's presence in Departure of
England, and the duke accepted his Governor
resignation. In New York there was Nicolls
universal sorrow at his departure; seldom has
a public man been so beloved. At the house
of the Dutch mayor, Cornelius Steenwyck, near
the Whitehall, there was a farewell banquet.

The *menu* has not come down to us, but an inventory of the things in the house has been preserved; and one feels that in those tapestried rooms, with their carved French cabinets, their velvet and Russia leather chairs, the muslin and " flowered tabby " curtains, the tall clock in the corner, and the paintings by Antwerp masters, there were the elements of refined comfort. The Netherlanders at that time lived more luxuriously in their houses than any other people, and their habits had been carried with them to the New World. From these last pleasant scenes the upright governor made his way back to England. He was soon to die a soldier's death. In the third naval war between the English and Dutch he served on the fleet and was killed at the battle of Solebay, May 28, 1672, at the early age of forty-seven.

Nicolls's successor, Francis Lovelace, a man of far less distinction for character and ability, Francis was nevertheless a worthy person, and Lovelace New York was prosperous under his rule. The year of his arrival is memorable for the abolition of the two classes of " great burghers " and " small burghers," introduced by Stuyvesant in 1657. The distinction was imitated from the custom in Amsterdam and other Dutch cities. Members of the council, burgomasters and schepens, officers of the militia, and ministers of the gospel, with their descendants

20

in the male line, were enrolled as great burghers; and other persons could be admitted to that class on payment of fifty guilders into the city treasury. These great burgh- ers were eligible to public offices, and in case of conviction for a capital offence were exempt from confiscation or attainder. The class of small burghers comprised all other persons born in the city, or who had dwelt there for a year and six weeks; all men who were married to the daughters of burghers; all salaried servants of the West India Company; and all persons who kept a shop or permanently transacted business in the city. Strangers temporarily in the city could be enrolled in this class by paying a fee of twenty-five guilders. The privileges pertaining to it scarcely extended beyond sundry facilities for trading.[1] This division into classes proved very unpopular, and it was abolished in 1668 with general satisfaction.

Great and small burghers

Several families from Boston now bought estates in New York and came there to live, willing perhaps, like Maverick, to escape from the saintly rule of the "lords brethren." The most important and memorable act of Lovelace's administration was the establishment of a regular monthly mail service through southern New England between New York and Boston. This event

The monthly mail between New York and Boston

[1] O'Callaghan, *History of New Netherland*, ii. 341.

may best be described by quoting the letter which Lovelace sent to Winthrop, at Hartford, in December, 1672 : " I here present you with two rarities, a pacquett of the latest intelligence I could meet withal, and a Post. By the first, you will see what has been acted on the stage of Europe; by the latter you will meet with a monthly fresh supply ; so that if it receive but the same ardent inclinations from you as at first it hath from myself, by our monthly advisoes all publique occurrences may be transmitted between us, together with severall other great conveniencys of publique importance, consonant to the commands laid upon us by His sacred Majestie, who strictly injoins all his American subjects to enter into a close correspondency with each other. This I look upon as the most compendious means to beget a mutual understanding ; and that it may receive all the countenance from you for its future duration, I shall acquaint you with the model I have proposed ; and if you please but to make an addition to it, or substraction, or any other alteration, I shall be ready to comply with you. This person that has undertaken the imployment I conceaved most proper, being both active, stout, and indefatigable. He is sworne as to his fidelity. I have affixt an annuall sallery on him, which, together with the advantage of his letters and other small portable packes, may afford him a handsome livelyhood. Hartford is the first stage I have designed him to change his horse, where constantly I expect he should have a fresh one lye. All the letters outward shall be delivered gratis, with a signification of *Post Payd* on the superscription; and reciprocally, we expect all to us free. Each first Monday of the month he sets out from New York and is to return within the month from Boston to us againe. The maile has divers baggs, according to the townes the letters are designed to, which are all sealed up till their arrivement, with the seale of the Secretarie's Office, whose care it is on Saturday night to seale them up. Only by-letters are in an open bag, to dispense by the wayes. Thus you see the scheme I have drawne to promote a happy correspondence. I shall only beg of you your furtherance to so universall a good work; that is to afford him directions where and to whom to make his application to upon his arrival at Boston; as likewise to afford him what letters you can to establish him in that imployment there. It would be much advantagious to our designe, if in the intervall you discoursed with some of the most able woodmen, to make out the best and most facile way for a Post, which in processe of tyme would be the King's best highway; as likewise passages and accommodation at Rivers, fords, or other necessary places." [1]

The first mail on the American continent started from New York for Boston on New Year's Day, 1673. The postman followed the Bowery Lane till it merged into the wagon-road just finished to the new village of Harlem, where even then the beer gave a foretaste of the preëminence in brewing to which Manhattan has since attained. After a cooling draught he The post-man's route was ready to go on his way past "Annie's Hook," or Pelham Manor, to Greenwich and Stamford, and so on to New Haven, Hartford, and Springfield, crossing all rivers and arms of the sea in boats, as was necessary until the last years of the eighteenth century. Now it was a stretch of newly built English wagon-road that our postman followed, but oftener a mere bridle-path, or an ancient Indian trail, and sometimes the way must needs be indicated by marking trees in the virgin forest. From Springfield eastward his path must have followed the same winding watercourses of which the Boston and Albany railroad now takes advantage, climbing near Quabaug (Brookfield) to a thousand feet above sea-level, then gently descending into the pleasant valley of the Charles. While our indefatigable carrier was

[1] *General Entries*, iv. 243; *Mass. Hist. Soc. Trumbull Papers*, MSS., xx. 110.

thus earning his "handsome livelyhood," a locked box stood in the secretary's office in New York awaiting his return, and in it from day to day the little heap of eastward bound letters grew. When the postman returned with his prepaid mail he emptied his New York bag on a broad table in the coffee-house where citizens most did congregate. That locked box and that coffee-house table had in them the prophecy of the great post-office that now stands in the City Hall Park, and indirectly of all the post-offices, urban and rural, in English-speaking America. There was admirable foresight in Governor Lovelace's scheme. That indefatigable horseman of his was an indispensable instrument in "begetting a mutual understanding;" he was one of the pioneers of our Federal Union.

Another prophetic incident of Lovelace's administration was the establishment of the first Merchants' Exchange, — a weekly meeting, on Friday mornings, at about the site where Exchange Place now crosses Broad Street. Some of the first American ships, moreover, were built at New York under this governor, and they were staunch craft.

Lovelace's rule, like that of Nicolls, was autocratic but in no wise oppressive. The change from Dutch to English rule had not yet bestowed English self-government upon the pro-

vince of New York. The despotism of Kieft and Stuyvesant was continued, only now, instead of the iron clutch, it was a stroke of velvet. This was simply due to the different personal qualities of the rulers. The most restive part of the population, under this prolonged autocracy, was to be found in the English towns on Long Island. Their people persistently grumbled at this sort of government, to which no Englishmen had from time immemorial been subjected. They wanted a representative assembly. In 1670 there was an approach toward an explosion. A tax was levied upon these Long Island towns to pay for repairs upon Fort James, in New York. The case was quite similar to that of the tax levied by the governor and council of Massachusetts in 1631 upon the men of Watertown, to pay for a palisadoed wall in Cambridge. The men of Watertown refused to pay the tax, on the ground that they had no share in electing the authorities who levied it; and this protest led at once to the introduction of representative government into the newborn commonwealth of Massachusetts. The first John Winthrop did not represent a would-be despotic authority in England, but Governor Lovelace did. Hence the protest of Long Island in 1670 was not so successful as that of Watertown in 1631. The towns drew up a remon-

The Long Island protest against arbitrary taxation

26

strance in which they declared that they would not yield to a demand for money to repair the fort; they might next be called upon to support the garrison, and there was no telling to what lengths the affair might go. They stoutly maintained that the principle of "no taxation without representation" — which England had asserted in 1265 and the Netherlands in 1477 — was their inalienable birthright. This remonstrance was pronounced seditious, and Lovelace ordered it to be publicly burned in the street before the City Hall. It is needless to add that Long Island remained disaffected and more or less turbulent.

Events in Europe were fast bringing about a fresh surprise for Manhattan. After the peace of Breda, Charles II. had entered into the famous Triple Alliance with Sweden and Holland, for the purpose of curbing the aggressive power of Louis XIV. As Bishop Burnet said, this was the best thing Charles II. ever did, and had he only adhered to this sound and manly policy it would have covered him with glory. But Louis well knew his cousin Charles's weaknesses. The blandishments of a new French mistress, and the promise of money enough to dispense with parliaments, were quite too much for the degenerate grandson of Henry of Navarre. He broke away from the Triple Alliance, scarcely two years old, and joined hands

with Louis XIV. for the destruction of Holland. There followed, in rapid sequence, the fall and shameful murder of De Witt, the stride of the third William of Orange into the historic foreground, and one more wicked and terrible war between Englishmen and their Dutch cousins.

War between England and Holland

And thus it happened that in the Christmas season of 1672, while the worthy Lovelace was setting afoot his postal scheme, a powerful Dutch fleet of fifteen ships, commanded by Cornelius Evertsen, was cruising in the West Indies to harass the English. By reinforcements this fleet was increased to three and twenty warships, carrying, besides their crews, 1600 troops. After finishing their business in the West Indies, these Dutchmen, in July, 1673, visited Chesapeake Bay, destroying merchant vessels; and thence they kept on for New York, which had from the outset been their ultimate destination. Its recapture had been planned in Holland. On the morning of August 7 the ships dropped anchor off Staten Island; the next day they came up through the Narrows; the next they were ready to proceed to extremities.

Admiral Evertsen's fleet

The case was virtually a repetition of that of 1664. Governor Lovelace was absent on business, over on Long Island, but had he been on the spot it would have made no difference.

28

The garrison of Fort James numbered scarcely eighty men. There was a brief exchange of volleys between the feeble fort and the majestic fleet, and a few lives were sacrificed, but resistance was hopeless. Before sunset of August 9 the ensign of the Dutch Republic floated over the fort, and the city on Manhattan passed once more under the sway of its founders. Once more there was a general change of nomenclature. The province resumed its old name of New Netherland, its eastern limit was pronounced to be that of the Hartford treaty of 1650,[1] and the whole of Long Island was declared to belong to it, but no claims were made upon Martha's Vineyard, Nantucket, or Pemaquid. Westward the claim took in whatever had been ruled by Stuyvesant, including New Sweden. Fort James was rechristened Fort Willem Hendrick, after the new stadholder, and the city was called New Orange. Esopus, which had exchanged its Indian name for Kingston, was now called Swanenburg. Albany received the name of Willemstadt, and its blockhouse that of Fort Nassau. As for Carteret's domain of New Jersey, it was baptized Achter Koll, or "Back Bay," from the broad sheet of water across which Elizabethtown was approached. A council of war was held by the officers of

Capture of New York by the Dutch

[1] See above, vol. i. p. 299.

the fleet, and they appointed Anthony Colve, a captain of infantry, to be governor of New

Anthony Colve, governor of New Netherland

Netherland. All the places mentioned as within his jurisdiction submitted gracefully, and some of them very cheerfully, except on Long Island. There the Dutch towns, such as Brooklyn and Flatbush, rejoiced in the change of rulers; even some of those towns where the English were a majority, such as Flushing and Jamaica, made no resistance. But the purely English towns in the East Riding — Southampton, Easthampton, Brookhaven, Southold, and Huntington — were extremely unwilling to yield; and although they succumbed for a moment to the inexorable situation,[1] yet Southampton published a protest and sent it all over New Eng-

[1] The "oath of fidellitj," which the inhabitants of these towns were required to take, is interesting as a quaint specimen of English written by a Dutch secretary: "Wee do sware in the presents of the Almightij God, that wee shall be true & faithfull to ye high & mighty Lords ye States Gennerall of ye united Belgick Provinces, & his Serene hignesse the Prince of Orange, & to their Govern^rs here for the time being, and to ye utmost of our power to prevent all what shall be attempted against the same, but uppon all occasions to behave ourselves as true & faitful subiects in conscience are bound to do, provided that wee shal not be forced in armes against our owne Nation if theij are sent bij a Lawful commission from his Majesty of England. Soo help us God." *N. Y. Colonial Documents*, ii. 602.

land, "in order to take off any aspersion cast upon us, as though we should freely submit to this foreign government." It became necessary for Governor Colve to "admonish" these froward eastern towns, but they did not cease to be thorns in the flesh. The appeal of Southampton was heard by sympathetic ears. Connecticut joined in the protest, angry letters passed between Colve and Winthrop, and presently Connecticut troops crossed the Sound. Scrimmages and reprisals on the high seas went on until Massachusetts also was aroused. Having seen some of her own ships *Danger of an attack by the New England Confederacy* captured and confiscated, Massachusetts decided that "God doth call them to do something in a hostile way for their own defence." Plymouth acquiesced in this policy, declaring that "just ground of a war" existed. Rhode Island, which was not a member of the Confederacy, took measures to defend her harbours against Dutch attacks; while the three confederated colonies were planning an expedition which might have threatened not only Long Island, but Manhattan itself, for Evertsen's great fleet had sailed for Europe, leaving one frigate and one sloop-of-war to sustain Colve's government.

It was indeed a precarious situation which depended upon the continued presence of a Dutch fleet in the midst of a European war that was

straining Holland's resources. Fort Willem
Hendrick, if good for anything, ought to be
able to make it dangerous for hostile ships to
enter either the East River or the North; but
as an instrument of war that fortress was now
but little better than on the day when Dominie
Megapolensis warned Stuyvesant of the folly of
using it. Houses had been built and gardens

How Gov-
ernor Colve
pulled down
houses

planted so close to it as to interfere
with firing. Colve felt bound to make
an effective weapon of it, and he decided that the offending houses must either be
moved away or be pulled down. It was done
as considerately as possible; and here perhaps
a few extracts from the contemporary records
will help to bring the situation vividly before us.

It was announced that all persons injured in
their property by the proposed work should be
indemnified, either in money or by a gift of real
estate in some other locality. At a meeting held
in the City Hall of New Orange, October 10,

The petitions

1673, at which were present Governor
Anthony Colve, Councillor Cornelius
Steenwyck, and three burgomasters, Johannes
van Brugh, Johannes de Peyster, and Ægidius
Luyck, a number of petitions were heard, of
which the following are samples:—

" Peter de Riemer is willing to remove his
house, but requests Muyen's lot or one at the
Water side instead.

32

"Lodewyck Pos requests the house next the City Hall; otherwise 't will be impossible for him to move.

"Jacobus van de Water requests Pattison's house in Pearl Street, or a lot as near his former residence as possible, with satisfaction.

"George Cobbett says he is unable to move unless assisted.

"Jan Dircksen Meyer says he knows not whither to turn, but finally requests a lot behind The Five Houses, in Bridge Street.

"Andrew Meyer in like manner requests a lot there.

"Gerritt Hendricks, butcher, says he has been ruined by the English and is unable to move; requests help and assistance.

"Peter Jansen Slott, by his father, requests a lot behind the City Hall.

"Simon Blanck requests accommodation for the winter, as his house cannot be moved; asks a lot behind the Five Houses.

"Peter Stoutenburgh, absent.

"Martin Jansen Meyer says he is not able to move; is offered the lot next to Kip in the valley, or recommended to look up another.

"Lysbeth Tyssen is told that her small houses will be examined, to see whether they cannot be spared.

"Peter Harmensen's little house is in like manner to be examined.

" Peter Jansen Mesier requests a place on the Water side ; otherwise cannot remove.

" Ephraim Herman requests satisfaction with others.

" Dr. Taylor's wife says that her husband is willing to risk his house, and to abide the result."

Steenwyck and the three burgomasters were then authorized to make an appraisal of the houses and lots which were to be destroyed or surrendered, and likewise of the houses and lots which they should think proper to bestow as indemnity. By permission, two carpenters were added to this committee of appraisal. After their work had been done a proclamation was issued, October 16 : —

" Whereas Fort Willem Hendrick and the city of New Orange situate on Manhatans Island is seriously encumbered and weakened by the houses, gardens, and orchards which lie so close under its walls and bulwarks that it is impossible to defend it properly when occasion

The procla-
mation

requires against its enemies, unless at least some of those houses, lots, and orchards be demolished and removed. It is therefore considered necessary by the Governor-General, by and with the previous advice of his Council, to demolish, pull down, and remove the undernamed houses, gardens, and orchards, and the owners thereof are hereby most strictly ordered and commanded instantly to commence demolishing and pulling down their houses, gardens, and orchards, and to remove them to such lots as are laid out within this city by the Governor's order to that end and shall be shown to each of them by the Burgomasters."

A list of the doomed estates follows. The penalty for non-compliance with the order was forfeiture of the indemnity. In order to meet this extraordinary public outlay, a temporary tax was imposed. "It is resolved and ordered to collect from now henceforth until said indemnity and damage shall be prompt paid to said persons and no longer, to wit : —

" From all Beavers and peltries which will be exported from this government to Patria [the Netherlands] or elsewhere after the publication hereof, two and one half per cent.

" From Duffels and Blankets imported from Patria or elsewhere into this government, two per cent.

"And from powder, lead, muskets, wines, brandies, distilled waters, and rum, five per cent."

To this general proclamation was added the following specific notice : —

" Willem van Vredenburgh :

" You are hereby required and ordered, pursuant to the Proclamation, to demolish from garret to cellar your house and lot lying and

35

being in Broadway, and to remove to the Company's garden, No. 1, for which removal you
The specific notice are allowed by arbitrators the sum of 330 florins, Wampum value, which shall be handed and paid you out of the extra duty which is ordered to be paid for that purpose."

A note in the records informs us that " a similar order is sent to the house of all the others mentioned in the Proclamation, except Dr. Taylor, Lysbet Tyssen, and Peter Harmsen, whose houses shall be still further examined, in order if possible to spare them." [1]

Colve was certainly a man of energy, for by the spring of 1674 his fortress was not only far advanced toward completion, but mounted 190 guns, collected from far and near, so that it might have made warm work for ships attempting to enter either of the rivers. To meet such expenses the treasury had recourse not only to extraordinary duties, but also to wholesale confiscations. As no articles of capitulation had been agreed upon when New York surrendered to Admiral Evertsen, and no fettering promises had been made, it was considered quite right and legitimate to confiscate all English and French property found in the city. Property belonging to persons actually living in Virginia, Maryland, or New England was exempted from

[1] *N. Y. Colonial Documents,* ii. 630–635.

this seizure. Those who suffered most were the friends and agents of the Duke of York, among them Lovelace, the ex-governor. This gentleman was of a speculating turn of mind, and had bought sundry snug bits of real estate and parcels of chattels, but without always paying for them on delivery ; so that quite naturally he became involved in a Cretan labyrinth of debt. One of his purchases has achieved fame as the initial step in one of the most pertinacious cases of litigation known to modern history. In 1671 he bought the greater part of the " Dominie's Bowery," a farm of sixty-two acres on the North River between the present Fulton and Christopher streets, and mostly west of West Broadway. Lovelace bought it of the heirs of Anneke Jans, the widow of the stout Dominie Bogardus, who has already played his part in our narrative. The hitch in the transaction, which afterward opened the sluices of litigation, was the fact that one of the heirs did not join in the sale to Lovelace. But for that worthy himself there was a more fatal hitch, when the Dutch governor confiscated this purchase with all the rest of his property in New Netherland. No sooner had Lovelace returned from Long Island to Manhattan after its capture by the Dutch, than his creditors arrested him for debt. Concerning the great catastrophe the unfortunate man thus wrote to

37

Governor Winthrop : " To be brief — it was *digitus Dei*, who exalts and depresses as he pleases, and to whom we must all submit. Would you be curious to know what my losses amount to — I can in short resolve you. It was my all which ever I had been collecting; too greate to misse in this wildernesse . . . I am now intending for England, with all the conveniency I may, unlesse prevented." [1] He was told that he might go within six weeks if he could first pay all his debts, but as this was impossible, and there seemed to be nothing to be gained by holding him in durance, he was allowed to sail in the fleet for Holland.

The burgomasters and schepens of New Orange had requested the States General to undertake the government of the province of New Netherland, so auspiciously won back. Their High Mightinesses assented to this, and appointed, for governor of the province, Joris Andringa, who had been secretary to Admiral de Ruyter. For the moment it looked as if New Netherland, set free from the narrow and selfish tyranny of the West India Company, was about to enter upon a period of enhanced prosperity under the more liberal and far-sighted policy of the States General. But it had been otherwise decreed. The prosperity was indeed to come,

[1] Brodhead, ii. 215.

but under other rulers. Diplomacy quickly undid the work of Admiral Evertsen.

This war, in which France and England were united against Holland, very closely concerned the interests of the House of Haps- The situation burg, in Spain and Austria. The pur- in Europe pose of Louis XIV. was to conquer and annex to France as much as possible of the ancient Middle Kingdom, or Lotharingia, and more especially Franche Comté and the Spanish Netherlands. It therefore became Spain's interest to defend her old adversary, the Dutch Netherlands; and the interest of the Empire was similar, since if France should succeed in swallowing Franche Comté she would next attempt to swallow Alsace. As for the Dutch, they were hard pressed by the united strength of France and England, and willing to pay something for relief. Under these circumstances Spanish diplomacy prevailed upon the States General to make peace with England upon the basis of a mutual restoration of conquests and the payment of a liberal war indemnity from the Dutch into the English treasury. Upon such terms Charles II. was willing to make peace, the more so since the recent events had brought about the rise of his nephew, the Prince of Orange, to the head of affairs and the downfall of De Witt. Moreover, since Spain and the Empire were coming into the lists against France, it became

possible for Charles to gain his personal ends
without the trouble of fighting. His abiding
New policy of Charles II. need was of money, to preserve as far
as possible his independence of Parlia-
ment, and to support his innumerable mis-
tresses. "There are two paymasters to whom
he may apply. The one is Parliament, the other
is Louis XIV. In these years he sets himself
up to auction. As the feeling against France is
constantly growing in Parliament, it becomes a
principle with Charles that by opposing Louis
he can obtain money from Parliament, and on
the other hand that on condition of restraining,
thwarting, or proroguing Parliament, he can obtain money from Louis. During this period
Louis is contending against a great coalition. It
lies with Charles to decide the issue of the European war, which is particularly dependent on
him. He has ceased to aid France ; what if he
should strike in on the other side ? If Louis
does not wish to see this happen, Louis must
pay ! " [1] In accordance with this Machiavellian
policy, Charles prorogued his Parliament in
1675, and got £100,000 from his French cousin ; in 1677 he made his demand greater and
got £180,000 for a similar service ; in 1678 he
wanted £600,000 for turning Parliament out of
doors, and upon Louis's refusal our merry monarch turned around and got £600,000 from Par-

[1] Seeley, *The Growth of British Policy*, ii. 213.

liament, in the expectation that it would be used in a war against Louis!

Such was the course upon which Charles was feeling inclined to enter at the beginning of the year 1674, and accordingly it became easy to detach him from the alliance with France. At the eleventh hour Louis came forward with a handsome offer of money, but it was too late. A treaty was signed at West-minster, February 19, between the British king and their High Mightinesses at the Hague, and among its provisions was one which finally shaped the destiny of New Netherland, and made it an English province. On the 11th of July following, the treaty was proclaimed at the City Hall of New Orange. It marked the beginnings of greater changes than anybody could foresee. The end of the unnatural estrangement between English and Dutch was approaching; children born that year in London and Amsterdam were still in the school-room when the Prince of Orange was hailed as King of England.

The treaty of Westminster, Feb. 19, 1674

The treaty of Westminster did not put New Netherland back into the hands of the Duke of York. The crown lawyers decided that his title was extinguished by the Dutch conquest, and that the treaty handed it over from the States General to Charles II. Accordingly that monarch granted it afresh to his brother. The

41

new grant was not a confirmation of the old grant of 1664; it made no allusion to it and took no heed of several important things that had been done under it. It gave to the Duke of York the whole territory between the Con-

Conflicting claims

necticut and Delaware rivers, in utter disregard alike of Nicolls's arrangements with Winthrop and of the claims of Berkeley and Carteret. Thus were the seeds of further vexation and bickering plentifully sown. As for the sturdy Carteret, he entered his protest immediately and with so much vigour that he quite won over Charles, and then James thought it best to yield. But like a true Stuart he could not do anything without creating fresh entanglements. He had once granted New Jersey to Berkeley and Carteret jointly; he now made a fresh grant of the eastern part to Carteret in severalty, while he took no notice of the western part, which Berkeley had sold to a couple of Quakers, and for which he had pocketed the purchase-money, £1000. Lord Berkeley had gone as ambassador to France; and as for such little folk as Friends Byllinge and Fenwick, the duke had apparently forgotten their existence. The boundary between East Jersey and West Jersey was declared in Carteret's patent to be a straight line running from Barnegat Creek on the seacoast to a small tributary of the Delaware River next below the

mouth of Rankokus Kill. The patent conveyed
the territory of East Jersey to Carteret, but
without any powers of sovereignty. As for
Staten Island, concerning which some question
had arisen, it was "adjudged to belong to New
York."

The next thing to be done was to send a governor to take possession of New York. Poor
Lovelace had fallen from favour. The Dutch
had once confiscated his property; Edmund An-
the Duke of York now confiscated it dros, the new
again, to satisfy debts due to himself, governor
amounting — as he said — to £7000. The unfortunate ex-governor died before his accounts
were settled. For his successor the duke's
choice fell upon an energetic young man whose
name has left behind it in America some harsh
and jarring memories: Edmund Andros, majo
in Prince Rupert's regiment of dragoons.

Massachusetts writers have been apt to
too severely with Andros, for it was in B
that his hand was felt most heavily. T
him with vulgar tyrants would be gro
just. As to his personal integrity and
eral rectitude of purpose there can be
no doubt. His administrative abilit
also was unquestionable; but
minded in some ways, there w
narrowness in his mind and he
tact and sympathy. He was

man who would find it easy to wield arbitrary power according to James Stuart's notions without making it oppressive. But he was immeasurably better in all ways than the princes whom he served; and if his career in the New World had ended with his governorship of New York, his name would have escaped the odium which has been visited upon it.

Andros belonged to a family eminent in the history of the little island of Guernsey, where his father was lord of the manor of Sausmarez and bailiff of the island. The father was also an officer of the royal household. Edmund was born in London in 1637, was brought up at court with the children of Charles I., and shared their exile. At that time he served for a while in the Dutch army, and became famil-

His early life

iar with the Dutch language, while he uld also speak French fluently. These were ul accomplishments in a governor of New . Of the dozen or more languages in there, next after Dutch and English rench, because of the large numbers enots and Walloons who had found Manhattan.

have occasion hereafter to comment culiar comradeship between Qua- an Catholics which signalized the st two Stuart kings. We may of it in some of James's ap-

44

pointments for New York. Governor Andros was a member of the Church of England. With him was joined, as lieutenant-gov- Quakers and Catholics ernor, Anthony Brockholls, who was a Roman Catholic, disqualified from holding office in England; while the collector of the port was William Dyer, formerly secretary of Rhode Island, whose Quaker wife had been cruelly hanged on Boston Common in 1660.

On an October day of 1674 the English frigates Diamond and Castle sailed into the bay of New York, bringing Major Andros and his companions, among whom was Philip Carteret returning to the governorship of New Jersey. The surrender of the city by Colve was an affair of bows and smiles and pretty speeches. Andros regaled the city officials in his Arrival of Andros in New York cabin with " yᵉ beste of vitayles and drink," and Colve, not to be outdone in hospitality, presented to his successor his own handsome carriage with three finely caparisoned horses. The liberal terms formerly granted by Colonel Nicolls were renewed; the " Duke's Laws " were proclaimed once more in force; city officers were appointed, of whom some were English, some Dutch, and some French; and the Andros government seemed to be going into peaceful operation. At Albany and Kingston there was no opposition, but on the eastern end of Long Island there was grumbling. On No-

vember 14 Andros issued a proclamation rein-
stating the magistrates of the several towns who
had been in office under Lovelace at the moment of the Dutch conquest. When this doc-
The Long ument was received on Long Island
Island towns the towns of Southold, Easthampton,
and Southampton held town meetings and instructed their magistrates to inform the governor that they were not under his jurisdiction,
but under that of Governor Winthrop of Connecticut. With the help of that colony they had
cast off the rule of the Dutch, and they did not
feel authorized to separate themselves from her
without her express consent. Andros replied
that if the three towns did not at once comply
with his proclamation they would be dealt with
as if in rebellion ; at the same time he thanked
Connecticut for her services in restoring these
towns to the Duke of York's allegiance ; and
thus Winthrop and the three towns, on the
whole, deemed acquiescence the best policy.

More serious trouble broke out at Manhattan in the following March, when Andros issued
a proclamation requiring all citizens of the province of New York to take the same oath of
allegiance which Nicolls had exacted in 1664.
The oath of The articles of capitulation between
allegiance Nicolls and Stuyvesant had contained
provisions that the Dutch might " enjoy the
liberty of their consciences in divine worship

46

and church discipline," that they might retain "their own customs concerning their in-
heritances," that all public records should be
respected, and various other safeguards against
oppression. When Nicolls demanded the oath
of allegiance, Cornelius Steenwyck and several
other burghers were unwilling to take it unless
Nicolls should expressly declare that the articles
of capitulation were "not in the least broken or
intended to be broken by any words or expressions in the said oath;" and to this Nicolls
readily assented. Now the same objection was
urged before Andros by eight leading burghers.
Four of these — Cornelius Steenwyck, Johannes van Brugh, Johannes de Peyster, and Jacob
Kip — had urged it before Nicolls; the others
were Nicholas Bayard, William Beekman, Ægidius Luyck, and Anthony de Milt. It was evi-
dent that the action of these gentlemen would
determine that of many other citizens, and
Andros saw fit to charge them with a wish to
stir up rebellion. He insisted that they should
take the oath without any qualification or proviso. Then the eight recusant burghers replied
that if they could not be allowed to take the
oath now as they had taken it for Nicolls, they
hoped they might be permitted to sell their
estates and move away from New York. The
governor answered by sending them to jail,
from which they were released only on giving

bonds to appear before the next court of assizes, to be tried for mutinous and inflammatory behaviour. The case came up in the following October, when the accusation was adroitly modified, and the defendants were charged with having violated an act of Parliament by engaging in trade without having taken the oath of allegiance. On this charge conviction was inevitable, and the penalty was forfeiture of goods. Thus driven to the wall the recusant burghers were fain to secure a remission of the penalty by taking the oath unconditionally; and such other citizens as had been waiting to follow their example presently came forward and took the oath likewise.[1]

The affair thus ended in a complete victory for Andros, but it was not to his credit for wisdom and tact that there should have been any such affair at all. His refusal to grant the very reasonable request of the burghers was indeed not a heinous act of tyranny; his inability to see anything but sedition in it was a kind of weakness not uncommon with arbitrary rulers; and his willingness to remit all penalties on carrying his point was surely not the mark of a truculent temper. The incident shows Andros in no worse light than that in which Stuyvesant often appeared,

Andros showed a want of tact

[1] *Minutes of Common Council,* i. 9–11 ; *Colonial Documents,* iii. 233–239.

48

but at the same time it plainly shows his inferiority to Nicolls. His want of tact was the more blameworthy in that Nicolls had once granted the same request that was now made, and no harm whatever had come of it. Andros showed himself in this instance incapable of profiting by his predecessor's experience.

The popular discontent, which in the city and throughout the province had so readily acquiesced in the first change from Dutch to English rule, was still far from abated. Many of the best citizens had hoped that the change would result in self-government with a regular legislative assembly. The question Demand for had been more or less talked about a representative as-under Nicolls and Lovelace; now it sembly was brought up afresh, and the demand for an assembly was so emphatic that Andros felt it necessary to consult his master about it. At first Andros was opposed to the demand, as we learn from the following letter written to him by the Duke of York, in April, 1675 : —

"Touching Generall Assemblyes wch ye people there seem desirous of in imitacõn of their neighbour Colonies, I thinke you have done well to discourage any mocõn of y^t kind, both as being not at all comprehended in yor Instructions nor indeed consistent wth ye forme The duke's of governm^t already established, nor letters necessary for ye ease or redresse of any grievance y^t may happen, since y^t may be as easily obtained by any peticõn or other addresse to you at their Generall Assizes (wch is once a yeare) where the same persons (as Justices) are usually present, who in all probability would be theire Representatives if another constitucõn were allowed." [1]

But apparently in the course of that year the views of Governor Andros underwent some change, for in January, 1676, the duke thus advises him : —

" I have formerly writt to you touching Assemblyes in those countreys and have since observed what severall of your lattest letters hint about that matter. But unless you had offered what qualificacõns are usuall and proper to such Assemblyes, I cannot but suspect they would be of dangerous consequence, nothing being more knowne then [$i. e.$ than] the aptnesse of such bodyes to assume to themselves many priviledges wch prove destructive to, or very oft disturbe, the peace of y^e governm^t wherein they are allowed. Neither doe I see any use of them wch is not as well provided for, whilest you and your Councell governe according to ye laws established (thereby preserving evary man's property inviolate) and whilest all things that need redresse may be sure of finding it, either at ye Quarter Sessions or by other legall and ordinary

[1] *Colonial Documents,* iii. 230.

wayes, or lastly by appeale to myselfe. *But how-soever if you continue of ye same opinion, I shall be ready to consider of any proposalls you shall send to y^t purpose."* [1]

The last sentence, which I have italicized, indicates that the governor had suggested the feasibleness and prudence of yielding to the popular demand for a legislature. It seems, moreover, to show the duke in one of his gracious moods. Nothing, however, came of the discussion, and the rule of Andros continued without constitutional check. There can be no question as to his faithfulness to his master, or as to his unflagging zeal for the interests of the city and province which had been committed to his care. In municipal reforms he was most energetic, and he found an able ally in the wealthy and accomplished Stephanus van Cortlandt,[2] the first mayor of New York who was born in the city. Van Cortlandt's beautiful wife, Gertrude Schuyler, was an especial favourite with Mrs. Andros, and there was warm friendship between the husbands, so that mayor supported governor with more than ordinary alacrity. Van Cortlandt laid out and graded Broadway for some distance beyond the city wall; and seven

Municipal improvements

[1] *Ibid.* iii. 235.

[2] His name is commemorated in Cortlandt Street, leading from Broadway down to the Pennsylvania Railroad's ferry.

wells were sunk, which proved useful in cases of fire, though the water was too brackish for drinking. Andros was a stickler for cleanliness, and obliged every householder on certain stated days to set out by the wayside his litter and garbage in barrels or tubs, for the city's carts to take away. Andros also built a market-house on Broad Street, and a wharf on the East River, and had decrepit houses thoroughly repaired, or if not worth repairing and liable to become dangerous, he had them pulled down. Tidy housekeeping was a hobby to which he was always ready to give personal supervision. When building was going on he would stand by and give orders to the workmen, or would even in his zeal pick up a foot-rule and measure a board to see if it would fit. It goes without saying that trade and currency would engage the attention of such a man. He pestered trades and tradesmen with rules and regulations until it was a wonder that New York had any trade left. Even the quantity of brine in which the

Currency farmer might immerse his blocks of fat pork was minutely prescribed. As for prices, they were of course fixed by ordinance. The currency of the province was in that unfathomable chaos which has always had so many admirers in the New World, — specie, beaver skins, white and black wampum, with relative values perpetually shifting, — and in

the attempt to introduce something like order
and stability Andros struggled manfully but in
vain. Another crying evil was intemperance.
It was said, perhaps with some exaggeration,
that one quarter of all the houses in the city
were places for retailing beer and
spirits, and it could not be denied   Dram-shops
that the streets were too noisy with tipplers.
The vehement mood in which Andros approached such matters is shown by his ordinance that if any man were to be seen drunk
on the street, and the magistrates should be
unable to discover where he had got his liquor,
they were empowered forthwith to clap a fine
upon every house in that street! How far
this superlative edict was enforced we do not
know.

In spite of his zeal and diligence the prosperity of New York did not come up to its governor's wishes and expectations, and although
inducements were held out to immigrants, yet
the population did not increase so rapidly as
was desired. It seemed to Andros necessary
for the general welfare that the thriving towns
and teeming fields of Connecticut should be
added to his province; or, as he him-   Andros
self would have honestly said, to as-   covets Con-
sert the duke's rightful authority over   necticut
this eastern portion of his province. At the
same time both Andros and the duke knew

53

that some discretion was needful in proceeding against a colony chartered by the king, to say nothing of the facts that Connecticut single-handed was stronger than New York, and that she was loosely confederated with Massachusetts and Plymouth, upon whose aid in certain emergencies she could count.

In the spring of 1675 Andros sent a message to Hartford, requesting the General Court to make arrangements for turning over that town and all the country west of the Connecticut River to the Duke of York. The court replied by alleging the award of the royal commissioners of 1664, which gave to Connecticut a and lays boundary twenty miles east of the claim to it Hudson River. Andros rejoined that the alleged award had never been confirmed by the king, and was now quite superseded by the new royal grant to the duke. The men of Connecticut refused to admit this claim, and their contumacy was declared by Andros and his council to be tantamount to rebellion. In June " hee sent home Capt^tn. Salisbury for England to let his Royal Highness know how impossible it was for this Government to subsist without the addition of Connecticut." [1]

[1] Governor Dongan's report of 1687 to the Lords of Trade, in O'Callaghan's *Documentary History of New York*, i. 187. Dongan goes on to say, " Much less can it subsist now without it, being at more expense than in the time of

In the answer to Salisbury's message, which did not come for nearly a year, the duke's secretary wrote to Andros: " Upon the whole you will see that His Roy[ll] H[ss] is willing things should rest as they are at present, but he is not sorry you have revived this clayme because possibly some good use may be hereafter made of it." [1]

But the ship that carried Captain Salisbury had scarcely sailed (July 2, 1675) when a courier from Hartford came spurring down the Bowery Lane (July 4) with the shocking news of the Indian massacre at Swanzey. The long-drawn chapter of horrors known as King Philip's War had begun. Andros at once wrote to Winthrop: " I am very much troubled at the Christians' misfortunes and hard disasters in those parts, being so overpowered by such heathen. Hereupon I have hastened my coming to your parts, and added a force to be ready to take such resolutions as may be fit for me upon this extraordinary occasion, with which I intend, God willing, to set out this evening, and to make the best of my way to Connecticut River, His Royal Highness' bounds there." [2]

Breaking out of King Philip's War

Sir Edmond, having lost Delaware, etc. . . . I hope his Ma[ty] will bee graciously pleased to add that Colony to this which is the Centre of all His Dominions in America."

[1] *Colonial Documents,* iii. 236.
[2] *Conn. Colonial Records,* ii. 579.

If the good people at Hartford had been at all slow to dread the coming of Andros with his Danaan gift of reinforcements, this last ominous allusion would have quickened them. They promptly recalled the force which they had despatched in aid of Plymouth, and they sent Captain Thomas Bull, with one hundred men, to hold the fort at Saybrook. The General Court was at once assembled, and unanimously adopted a protest against " Major Andros and all his aiders and abettors, as disturbers of the public peace of his Majesty's good subjects." It was resolved that they should " use their utmost power and endeavour (expecting therein the assistance of Almighty God) to defend the good people of the Colony from the said Major Andros's attempts."

On the 8th of July Andros arrived at Saybrook with three sloops-of-war, and found the fort already occupied by Captain Bull, and the royal standard floating over it, upon which it was neither prudent nor proper to fire. Andros sent a message up to Hartford, renewing his demand for territory, and asking for a " direct and effectual answer," for which he said he should wait. As for his aid against Indians, he hinted that the Connecticut people did not seem over eager for it. Captain Bull told him that if he wished to be helpful against Philip's Indians he had better lose no time

56

in sailing to Mount Hope Bay. After two days Andros came ashore and had an interview on the river's bank with Bull and his officers. Andros insisted upon having the duke's patent read aloud, but Bull's party refused to listen and walked away, saying it was no business of theirs. When the reading was finished, Andros said he should now depart unless they wished him to stay. The officers replied that they were not instructed to ask him to stay, but they had something to read aloud for his benefit, and they went on to read the protest of the General Court in which Andros was set down as a disturber of the public peace. He exclaimed that this was a poor requital for his kindness in offering aid against the savages; and so the colloquy ended. As his vessels got under weigh he was courteously saluted by the guns of the fort, and the salute was returned. Then with swelling canvas the governor's ships sailed out of the beautiful river and sped away over the majestic waters of the Sound with prows turned southward for Long Island. When the affair was reported to the Hartford magistrates, they commended Bull and his officers for what they had done, but wished that it might have been done less mildly. It would have been well, they said, if the reading of the patent had been drowned in a boom and clatter of drums.[1] Eighteen years later, as

[1] *Conn. Colonial Records*, ii. 262, 334, 339–343, 579–

Governor Nicolls held that this French invasion of the Mohawk country was a trespass on the territory of New York, since he recognized a kind of Dutch overlordship over the Long House, and held that their rights of suzerainty had now passed over to the English. For a moment Nicolls dreamed of a general attack upon Canada, in which the New England colonies should take part, but such a scheme found little favour. A war against New France meant a war against Algonquins and in aid of Iroquois, and was likely to infuriate the Algonquins of New England, whose love for their brethren of Canada may not have been strong, but whose hate for the Iroquois surpassed the hatreds of hell. Nicolls encouraged the Mohawks to resist the French, but neither under his administration nor that of Lovelace were adequate measures taken for securing a permanent Anglo-Iroquois alliance.

Meanwhile the sagacious and indefatigable rulers of New France were as ready to try persuasion as violence, and they found consummate instruments in the Jesuits. These devoted missionaries addressed themselves to the task of converting the Iroquois to Christianity and turning their hearts to an alliance with Onontio. With the Mo-

French intrigues with the Long House

Quill, and is a translation of the name Penn. See Parkman's *Jesuits*, ii. 102.

hawks, who had suffered the chief damage from
the French, the case was hopeless ; but the
other tribes — Oneidas, Onondagas, Cayugas,
and Senecas — were more ready to listen. Some
headway was made, and a few tawny warriors
were baptized, while Courcelle began building
a fortress at Cataraqui, where the river St. Lawrence flows out of Lake Ontario. This stronghold, which was finished in 1673 by Frontenac,
and bore his name for more than eighty years,
stood on the site of the present city of Kingston.
Its immediate purpose was to serve as a base
for expeditions across Lake Ontario against the
central and western tribes of the Long House,
and to cut off the lucrative fur-trade in which
these barbarians were the purveyors for the
Dutch and English in New York.

The moment when Andros was governor of
New York was therefore a critical moment. If
the Jesuit missionaries had won over the Long
House, it is not improbable that New York
would have become, and might perhaps have
remained, a French province. Possibly the formation of the American Union might **A critical**
have been prevented. Certainly the **moment**
history of the eighteenth and nineteenth centuries would have been modified in many important particulars.

There was imminent danger that the short-
sighted policy of the Duke of York would play

transferred to it the Iroquois name Schenectady, which was originally applied to the country Corlear's about the site of Albany.[1] At this village, Dutch village of Schenectady, the re- Schenectady motest western outpost of civilization, the governor and his retinue made a brief halt. At that fording-place the trail divided, one branch crossing the river, the other following its windings closely upon the southern bank. This southern trail would bring Andros through the three principal Mohawk castles; the first one being on the west bank of Schoharie Creek at its junction with the river, the second at Canajoharie; and the third on the site of the present town absurdly named " Danube," in Herkimer County. Soon after leaving this stronghold the trail passed from the territory of the Mohawks Andros ar- into that of the Oneidas, and there was rives in the no other stopping-place until the party Oneida country arrived at a hill around the base of which the trail made a very noticeable curve. Here at the Oneida stronghold known as Nun-

---

[1] The meaning of Schenectady is variously rendered. Morgan, whose familiarity was greatest with the Seneca dialect, makes it mean " Beyond-the-openings " (*i. e.* in the hills) ; see his *League of the Iroquois*, Rochester, 1851, p. 415. David Cusick the Tuscarora (in his *History of the Six Nations*, Lockport, 1848) makes it mean " Beyond-the-pine-plains," and Beauchamp (*Indian Names in New York*, Fayetteville, 1893) got the same interpretation from some Onondagas.

64

dadasis, or " around the hill," hard by the site of the city of Utica, this inland journey ended.

To this rendezvous in the depths of the primeval forest came chiefs from all the Five Nations, even from the furthest Seneca villages on the southern shore of Lake Erie. There was a grand powwow which lasted for several days. It was the season for green succotash and for mallards and teal, with the red man's inevitable gala dish of boiled dog. Solemn speeches were made, wampum belts were exchanged, and many a ring of blue smoke curled from the pipe of peace, as it was made clear to all that the wicked Onontio sought to bring ruin upon the Long House, while the English were its steadfast friends, even as the Dutch had been before them. The Indians' vivid sense of the continuity between these two was shown when they bestowed upon Andros the name of their old friend Corlear. As in their minds the Dutch power whose friendship they valued was personified in Corlear, the particular Dutchman with whom they chiefly had dealings on matters of public interest, so now the English power was personified in Andros. Since he stood for exactly the same things as their former ally, he too was Corlear, and by that name the governors of New York were henceforth known in the Long House for more than a hundred years.

Great conference with the Indians

An immediate result of this auspicious conference with the Five Nations was the organization of a Board of Commissioners of Indian Affairs, with its headquarters at Albany. From that time forth the proximity of Albany to the Long House made it one of the most important towns in English America, as was shown in 1754, when it was selected as the place of meeting for the famous Congress at which Benjamin Franklin's plan for a Federal Union was propounded. For secretary of his Board of Commissioners Andros appointed a young Scotchman, the scion of a family long famous in Scotland and destined to further fame in America. Robert Livingston was the son of an eminent Presbyterian minister of Roxburghshire, who migrated to Rotterdam soon after Charles II. came to the throne. At about the age of twenty Robert came to America and settled in Albany, where he was almost immediately made town clerk. His appointment within another year to such a responsible post on the Indian Commission was an early testimony to the ability and force of character that were afterward shown in many ways. In 1679 he married Alida, sister of Peter Schuyler and widow of Dominie Nicholas van Rensselaer, — an alliance of three names potent in the history of the New World. Peter Schuyler, who was after-

The board of Indian Commissioners

Robert Livingston

Robert Livingston

with this large force he may have hoped to destroy Albany.[1] The alarm was sent to New York, and the governor at once wrote to Hart-

than Edwards. See Davidson, *Muh-he-ka-ne-ok : a History of the Stockbridge Nation,* Milwaukee, 1893.

[1] Increase Mather credits him with a more Machiavellian purpose : "We hear that Philip, being this winter entertained in the Mohawk country, made it his design to breed a quarrel between the English and them ; to effect which, divers of our returned captives do report that he resolved to kill some scattering Mohawks, and then to say that the English had done it. But one of those whom he thought to have killed was only wounded, and got away to his countrymen, giving them to understand that not the English, but Philip, had killed the men ; so that, instead of bringing the Mohawks upon the English, he brought them upon himself. Thus the heathen are sent down into the pit that they made ; in the net which they had laid is their own foot taken ; the Lord is known by the judgment which he executeth ; the wicked is snared in the work of his own hands." Mather's *Brief History of the War with the Indians,* Boston, 1676, p. 38. I agree with Dr. Palfrey in suspecting this to be a "wild story," and I doubt if anything could have induced the Wampanoag chief to risk his scalp in the Mohawk country ; nevertheless the diplomacy ascribed to him is characteristically Indian, and the tale may be based upon facts. No such explanation, however, is needed for the Mohawk attack upon Philip, since the Mohawks were in close alliance with the English. My statement (*Beginnings of New England,* p. 290), "what Philip had been doing, or where he had been since the Brookfield fight in August, was never known," needs some modification. When I wrote it, I knew Mather's story, to which I attached no importance, but I had not seen the paper in the New York archives.

ford and to Boston for permission to bring a
force of English and Iroquois into New England to attack their Algonquin foes. The request was refused, which indicates that it was
suspected of being a ruse to cover a real design
upon the west bank of the Connecticut River.
Then Andros went up to Albany with six
sloops and there met a large force of exulting
Mohawks, loaded with the scalps of Philip's
warriors whom they had defeated and chased
through Berkshire.[1] It was immediately after
this defeat that Philip, moving eastward, attacked Lancaster with a strong party of Nipmucks.

After the summer of 1676 the war came to
an end in southern New England, with the
almost complete extermination of Narragansetts,
Wampanoags, and Nipmucks, but it was kept
up two years longer by the Tarratines on the
Maine coast. Massachusetts and Connecticut
wished to deal directly with the Mohawks, to
obtain military aid from them, but Andros
would not allow this. He was willing, however,
to have envoys from Boston and Hartford
meet envoys from the Long House in his presence at Albany and negotiate to their hearts'
content. Sundry questions connected with the
Indian troubles at the South, which had ensued
after the overthrow of the Susquehannocks by

[1] *N. Y. Colonial Documents*, iii. 255.

the Senecas, brought envoys likewise from Virginia and Maryland to Albany. In 1677 Andros dealt a blow at the Tarratines War with the in the interest of the Duke of York. Tarratines He sent a force which took possession of Pemaquid and built a fort there; but here he contrived to irritate Massachusetts by forbidding the curing of fish except upon the islands and one small spot near the fort.

In the autumn of 1677 Andros went to England on private business, leaving Brockholls in charge of his province. He Andros visits was knighted in approval of his offi-England, is cial conduct, and returned to New knighted, and York in the autumn of 1678. With New York him came Rev. Charles Wolley, a young Cambridge graduate, who, after his return to England three years later, published a book which was widely read, entitled "A Two Years' Journal in New York." It was in the next year, moreover, that New York was visited and carefully described by two very keen and intelligent Dutch observers, the so-called Labadist emissaries, Jasper Dankers and Peter Sluyter. Let us seize this occasion for taking a survey of the city as it appeared in the days of the Duke of York's autocratic governors. For this purpose, we shall do best to take our start in a new chapter.

XI

NEW YORK IN THE YEAR 1680

LATE in the autumn of 1680 the good people of Manhattan were overcome with terror at a sight in the heavens such as has seldom greeted human eyes. An enormous comet, perhaps the most magnificent one on record, suddenly made its appearance. At first it was tailless and dim, like a nebulous cloud, but at the end of a week the tail began to show itself and in a second week had attained a length of 30 degrees; in the third week it extended to 70 degrees, while the whole mass was growing brighter. After five weeks it seemed to be absorbed into the intense glare of the sun, but in four days more it reappeared like a blazing sun itself in the throes of some giant convulsion, and threw out a tail in the opposite direction as far as the whole distance between the sun and the earth. Sir Isaac Newton, who was then at work upon the mighty problems soon to be published to the world in his " Principia," welcomed this strange visitor as affording him a beautiful instance for testing the truth of his new theory

The great comet

72

of gravitation.[1] But most people throughout the civilized world, the learned as well as the multitude, feared that the end of all things was at hand. Every church in Europe, from the grandest cathedral to the humblest chapel, re-sounded with supplications, and in the province of New York a day of fasting and humiliation was appointed, in order that the wrath of God might be assuaged. Let us take a brief survey of the little city on Manhattan Island, upon which Newton's comet looked down, while Dominie Nieuwenhuysen and Dominie Frazius were busy with prayers to avert the direful omen.

To a visitor sailing up the harbour the most conspicuous objects would have been Fort James, standing on the present Bat- Fort James tery and mounting forty-seven guns, and a little to the west of it the principal town windmill.[2] On the other side, near the present South Ferry, scarcely less conspicuous, was the stone Government House, built by Stuyvesant, the name of which was afterward changed by Governor Dongan to Whitehall. Hard by was the governor's dwelling-house. Going up White-

[1] Newton's *Principia*, book iii. prop. 41.

[2] This description partly follows the map of " The Towne of Mannados, or New Amsterdam, in 1661," of which the original is in the British Museum.

hall Street, one would espy the warehouse and bakery that had once belonged to the West India Company, and the brewery, convenient for governor and dominie. Near it stood the Dutch parsonage with its quaint flower-beds gorgeous in colours and bordered with closely trimmed box. Coming to the Bowling Green, the belfry of Kieft's church of St. Nicholas would be seen peering over the walls of the fort at the grave-yard on the west side of Broadway. Just north of the wall stood the town pump. Stepping back to Whitehall and turning eastward, we come upon the jail and the stocks. Pearl Street, the oldest in the city, was then the river bank, and was often called Waterside or the Strand, but the old name has prevailed, which is said to have been given it from the abundant heaps of oyster-shells, highly prized for the excellence of their lime. The quaint Dutch houses, with their gables and weathercocks and small-paned dormer windows, were built of bricks baked in Holland, cemented with mortar made from this lime. They retained the high stoop (*stoep*, *i. e.* steps), which in the Fatherland raised the best rooms above the risk of inundation, and thus bequeathed to modern New York one of its most distinctive architectural features.

From Pearl Street in a gentle curve ran north-ward to the city wall a street most suggestive of Holland, with a stream flowing through its cen-

tre diked on both sides like a Dutch canal.
This was rightly called Broad Street, for it was
seventy-two feet in width. Its canal Broad Street
was spanned by several wooden foot-
bridges and one " for cattell and waggons." At
about the time which our narrative has reached,
Governor Andros had the canal effaced and the
road built solidly over it, and from that day to
this the stream has continued to flow under
Broad Street, doing duty as a sewer.[1] Two spacious docks were then built at the foot of the
street, between the jail and Whitehall, which
greatly increased the facilities for shipping.
Walking up Pearl Street as far as the present
No. 73, opposite Coenties Slip, one would come
upon the old Stadt Huys, which served as a
city hall until 1699, when a new one was built
on Wall Street, facing the head of Broad. In
that new City Hall the eccentric Charles Lee
spent the year 1777 as a prisoner, and on its
balcony in 1789, the object of his jealous hatred,
George Washington, was inaugurated President
of the United States.

Where Pearl Street crossed Wall, there was
the Water Gate through the tall palisadoed
structure. A little below, the burgher's The Water Gate
battery of ten guns frowned upon
the river ; just at the gate was a demi-lune called

[1] Hill and Waring, *Old Wells and Water-Courses of the
Island of Manhattan*, p. 310.

75

the Fly (V'lei) blockhouse ; and a short distance
above stood the slaughter-houses, which Andros
had banished from the city. Proceeding northward, we enter a bright green marshy valley
drained by a brook, where groups of laughing
women might be seen washing clothes, as one
often sees them to-day in France. The brook
and the verdure have long since departed, but
Maiden Lane the brookside path still keeps the
name of Maiden Lane. On the East
River, at the foot of this path, is a busy blacksmith's forge, from which the valley is known
as Smit's Vallei, shortened in common parlance
to V'lei. A few steps above the smithery bring
us to the site of Peck Slip, where a boat is
moored to a tree growing on the bank. A horn
hangs upon this tree, and if we take it down and
blow, a farmer will emerge from his house near
by and ferry us over to Brooklyn for three
stivers in wampum, or about six cents in our
modern reckoning. But we will leave the horn
unsounded, for after a brief visit to Isaac Aller-
ton's big tobacco warehouse, between the present Cliff Street and Fulton Ferry, we must
Shoemakers' walk through Shoemakers' Land.
Land Until 1676 the tanneries were on
Broad Street, but Andros then declared them
a nuisance and ordered them out of the city ;
whereupon their owners bought the land now
inclosed between Broadway, Ann, Gold, and

John streets, and did there tan hides and make boots. After twenty years this odorous business was removed somewhat further north, to Beekman's Swamp, which has remained for two centuries the principal home of the city's leather trade.

From the western border of Shoemakers' Land a southward walk on Broadway outside the wall, a country road among woods and fields, brings us down to the Land Gate. Of peril from savage foes or from wild beasts in this open country, not much was to be apprehended in 1678, although the young parson Wolley tells with much unction of the part which he took in a bear hunt near Maiden Lane. But the military defences were kept up and increased until the end of the century, The Land Gate chiefly in view of possible danger from France. At the Land Gate (Broadway and Wall Street) a large stone salient was added, mounting several guns, and known by the name "Hollandia;" while a similar structure, called "Zealandia," stood where Wall was crossed by King (now William) Street. The site of Greenwich Street was then a long steep bluff with its base washed by the North River, and presently the wall was continued and carried southward, crowning the bluff and reinforced by three stout bastions, until it reached Fort James. There were no buildings of note west of Broadway except the

77

Lutheran church and parsonage, near the Land
Gate.

Manhattan north of the city wall was an undu-
lating woodland, with many rocky hills and considerable areas of salt marshes partially drained
by sluggish streams. In several favoured localities were flourishing boweries (Dutch *bouweries*,
i. e. farms) with smiling orchards and gardens.
The main thoroughfare started at the Land
Gate as the northward extension of Broadway ;
at the site of Ann Street it was deflected eastward and followed the direction of Park Row
and Chatham Street into the Bowery Lane, so
called from Stuyvesant's country seat, which
it passed. Walking northward from the point
of deflection, one would have on the right hand
Beekman's Swamp and on the left hand the
grazing-ground long known as the Flats, then
The   as the Common or the Fields, now as
Common   the City Hall Park. In time it came
to supersede the Bowling Green as a place for
great open-air assemblies ; there it was, in 1774,
that the youthful Alexander Hamilton, a student at King's College, began his public career,
just a century after the first coming of Andros
to govern New York. During those hundred
years the changes of landscape in that neighbourhood were not great. The most notable feature
was the large pond which covered the area now
bounded by Baxter, White, Elm, Duane, and

78

Park streets. Around the shores of this bright and sparkling sheet of water stood a village of Manhattan Indians before the white The Collect, intruders came to their island. For or Fresh Indians, Dutch, and English it was Water a bountiful reservoir of dainty fish, and in the winter it was the gay scene of skating parties. It was sometimes called the Fresh Water, sometimes the Collect, of which more anon. To the south of it was a much smaller pond known as the Little Collect, and on the narrow isthmus between, about at the present junction of Duane and Centre streets, the City Magazine or Powder House was built in 1728. There it has been supposed that the French fort of Norumbega may have stood in 1542, when it was visited by Jean Allefonsce.[1]

This deep and limpid lake, the Collect, was at the divide between the two watersheds into the East and North rivers. Its surface was at the level of a ridge of high land, from which, in the southeast and northwest directions, there ran two deep depressions, separating the lower end of Manhattan from the broader region above. These depressions were salt marshes. The easterly one, called Wolfert's Wolfert's Marsh, extended to the East River, Marsh and through it flowed the Old Kill on about the line of Roosevelt Street. The wayfarer on

[1] See above, vol. i. p. 89.

his way up from the city, just before reaching the brink of Wolfert's Marsh, might quench his thirst at a copious spring, called the Tea Water Pump, which remained famous until the middle of the nineteenth century. After passing this natural fountain, he would come to the descent into the marshy ravine, a descent so steep that the high-road was constrained to make a sharp curve from the line of Park Row eastward through a bit of William and Pearl, and back again. After the descent, he would cross the The Kissing Bridge Old Kill upon the Kissing Bridge, where, if he happened to be walking or driving with a lady companion it was his privilege to kiss her. On the further side of the stream another sharp curve (the cause of the opening at Chatham Square) was made necessary by the abrupt ascent.[1] At the top of the hill stood Wolfert Webber's tavern, and a little beyond it a tall windmill built in 1662. In this neighbourhood were a few farms kept by free negroes. Some distance further out one would pass the ancient milestone, which still stands on the Bowery opposite Rivington Street, " on which, if it does not happen to be covered over with bills, one may still read the legend,

---

[1] In this account I have been much assisted by Hill and Waring, *Old Wells and Water-courses*, an admirable monograph.

2 miles to City Hall."[1] Still further north, near the Ninth Street station of the Third Avenue elevated railroad, came the cluster of settlements known as the Bowery Village, founded by Stuyvesant on his own territory. The Bowery Village There were the clanking smithery, the church where the town schoolmaster, Dominie Selyns, preached on Sundays, and the inn where good entertainment was furnished for man and beast.

About a mile above the Bowery Village, the road began to make its way over wild and rugged hills, with few traces of human occupation save at the well-kept farm of Jacobus Kip, at that deep bight of the East River between Thirty-third and Thirty-seventh streets which is still known as Kip's Bay. Kip's Kip's Bay massive and stately house, which he built in 1655, being then secretary of New Netherland, was demolished in 1851, because it occupied the space where Thirty-fifth Street now crosses Second Avenue. After leaving this farm behind and proceeding for another half mile, one would come upon another indentation of the river, which the Dutch called Deutel (*i. e.* Wedge) Bay, a name which in English mouths soon became Turtle Bay. Into it, near Turtle Bay the foot of Forty-seventh Street, emptied a brook which, from its sources near Ninth Ave-

[1] Hewitt's *The Bowery*, p. 372.

nue and Seventy - second Street, meandered across the island, leaving a modern vestige of itself in the lake near the Plaza in Central Park. Some of this brook's water was utilized in turning the wheels of Mynheer de Voor's grist-mill, whereby it was commonly known as Voor's Mill-stream. The bridge on which our high road was carried over it afforded our wayfarer a second opportunity for kissing the damsel beside him without fear of rebuke. Just above this bridge there stood for more than a century Old Cato's Inn, famous for suppers of fish and game. Nothing else do we encounter that calls for mention here until we arrive at the Flats, where the village of Harlem had reached a flourishing condition by 1660.

Harlem

We may now return to the place where Broadway was deflected into Park Row, and thence take a fresh northward start on the other side of the Common, along the present line of Broadway. In the days of Andros this was merely a walk across the fields, but afterwards the prolongation of Broadway began as a ropewalk. By 1776 that thoroughfare, with the streets west of it, had been laid out and partially occupied with houses as far up as Reade Street. There the land descended into the great hollow through which flowed the Collect's western outlet down to the Hudson River. Its breadth was rather more than half a mile, from

the line of Duane to that of Spring Street, which
received its name from one of the rivulets which
swelled the volume of the Groote The Great
(*i. e.* Great) Kill, as the main outlet Kill, and
was called. Up this Groote Kill the Meadows
red men used to paddle their canoes laden with
oysters, and from the heaps of shells on the
shores of the pond came the Dutch name Kolch
Hoek (*i. e.* Shell Point), which the English cor-
rupted into Collect. The wide region which the
stream imperfectly drained was afterward long
known as Lispenard's Meadows. Part of it was
excellent grazing-land, but it was largely swamp,
with treacherous quagmires here and there in
which cattle were engulfed. Its perils were
illustrated by gruesome incidents, as when a
puzzled pedestrian after nightfall, losing his way
where Greene Street now crosses Grand, stepped
into a deep pool and was drowned. Through
its insidious and spongy wastes, musical with
bull-frogs, many a zealous angler made his way,
while the fowler with his shot-gun was sure to
find woodcock and snipe abounding. After
1730 the region was regarded as a lurking-place
of miasma, and from time to time portions were
filled in by dumping stones and earth. At
length the whole space was filled up, while the
Groote Kill was straightened and deepened and
confined between plank walls, so as to become
a canal in a street one hundred feet wide. Such

was the origin of Canal Street. Early in the nineteenth century the city had come to envelop the beautiful Collect, which became a receptacle for rubbish and filth until it was voted a nuisance and obliterated. On a rising ground to the west of the water had formerly stood the gallows. In 1838, on a spot which had been in the central portion of the lake, was built the city prison, that noble but dismal specimen of Egyptian architecture commonly known as The Tombs.

Canal Street

On the bank of the North River, half a mile or so above the northern confines of Lispenard's Meadows, there was an interesting hamlet, at first accessible only by the river and afterward by foot-paths. It was originally an Indian village rejoicing in the name of Sappokanican, and occupied a very defensible position between the steep river bank and Minetta Brook, a stream which still flows in its old course, though no longer visible. Two rivulets, arising the one near the site of Calvary Church and the other at Sixth Avenue and Seventeenth Street, came together between Fifth and Sixth avenues a little below Twelfth Street. Their junction formed Minetta Brook, which, after curving eastward enough to touch Clinton Place, flowed across Washington Square and down into the North River, through a small swamp between Charlton and West

Sappokani-can, or Greenwich

Houston streets, known as Minetta Water. It was a clear swift brook abounding in trout, and its left bank was high and covered with dense forest. The space inclosed between its right bank and the North River (through the centre of which Christopher Street now runs) was a vast and smiling field, salubrious and fertile. Indian hamlets not infrequently migrate with very little ado, and as to what became of Sappokanican we are not informed, but it is on record that Director Van Twiller procured it for his own behoof in 1633 and made it a tobacco plantation. It was known in his time as the Bossen Bouwerie (*i. e.* Forest Farm), and the quality of its tobacco was highly esteemed. By 1727 there was a flourishing village there and the English had begun to call it Greenwich. It was then connected with the city by a good road, nearly identical with Greenwich Street, crossing Lispenard's Meadows and the Minetta Water on causeways.

In the time of Andros, and long after, there was nothing on the west side of the island above Greenwich that calls for special mention in our narrative. Greenwich is mentioned, by its old Indian name, in the journal of the two Labadist emissaries, Jasper Dankers and Peter Sluyter, who visited New York in the autumn of 1679. They were representatives of a small sect of Mystics or Quietists

Dankers and Sluyter

lately founded by one Jean de Labadie. While their theology was mainly that of the Reformed Dutch Church, their aim was to restore sundry customs of primitive Christians, including community of goods. The result of this visit to New York was the grant of a large tract of land on Bohemia Manor, in Maryland, on which a company of Labadists settled in 1683.[1] The worthy brethren, Dankers and Sluyter, left an interesting journal of their visit, which was discovered a few years ago ; and they made some quite artistic pencil sketches of the city withal, which are extremely precious as historical documents.[2] A few extracts from their diary will be found instructive.

The ancient custom of robbing innocent travellers for the gratification of thick-witted and sordid hucksters, which still prevails at the port of New York, was attended with more or less delay and personal inconvenience, as it is to-day. If all the curses upon "protectionism" that have been wasted during two and a half centuries on those inhospitable docks could some day take effect and bury the foul iniquity

[1] See *Old Virginia and Her Neighbours*, ii. 165.

[2] An English translation of their Journal, edited by H. C. Murphy, forms the first volume of the *Memoirs of the Long Island Historical Society*, Brooklyn, 1867. It contains excellent engravings of the pictures.

86

deeper than Malebolge, what a gain for civilization it would be!

> " S' io avessi le rime aspre e chiocce,
>   Come si converrebbe al tristo buco ! " [1]

It would indeed take rhymes rough and hoarse to do justice to such a theme. The unvarnished tale of Messrs. Dankers and Sluyter has a familiar sound. Arriving in the harbour on Saturday evening, they were allowed to go ashore for Sunday and hear some New World preaching. On Monday morning " we went on board ship in order to obtain our travelling bag and clothes for the purpose of having them washed, but when we came on board we could not get ashore again before the afternoon, when the passengers' goods were to be delivered. All our goods which were between decks were taken ashore and carried to the public storehouse, where they had to be examined, but The custom-some time elapsed before it was done, house in consequence of the examiners being elsewhere. At length, however, one Abraham Lennoy, a good fellow apparently, befriended us. He examined our chest only, without touching our bedding or anything else. I showed him a list of the tin which we had in the upper part of our chest, and he examined it and also the tin, and turned up a little more what was in the

[1] Dante, *Inferno*, xxxii. 1.

chest and with that left off, without looking at it closely. [A little shamefast wert thou then, worthy Lennoy, at the dirty work for which government hired thee? or, perchance, did a Labadist guilder or two, ever so gently slipped into thy palm, soften the asperities?] He demanded four English shillings for the tin, remarking at the same time that he had observed some other small articles, but would not examine them closely, though he had not seen either the box or the pieces of linen. This being finished, we sent our goods in a cart to our lodgings, paying for the two heavy chests and straw beds and other goods from the public store-house to the Smit's Valey, 16 stivers of zeawan (*i. e.* wampum), equal to $3\frac{1}{2}$ stivers in the money of Holland. This finished the day, and we retired to rest. On Tuesday we remained at home for the purpose of writing, but in the afternoon, finding that many goods had been discharged from the ship, we went to look after our little package, which also came. I declared it, and it was examined. I had to pay 24 guilders in zeawan, or 5 guilders in the coin of Holland. I brought it to the house and looked the things all over, rejoicing that we were finally rid of that miserable set and the ship, the freight only remaining to be paid, which was fixed at 4 guilders in coin.

" As soon as we had dined we sent off our

letters, and this being all accomplished we started
at two o'clock for Long Island. . . . The water
by which it is separated from the
Manhattans is improperly called the East River
East River, for it is nothing else than an arm
of the sea, beginning in the Bay on the west
and ending in the sea [*i. e.* the Sound] on the
east. After forming in this passage several
islands, this water is as broad before the city as
the Y before Amsterdam,[1] but the ebb and
flood tides are stronger. . . . We three crossed,
my comrade and self, with Gerrit [a fellow-
passenger returning from Holland] for our
guide, in a rowboat, which in good weather and
tide carries a sail. When we had crossed . . .
we went on up the hill along open roads slightly
wooded, through the first village,
called Breuckelen, which has an ugly Brooklyn
little church standing in the middle of the road.
Having passed through here, we struck off to
the right in order to go to Gowanes. We went
upon several plantations where Gerrit was acquainted with almost all the people, who made
us very welcome, sharing with us bountifully
whatever they had, whether milk, cider, fruit,
or tobacco, and especially and most of all, mis-

---

[1] A slight exaggeration. The Y or Ij, an arm of the
Zuyder Zee, is considerably more than a mile in breadth
before Amsterdam, while the East River, at Peck Slip, in the
seventeenth century, was about three fifths of a mile.

erable rum or brandy brought from Barbadoes and the other islands, and called by the Dutch *kill-devil*. All these people are very fond of it, most of them extravagantly so, although it is very dear and has a bad taste. It is impossible to tell how many peach-trees we passed, all laden with fruit to breaking down, and many of them actually broken down. We came to a place surrounded with such trees from which so many had fallen off that the ground could not be discerned, and you could not put your foot down without trampling them, and notwithstanding such large quantities had fallen off, the trees were still as full as they could bear. The hogs and other animals mostly feed on them. This place belongs to the oldest European woman in the country. We went into her house where she lives with her children. She was sitting by the fire, smoking tobacco incessantly, one pipe after another. We inquired after her age, which the children told us was about a hundred years. . . . She had been about fifty years now in the country, and had above seventy children and grandchildren. We tasted here for the first time smoked twælft [*i. e.* twelfth, meaning striped bass], a fish so called because it is caught in season next after the elft [*i. e.* eleventh, meaning shad]. It was salted a little and then smoked, and although now a year old, it was still perfectly good and in flavour not inferior to smoked salmon. We drank here also the first new cider, which was very fine.

"We proceeded on to Gowanes, . . . where we arrived in the evening at one of the best friends of Gerrit, named Symon.[1] He was very glad to see us, and so was his wife. He took us into the house and entertained us exceedingly well. We found a good fire, halfway up the chimney, of clear oak and hickory, of which they made not the least scruple of burning profusely. We let it penetrate us thoroughly. There had been already thrown upon it, to be roasted, a pailful of Gowanes oysters, which are the best in the country. They are quite as good as those of England, and better than those we ate at Falmouth. I had to try some of them raw. They are large and full, some of them not less than a foot long. . . . Everybody keeps the shells for the purpose of burning them into lime. They pickle the oysters in small casks, and send them to Barbadoes and the other islands. We had for supper a roasted haunch of venison, which he had bought of the Indians for 3½

Gowanus

---

[1] This was Simon de Hart. Our Labadists follow the ancient usage in which the forename was of more importance than the surname. The house where they were so well regaled "is still standing, having been in the possession of the descendants of Simon de Hart ever since." Mrs. Lamb's *History of the City of New York*, i. 287.

guilders of zeawan [*i. e.* 15 cents] and which
weighed 30 lbs. The meat was exceedingly
tender and good, and also quite fat. It had a
slight spicy flavour. We were also served with
wild turkey, which was also fat and of a good
flavour; and a wild goose, but that was rather
dry. . . . We saw here, lying in a heap, a
whole hill of watermelons as large as pumpkins,
which Symon was going to take to the city to
sell. . . . It was very late at night when we
went to rest in a Kermis bed, as it is called,[1] in
the corner of the hearth, alongside of a good
fire."

Next morning, after their host and hostess
had gone with their marketing to the city, our
Fort three friends made their way on foot
Hamilton to Najack (Fort Hamilton), where
they came upon a great field of ripe maize,
which their diary calls " Turkish wheat." The
epithet is interesting as a survival from the time
when America was supposed to be Asia. Just
as the American bird which in French is called
" Indian fowl " is called in English a " turkey,"
so this " Turkish wheat " is only another name
for " Indian corn." The adjective occurs with
the same meaning in the next sentence: " We

1 Kermis was a great fair or festival, in the Low Countries,
with much dancing and frolic. A Kermis bed would be an
extra bed for such occasions when the house was full of
company.

soon heard a noise of pounding, like threshing, and went to the place whence it proceeded, and found there an old Indian woman busily employed beating Turkish beans out of the pods by means of a stick, which she did with astonishing force and dexterity. Gerrit inquired of her, in the Indian language which he spoke perfectly well, how old she was, and she answered eighty years; at which we were still more astonished that so old a woman should still have so much strength and courage to work as she did. We went thence to her habitation, where we found the whole troop together, consisting of seven or eight families, and twenty or twenty-two persons. Their house was low and long, about sixty feet long and fourteen or fifteen wide. The bottom was earth, the sides and roof were made of reed and the bark of chestnut trees; the posts or columns were limbs of trees stuck in the ground and all fastened together. The ridge of the roof was open about half a foot wide from end to end, in order to let the smoke escape, in place of a chimney. On the sides of the house the roof was so low that you could hardly stand under it. The entrances, which were at both ends, were so small that they had to stoop down and squeeze themselves to get through them. The doors were made of reed or flat bark. In the whole building there was no iron, stone, lime, or lead.

An Algonquin household

"They build their fire in the middle of the floor, according to the number of families, so that from one end to the other each boils its own pot and eats when it likes, not only the families by themselves, but each Indian alone when he is hungry, at all hours, morning, noon, and night. By each fire are the cooking utensils, consisting of a pot, a bowl or calabash, and a spoon also made of a calabash. These are all that relate to cooking. They lie upon mats, with their feet towards the fire on each side of it. They do not sit much upon anything raised up, but, for the most part, sit upon the ground, or squat on their ankles. Their other household articles consist of a calabash of water, out of which they drink, a small basket in which to carry their maize and beans, and a knife. The implements are, for tillage, merely a small sharp stone; for hunting, a gun and pouch for powder and lead; for fishing, a canoe without mast or sail, and not a nail in any part of it, though it is sometimes full forty feet in length, fish-hooks and lines, and scoop to paddle with in place of oars. . . .

"All who live in one house are generally of one stock, as father and mother, with their offspring. Their bread is maize pounded in a block by a stone, but not fine; this is mixed with water and made into a cake, which they bake under the hot ashes. They gave us a small piece when we entered, and although the grains were not ripe, and it was half-baked and coarse grains, we nevertheless had to eat it, or at least not throw it away before them, which they would have regarded as a great sin, or a great affront. We chewed a little of it and managed to hide it. We had also to drink out of their calabashes the water, which was very good.

" Here we saw the Indians who had come on board the ship when we arrived. They were all joyful at the visit of our Gerrit, who had long dwelt thereabouts and was an old acquaintance of theirs. We gave them two jews-harps, whereat they were much pleased and at once began to play them, and fairly well. Some of their chiefs — who are their priests and medicine-men and could speak good Dutch — were busy making shoes of deer-leather, which they make soft by long working it between the hands. They had dogs, besides fowls and hogs, which they are gradually learning from Europeans how to manage. Toward the last we asked them for some peaches, and their reply was ' Go and pick some,' which shows their politeness ! However, not wishing to offend them, we went out and pulled some. Although they are such a poor miserable people, they are licentious and proud, and much given to knavery and scoffing. As we noticed an extremely old woman (not less than a hundred, one would think), some saucy young fellows jeeringly answered, 'Twenty years.' We observed the manner in which they travel with their children, a woman having one which she carried on her back. The little thing clung tight around her neck like a cat, and was held secure by a piece of duffels, their usual garment."

A most admirable and lifelike description of an aboriginal dwelling! Our Labadist friends were keen observers, and deft with pen as well as pencil. We cannot recount all their experiences, but may follow them on their trip to the extreme north of Manhattan. After leaving

A night at Harlem

the Bowery Tavern they proceeded "through the woods to New Harlem, a rather large village directly opposite the place where the northeast creek [Harlem River] and the East River come together, situated about three hours' journey from New Amsterdam, like as the old Harlem in Europe is situated about three hours' distance from the old Amsterdam. As our guide, Gerrit, had some business here, and found many acquaintances, we remained over night at the house of a man named Geresolveert,[1] the schout of the village, who had formerly lived in Brazil, and whose heart was still full of it. His house was all the time filled with people, mostly drinking that execrable rum.

[1] Oh, delicious! — a Dutch translation of Resolved, a Puritan forename by no means uncommon in those days. The person meant was Resolved Waldron, constable of Harlem.

He had also the best cider we have tasted. Among the crowd we found a person of quality, an Englishman, namely, Captain Car- James teret,[1] whose father is in great favour Carteret with the king, and he himself had assisted in sundry exploits in the king's service. He commanded the English forces which went in 1660 to retake St. Kitts. . . . The king has given to his father, Sir George Carteret, the entire government of the lands west of the North River, in New Netherland, with power to appoint as governor whom he pleases ; and at this present time there is a governor over it by his appointment, another Carteret, his nephew, I believe,[2] who resides at Elizabeth, in New Jersey. . . . This son is a very profligate person. He married a merchant's daughter here, and has so treated his wife that her father has been compelled to take her home again. He runs about among the farmers, and stays where he can find most to drink, and sleeps in barns on the straw.

---

[1] See above, p. 18. James Carteret was a legitimate younger son of Sir George, not an illegitimate son, as has sometimes been said. See Burke's *Dormant and Extinct Peerages,* p. 108.

[2] W. L. Stone (*Hist. New York City,* p. 63) makes him a brother of Sir George ; Brodhead (*Hist. New York,* ii. 84) makes him a cousin ; and Burke does not elucidate the matter. The names Philip and George had for at least four centuries been so thickly iterated among the Carterets that their use as distinctive appellations was lost.

If he would conduct himself properly he might hold the highest positions, for he has studied the moralities, and seems to have been of a good understanding; but that is all now drowned. His father, who will no longer acknowledge him as his son,[1] allows him yearly as much only as is necessary to live."

The morning after this hilarious night at the schout's, our friends set out from Harlem village to go up to the end of the island, and perhaps it may have been the thirst which sometimes ensues upon such nights that made them exclaim over the deliciousness of the juicy morning peaches. "When we were not far from the point of Spyten Duyvil we could see on our left hand the rocky cliffs of the mainland on the other side of the North River, these cliffs standing straight up and down, with the grain, just as if they were antimony. We crossed over the Spyten Duyvil in a canoe, and paid nine stivers fare [or about eighteen cents] for us three, which was very dear. We followed the opposite side of the land, till we came to the house of one Valentyn, a great acquaintance of our Gerrit's. He had gone to the city, but his wife, though she did not know Gerrit or us, was so much rejoiced to see Hollanders that she hardly knew what to do for us. She set before us what she had. We

Spyten
Duyvil

[1] Hence probably the rumour of illegitimacy.

left after breakfasting. Her son showed us the
way, and we came to a road entirely covered
with peaches. We asked the boy why they left
them to lie there, and why the hogs did not eat
them. He answered, we do not know what to
do with them, there are so many; the hogs are
satiated with them and will not eat any more.
. . . We pursued our way now a small distance through the woods and over the hills,
then back again along the shore to a point
where lived an Englishman named Webblingh,
who was standing ready to cross over. He carried us over with him, and refused to take any
pay for our passage, offering us at the same
time some of his rum, a liquor which is every
where.

"We were now again at New Harlem, and
dined with Geresolveert, at whose house we had
slept the night before, and who made us welcome. It was now two o'clock; and leaving
there we crossed the island, which takes about
three quarters of an hour to do, and came to
the North River, which we followed   The good
a little within the woods, as far as   beer of
Sappokanican, where Gerrit had a sis-   Greenwich
ter and some friends. There we rested ourselves and drank some good beer, which was
very refreshing. We then kept on our way
along the shore to the city, where we arrived
in the evening very tired, having walked this

day about forty miles. I must add, in passing through this island we sometimes encountered such a sweet smell in the air that we stood still, because we did not know what it was we were meeting."

In the course of their adventures our worthy friends inform us that they talked with " the first male born of Europeans in New Netherland," a brewer named Jean Vigné. His parents were from Valenciennes, and he was now about sixty-five years of age." Their pictures Three of the clergy are not flattering. They dominies heard a venerable minister "from the up-river country at Fort Orange," who was called Dominie Schaats, whose demeanour was so rough and outlandish that they suspected him of indulgence in the ubiquitous rum. They tell us that Dominie Nieuwenhuysen was " a thick, corpulent person, with a red and bloated face, and of very slabbering speech." On one Sunday they went at noon " to hear the English minister, whose service took place after the Dutch church was out. There were not above twenty-five or thirty people in the church. The first thing that occurred was the reading of their prayers and ceremonies out of the prayer-book, as is done in all Episcopal churches. A young man then went into the pulpit and preached, who thought he was performing wonders ; but

he had a little book in his hand out of which he read his sermon, which was from a quarter to half an hour long. With this the services were concluded, whereat we could not be sufficiently astonished."

This young parson was Mr. Charles Wolley, who came in 1678 with Andros. We may now let him speak for himself, and first as to the climate: " It is of a sweet and wholesome breath, free from those annoyances which are commonly ascribed by naturalists for the insalubriety of any Country, viz. . . . stagnant Waters, lowness of Shoars, inconstancy of Weather [!], and the excessive heat of the Summer [!!]; it is gently refreshed, fanned, and allayed by constant breezes from the Sea. . . . Nature kindly drains and purgeth [the land] by Fontanels and Issues of running waters in its irriguous Valleys, and shelters it with the umbrellas of all sorts of Trees . . . ; which Trees and Plants do undoubtedly, tho' insensibly, suck in and digest into their own growth and composition those subterraneous Particles and Exhalations, which otherwise wou'd be attracted by the heat of the Sun, and so become matter for infectious Clouds and malign Atmospheres. . . . I myself, a person of a weakly Stamen and a valetudinary Constitution, was not in the

Mr. Wolley on the New York climate

least indisposed in that Climate during my residence there, the space of three years."

Allowing for a somewhat too roseate tint
in the references to the freedom from fickle
weather and torrid heat, this is an excellent
description of the breezy and salubrious air
of Manhattan. As for the people, they im-
pressed Mr. Wolley as extremely " high-flown
religionists," but he had never visited Boston
or New Haven. Even in this comparatively
tolerant New Netherland, the ministers of different churches sometimes would not take tea
together, and our young Cambridge friend did
not relish such narrowness.

" There were two Ministers, or Dominies
as they were called there, the one a Lutheran
or High-Dutch,[1] the other a Calvinist or Low
Dutchman,[2] who behaved themselves one towards another so shily and uncharitably as if
Luther and Calvin had bequeathed and entailed their virulent and bigoted Spirits upon
them and their heirs forever. They had not
visited or spoken to each other with any respect for six years together before my being
there, with whom I being much acquainted, I
invited them both with their Vrows
to a Supper one night unknown to
each other, with an obligation that they should

A Latin
supper

---

[1] Dominie Bernhardus Frazius.
[2] Dominie Nieuwenhuysen.

102

not speak one word of Dutch, under the penalty of a bottle of Madeira, alledging I was so imperfect in that Language that we could not manage a sociable discourse. So accordingly they came, and at the first interview they stood so appalled as if the Ghosts of Luther and Calvin had suffered a transmigration, but the amaze soon went off with a *salve tu quoque* and a Bottle of Wine, of which the Calvinist Dominie was a true Carouzer, and so we continued our *Mensalia* the whole evening in Latine, which they both spoke so fluently and promptly that I blushed at myself with a passionate regret that I could not keep pace with them. . . . As to the Dutch language, in which I was but a smatterer, I think it lofty, majestic, and emphatical." [1]

The intemperate zeal of red-faced Dominie Nieuwenhuysen sometimes hurried him into a pace which he could not keep up. Dominie Nicholas van Rensselaer, having been ordained in England by a bishop, had come to be minister at Albany as colleague to the aged Dr. Schaats, whose oratory seemed to our Labadist visitors so uncouth. Nieuwenhuysen denied that ordination by an English bishop could confer the right to administer sacraments in the Dutch Reformed Church, and he therefore insisted that Van

Dominie Van Rensselaer

[1] Wolley's *Journal*, pp. 55, 56.

Rensselaer should be forbidden to baptize children; but when the point was argued before Andros and his council, the zealous Calvinist was obliged to recede from his position. An attempt was soon afterward made to convict Van Rensselaer of doctrinal heresy. Charges of "false preaching" were brought against him by Jacob Leisler, a wealthy German, one of Nieuwenhuysen's deacons, and a young English protégé of his, named Jacob Milborne. The result of the trial was the acquittal of Van Rensselaer, while Leisler and Milborne were obliged to pay the costs. We shall by and by meet the deacon and his friend under very different circumstances. Already this incident shows the existence of two mutually repugnant trends of feeling in the Dutch church at New York: the one aristocratic, liberal, mellow, and inclined to fraternize with Episcopacy; the other democratic, fanatical, bitter, and Puritanical. Such antagonisms were to bear fruit in deadly feuds.

According to Andros's own report, the province of New York consisted of twenty-four towns, villages, or parishes, divided into six precincts for courts of quarter sessions. The total value of the estates was about £150,000, equivalent to at least $3,000,000 of the present day. A merchant worth £1000 ($20,000) was deemed rich, and a planter with half that amount in chattels was accounted very well off. The population of the city since 1664 had increased from about 1600 to about 3500. Three ships, eight sloops, and seven boats were owned in the city, and of these craft four had been built there. The revenue of the province Estate and revenue was £2000, not enough " by a greate deale," which was a source of worry to the Duke of York. The lack of servants was also quite generally felt; there were a few black slaves, chiefly from Barbadoes, worth about £30 a head. The principal exports were furs, lumber, tar, and bolted flour; which paid for £50,000 of manufactured goods imported from England. There were no beggars in the province, but of all poor and disabled persons due care was taken. There were twenty churches — Reformed Dutch, Lutheran, Independent, Presbyterian, Baptist, Quaker, and Jew — all self-supporting; but there was a scarcity of ministers, which was an inconvenience in respect of funerals, weddings, and christenings.[1]

The scarcity of clergymen led the way to an interesting development. We have already seen that the Reformed Dutch Church in New York accepted ordination at the hands of an English bishop as sufficient qualification for the ministry; but this was not enough. The methods of the Dutch Church must be expanded to fit

[1] *N. Y. Colonial Documents,* iii. 245, 260–262.

the occasion. In 1678 Laurentius van Gaas-
beeck was sent out to be minister at Esopus,

Formation
of an inde-
pendent
Classis

under the authority of the Classis, or
supreme ecclesiastical body, of Amsterdam. Before his arrival the spiritual interests of Esopus were cared for temporarily by Petrus Tesschenmaeker, a young
graduate of Utrecht, who had lately come over.
Tesschenmaeker was a bachelor of divinity, but
had not been ordained. Upon the arrival of
the new dominie at Esopus, this young man received a call to the church at Newcastle on the
Delaware, which furthermore requested that he
might be ordained without the cumbrous for-
mality of crossing the ocean to Holland. Hereupon Andros directed Nieuwenhuysen with any
three or more clergymen to form themselves
into a Classis, and after duly examining Tesschenmaeker to ordain him if they saw fit. This
was done, the action of the New York dominies was approved by the Classis of Amsterdam, and thus in a most pleasant and sensible
fashion was the Dutch Church in America made
practically independent of the fatherland.[1]

The insufficiency of revenue was to a great
extent remedied by the ordinances concerning
the bolting of flour. First it was ordered that

[1] Dankers and Sluyter's *Journal*, iii. 222 ; *Book of General Entries*, xxxii. 61; Demarest, *History of the Reformed
Dutch Church*, p. 183.

all flour for exportation should be bolted and duly inspected and the barrels properly marked before they could be shipped. Then The flour it was further ordered that all in- monopoly spection of flour must take place in the city of New York. These arrangements conferred upon the city for some years a lucrative monopoly.

One order, to which the duke attached great importance, required that all vessels with cargoes bound for any port within the original territory of New Netherland should enter at the New York custom-house. The duke insisted that Sir Edmund should rigorously enforce this order, and the immediate result was trouble with New Jersey.

It will be remembered that in 1664 the Duke of York had granted New Jersey jointly to Sir George Carteret and Lord Berkeley as lords proprietary, and under this grant had exercised powers of sovereignty in the eastern and northern parts of that fine province. Practically there had come about an ill-defined separation Affairs in between Carteret's actual domain and New Jersey the southwestern region, which Berkeley soon sold to a couple of Quakers. The Dutch conquest of 1673 was held to have extinguished all these rights, and apparently vested them in the States General, which by the treaty of Westminster next year handed them over to Charles II.,

murred to its jurisdiction, but was overruled. Then he argued that his conduct as governor of East Jersey had been entirely legal " and by virtue of power derived from the king." His arguments and proofs convinced the jury, and they acquitted him. Andros could not conceal his chagrin; he tried to browbeat the jurors, and sent them out twice to reconsider their verdict, but they were immovable, and Carteret scored a triumph. Even now, however, Andros would not allow him to return to New Jersey until he had extorted from him a promise that he would not " assume any authority or jurisdiction there, civil or military." [1]

At length, early in June, the deposed governor was escorted back to Elizabethtown, with much politeness and ceremony, by his loving friends, Sir Edmund and Lady Andros. One would like to know how the dinner passed off at Mrs. Carteret's, and what Sir Edmund had to Carteret's say about the conduct of his ruffians. return to Elizabeth- Attempts have been made to excuse town him for his part in the transaction, on the ground that he was only carrying out the duke's orders. Nevertheless, while it would be hardly just to charge upon Andros all the brutality of his myrmidons, the whole affair helps

[1] Leaming and Spicer, *Grants, Concessions, etc.*, pp. 678–684 ; Dankers and Sluyter, *Journal*, pp. 347–351 ; Whitehead's *East Jersey*, pp. 73, 74.

us to understand the intense hatred which he inspired in people at a later period. In his eagerness to serve his master, we see him carrying out orders with needless violence and even behaving most reprehensibly, as in his attempt to overawe the jurymen. Our old comparison recurs to us as we feel that such was not the way in which Nicolls would have given effect to the duke's orders.

The people of East Jersey submitted to the appointment of sundry officers by Andros, but their Assembly refused to adopt the Duke's Laws. News of all these proceedings was sent by the deposed governor to Lady Carteret, widow of Sir George, who had lately died. These were people of great influence at court, and accordingly the duke deemed it best not to take to himself too much responsibility for the acts of his agent. He told Lady Carteret that he "doth wholly disown and declare that Sir Edmund Andros had never any such order or authority from him for the doing thereof," — a characteristic specimen of Stuart veracity. Presently James executed a paper relinquishing his claim upon East Jersey, and confirming it in the proprietorship of young Sir George Carteret, grandson and heir of the original grantee ; and so the quarrel ended in the discomfiture of Andros.

The duke relinquishes East Jersey to the Carterets

Questions of ownership and jurisdiction had

been coming up in West Jersey likewise, which ended in this same year 1680 in the duke's relinquishing all his claims in favour of

and West Jersey to Byllinge and his friends Friend Byllinge and other Quakers. But I must reserve this story for a while until it can fall into its proper place in the line of causation which led to the founding of Pennsylvania. We must bid adieu for a season to the pleasant country between the North and South rivers of New Netherland. We have to view the career of a man of extraordinary and varied powers, uniting after a fashion all his own the wisdom of the serpent with the purity of the dove,[1] who was able at once to be a leader of one of the most iconoclastic and unpopular of Christian sects, and to retain the admiring friendship of one of the most bigoted kings that ever sat upon a throne. We must make the acquaintance of William Penn, who, take him for all in all, was by far the greatest among the founders of American commonwealths.

---

[1] I leave this sentence as I first wrote it in 1882. I was not then aware that Benjamin Franklin had alluded to Penn as uniting "the subtlety of the serpent with the innocence of the dove." (See his *Works*, ed. Sparks, iii. 123.) Franklin's phrase, however, is intended for a sneer, as his context shows, while mine is meant to convey accurate but unstinted praise.

XII

PENN'S HOLY EXPERIMENT

AT the time of our Declaration of Independence the only states in which all Christian sects stood socially and politically on an equal footing were Pennsylvania and Delaware, the two states which had originally constituted the palatinate or proprietary domain of William Penn. Rhode Island, indeed, had been founded upon equally liberal principles, but during the strong wave of anti-Catholic feeling that passed over the country in the time of James II., a clause depriving Papists of the franchise found its way into the statute book, and it was not repealed until 1783. If Roger Williams had lived a few years longer, it is not likely that this one stain upon the noble record of Rhode Island would have been permitted. As for Pennsylvania, if there was anything which she stood for in the eyes of the world, it was liberty of conscience. Her fame had gone abroad over the continent of Europe. In Voltaire's writings Pennsylvania more than once receives admiring mention as the one fa-

Religious liberty in Pennsylvania and Delaware

voured country in the world where men can be devoutly religious and still refrain from tearing one another to pieces.

There was something more than satire in the suggested antithesis; as with most of Voltaire's keen-edged remarks, there was deep and earnest meaning behind it. Until quite modern times toleration was found only in union with indifference. In religious matters the Gallio, who "cared for none of those things," might refuse to play the part of a persecutor, but the most devout and disinterested zeal for religion was apt to be combined with more or less fanatical intolerance. Various causes from time to time contributed to this, but the deepest and most abiding cause was the imperfect separation between religion and politics. If we carry our thoughts back to primeval ages, we see that there was no such separation; religious life and civil life were identical. The earliest glimpses we can get of the human race show us nowhere anything like a nation, but everywhere small tribes perpetually encroaching upon one another and perpetually fighting to escape annihilation. The state of things among the American Indians of the seventeenth century may serve to illustrate what had been going on over a large part of the earth's surface for at least 300,000 or 400,000 years. From the Australian stage

Identity of civil and religious life in primitive ages

116

of human existence up to the Iroquois stage there was in many respects an enormous advance toward civilization, but the omnipresence of exterminating warfare continued, and enables us to understand that feature of primeval times. In such a stage of society almost every act of tribal life is invested with religious significance, and absolute conformity to tribal rules and observances is enforced with pitiless rigour. The slightest neglect of an omen, for example, might offend some tutelar deity and thus bring on defeat; it is therefore unhesitatingly punished with death. It is an important part of the duties of medicine-men to take cognizance of the slightest offences and lapses. In early society the enforced conformity relates chiefly to matters of ritual and ceremony; questions of dogma arise at a later stage, after a considerable development in human thinking. But to whatever matter the enforcement of conformity relates, there can be no doubt as to the absolute necessity of it in early society. No liberty of divergence can be allowed to the individual without endangering the community.

As a kind of help toward the illustration of this point, let me cite a familiar instance of persecution in modern times and in a highly civilized community, where some of the conditions of primitive society had been temporarily reproduced. In 1636 there were about five thousand

Englishmen in New England, distributed in more than twenty villages, mostly on the shores of Massachusetts Bay, but some as remote as the Connecticut River. Such a concerted Indian assault upon them as was actually made forty years later, in King Philip's war, might have overwhelmed them. Such an assault was contemplated by the Pequots and dreaded throughout the settlements, and the train-bands were making ready for war, when a certain number of Boston men refused to serve. There were a few persons of influence in Boston, called Antinomians, of whom the one best remembered is Anne Hutchinson. According to them it made a great difference to one's salvation whether one were under a " covenant of grace " or only under a " covenant of works." The men who in a moment of supreme peril to the commonwealth refused to march against the enemy alleged as a sufficient reason that they suspected their chaplain of being under a " covenant of works," and therefore would not serve with him. Under such circumstances Mrs. Hutchinson and the other Antinomians were banished from Boston. A disagreement upon a transcendental question of theology was breeding sedition and endangering the very existence of the state. Those who defend the government of Massachusetts for banishing Mrs. Hutchinson

The Antinomians and the Pequot war

118

rest their defence upon such grounds. Without feeling called upon to decide that question, we can see that the case is historically instructive in a high degree.

Now when we come to early society, the military urgency is incessant and imperative, and all other things must yield to it. It is sustained by the feeling of corporate responsibility which is universal among tribal communities. The tribe is regarded as responsible for the acts of each one of its individuals. Religious sanctions and penalties are visited upon everything. What we call conventionalities are in the tribal stage of society regarded as sacraments, and thus the slightest infringement is liable to call down upon the whole tribe the wrath of some offended tutelar deity, in the shape of defeat or famine or pestilence. In such a stern discipline there is no room for divergence or dissent. And such was undoubtedly the kind of training under which all our ancestors were reared, from far-off ages of which only a geologic record remains down to the mere yesterday that witnessed the building of the Pyramids. Under such rigid training were formed, through wave after wave of conquest, the great nations of prechristian times.

It is not strange that it has taken the foremost races of men three or four thousand years to free themselves from the tyranny of mental

Corporate responsibility

119

habits which had been ingrained into them for three or four hundred thousand. A careful study of the history of religious per-secution shows us that sometimes politics and sometimes religion have been most actively concerned in it. The perse-cution of Christians by the Roman emperors was chiefly political, because Christianity asserted a dominion over men paramount to that of the emperor. The persecution of the Albigenses by Pope Innocent III. was largely political, because that heresy threatened the very continu-ance of the Papacy as part of the complex gov-ernment of mediæval Europe. Innocent, like the heathen emperors, was fighting in self-defence. So, too, a considerable part of the mutual persecutions of Catholics and Protestants in the sixteenth and seventeenth centuries was simply downright warfare in which A kills B to prevent B from killing A. But if we consider the nature of the religious motives that have entered into persecution, whether they have been dominating motives or have simply been enlisted in furtherance of political ends, we find that they have always been rooted in the ancient notion of corporate responsibility. Let us get rid of the unclean thing lest we be cursed for its sake; such has been the feeling which has more than anything else sustained persecution. The Spanish prelates, for example, who urged

Political and religious per-secutions

the banishment of the Moriscos, loudly assev-
erated that the failure to suppress the Dutch
Netherlands was a mark of God's displeasure
that such people were allowed to stay in Spain.
Was God likely to aid the Spaniards in exterminating infidels abroad while they were so sin-
ful as to harbour infidels in their own country?
So when Queen Mary Tudor was led by domestic disappointments to fancy herself under-
going divine punishment, she quickly reached
the conclusion that she had not been sufficiently
zealous in purging the kingdom of heresy, and
this particular act of logic kindled the flames
for more than fifty Protestants. In the sixteenth century this way of looking at things
(which I now take pains to explain to my
readers) would not have needed a word of explanation for anybody; it was simply a piece
of plain common sense, self-evident to all!

Now inasmuch as this notion of corporate
responsibility is a survival from the very infancy
of the human race, since the rigorous restriction
of individuality persisted through countless
generations of men to whom it proved *Reasons for*
indispensably useful, it is not strange *the prolonged*
that, since it has come to be recog- *vitality of the*
nized as harmful and stigmatized as *persecuting*
spirit
persecution, it has been found so hard to kill.
The conditions of tribal society long ago ceased
to exist in Europe. Instead of tribes, the fore-

most races of men are organized in a complicated fashion as nations; instead of tutelar deities they have reached sundry more or less imperfect forms of monotheism; and with the advance of knowledge the conception of natural law has destroyed a host of primitive superstitions. Religion is no longer in the old materialistic way but in a much higher and more spiritual way implicated with each act of life. Part of this great change is due to the mighty influence exerted by the mediæval Church as a spiritual power distinct from and often opposed to the temporal power. In Christianity the separation of church from state took its rise; and while religion was made an affair of mankind, not of localities or tribes, the importance of the individual was greatly increased.

Now if we look at religious persecution from the point of view of modern society, it is easy

Importance of preserving variations

to see that it is an unmitigated evil. The evolution of a higher civilization can best be attained by allowing to individual tastes, impulses, and capacities the freest possible play. Procrustes-beds are out of fashion; we no longer think it desirable that all people should act alike. From a Darwinian standpoint we recognize that an abundance of spontaneous variation is favourable to progress. A wise horticulturist sees signs of promise in many an aberrant plant and carefully nurtures it. If you wish to produce a race of self-reliant, inventive, and enterprising Yankees, you must not begin by setting up a winnowing machine for picking out and slaughtering all the men and women who are bold enough and bright enough to do their own thinking, and earnest enough to talk about it to others. Such an infernal machine was the Inquisition ; it weeded out the sturdiest plants and saved the weaker ones, thus lowering the average capacity of the people wherever it was in vigorous operation. As a rule it has been persons of a progressive type who have become objects of persecution, and when they have fled from their native land they have added strength to the country that has received them. In the history of what has been done by men who speak English, it is a fact of cardinal importance that England has never had an Inquisition, but has habitually sheltered religious refugees from other countries.

Such is the scientific aspect of the case. But it has a purely religious aspect from which we are brought to the same conclusion. The moment we cease to regard religious truth as a rigid body of formulas, imparted to mankind once for all and incapable of further interpretation or expansion ; the moment we come to look upon religion as part of the soul's development under the immediate influence of the

From a religious point of view the innovator should be welcomed

Spirit of God ; the moment we concede to individual judgment some weight in determining
what the individual form of religious expression
shall be, — that moment we have taken the
first step toward the conclusion that a dead
uniformity of opinion on religious questions
is undesirable. In the presence of an Eternal
Reality which confessedly transcends our human
powers of comprehension in many ways, we are
not entitled to frown or to sneer at our neighbour's view, but if we give it due attention we
may find in it more or less that is helpful and
uplifting which we had overlooked. Thus, instead of mere toleration we rise to a higher
plane and greet the innovator with words of
cordial welcome. Such a state of things, on any
general scale, can hardly yet be said to have
come into existence, but in the foremost communities many minds have come within sight
of it, and some have attained to it. So in past
times we find here and there some choice spirit
reaching it. Especially in the seventeenth century, when Protestantism was assuming sundry
extreme forms, and when one of the symptoms
of the age was the demonstration, by Hobbes
and Locke, of the relativity of all knowledge,
there were active leaders of men who attained
Vane's hea-
venly speech to this great breadth of view. For
example, Sir Henry Vane, whom Mil-
ton, in that sonnet which is the most glorious

124

tribute ever paid by a man of letters to a statesman, calls Religion's " eldest son," — Sir Henry
Vane once exclaimed in Parliament, " Why
should the labours of any be suppressed, if
sober, though never so different? We now
profess to seek God, we desire to see light!"
Roger Williams called this a " heavenly speech."
It merited Milton's encomium : —

> . . . " To know
> Both Spiritual and Civil, what each means,
> What serves each, thou hast learn'd, which few have done."

It was greatly to the credit of Oliver Cromwell
as a statesman that he usually exhibited this
large-minded and generous tolerance. Cromwell's
tolerance
It was Cromwell, for example, who
encouraged Jews to come to England, where
they had not been allowed since 1290.[1] So a
Rhode Island statute of 1684, the year after
Roger Williams's death, and in accordance with
his principles, expressly admits Jewish immigrants to all the rights and privileges of citizens.
These men — Vane and Williams, Milton and
Cromwell — had reached a very modern standpoint in such matters.

Just at the zenith of Cromwell's career that
notable phase of religious development known
as Quakerism appeared upon the scene. Quakerism was the most extreme form which Protestantism had assumed. In so far as Protest-

[1] Masson's *Milton*, p. 71.

antism claimed to be working a reformation in Christianity by retaining the spiritual core and dropping off the non-essential integuments, the Quakers carried this process about as far as it could go. There have always been two sides to Quakerism, the rationalistic side, whereby it has sometimes drawn upon itself the imputation of Socinianism or Deism, and the mystic side, whereby it shows traces of kinship with various sects of Quietists. John Tauler, the mighty Dominican preacher in the days of the Black Death, seems in many respects a forerunner of the Quakers. Thomas à Kempis, author of the most widely read Christian book after the Bible, belonged to the same class of minds. Without much organization or machinery as a sect, such men were known in the thirteenth and fourteenth centuries as "Friends of God." A group of them which attained to some organization in Holland about 1360 came to be known as "Brethren of the Common Life." It was among these people that Thomas à Kempis was trained at Deventer; their influence upon Dutch culture was very great, and I dare say the mildness and tolerance of the Netherlands in matters of religion owes much to them.

The founder of Quakerism, George Fox, was born in Leicestershire, in 1624, the son of a prosperous weaver, known to his neighbours as

Quietists and Quakers

126

George Fox

"righteous Christopher Fox." An origin among Leicester weavers is suggestive of Dutch influences, but in the lack of detailed evidence it is easy to make too much of such suggestions. At an early age and with scanty education, George Fox became a lay preacher. His aim was not to gather disciples about him and found a new sect, but to purify the Church from sundry errors, doctrinal and practical. The basis of his teaching was the belief that each soul is in religious matters answerable not to its fellows, but to God alone, without priestly mediation, because the Holy Spirit is immediately present in every soul, and is thus a direct source of illumination. From this central belief flowed two important practical consequences, both essentially modern : one was complete toleration, the other was complete equality of human beings before the law, and hence the condemnation of slavery, in which Quakers have generally been foremost. Fox's extreme democracy was shown in the refusal to take off his hat, and in the avoidance of the plural pronoun of dignity. His rejection of a priesthood extended to all ordained and salaried preachers. He cared little for communion with bread and wine in comparison with communion in spirit, and set more value upon the baptism of repentance than upon the baptism of water. He regarded the inner light as a more authori-

George Fox

tative guide than Scripture, since it was the
interpreter to which the sacred text must ultimately be referred; but he was far from neg-
lecting the written word. On the contrary, his
deference to it was often extremely scrupulous,
as when he understood the injunction, " Swear
not at all," as a prohibition of judicial oaths,
and the commandment, " Thou shalt not kill,"
as a condemnation of all warfare. Fox was a
man of rare executive power; " I never saw the
occasion," said Penn, " to which he was not
equal." He was a man of lofty soul and deep
spiritual insight; and before his commanding
presence and starlike eyes the persecutor often
quailed.

It was customary at that moment of religious
upheaval for independent preachers and lay-
men to invade the pulpits and exhort the con-
gregations after the unceremonious manner
described by Sir Walter Scott in " Woodstock."
Unseemly brawls were apt to result, in the
course of which the preacher was dragged before the nearest magistrate. Fox tells
us how on one of these occasions, at
Derby in 1650, he was taken before
Justice Bennett, " who was the first that called
us Quakers, because I bade him tremble at the
word of the Lord." Fox and his early followers were often put in jail, not so much for
teaching heresy as for breaking the peace. The

Origin of
the epithet,
" Quaker"

128

absence of ecclesiastical organization made them seem like vagrant ranters, and their refusals to pay tithes, or to testify under oath, or to lift their hats before a magistrate, kept them perpetually liable to punishment for contempt of court. Cromwell was indisposed to annoy them, and his relations with Fox were friendly, yet between 1650 and 1658 several hundred Quakers were put into jail, usually for such breaches of custom and etiquette.

It was, moreover, not always possible to distinguish off hand between the followers of George Fox and those of other enthusiasts who were swarming in England. Such a preacher was James Nayler, who had been a cavalry officer in Cromwell's army, but turned prophet _{Crazy} and went stark mad, calling himself _{enthusiasts} "the Prince of Peace, the Fairest among Ten Thousand, and the Altogether Lovely." This Nayler marched through the streets of Wells and Glastonbury, while the people threw down their cloaks to serve as mats for his feet, and sang "Hosanna in the highest." On one occasion he was believed to have raised a dead woman to life. Other prophets, not easy to deal with, were those who thought it needful to remove all their clothing in order to "testify in the sight of the Lord." In a very few instances disciples of Fox seem to have taken part in such performances, but so little care was taken to discriminate that Quakers had to bear the odium of the whole. They were regarded as a set of ignorant and lawless fanatics, like John of Leyden and the Anabaptists of Münster ; and until the truth about them came to be better understood, the general feeling toward them was one of horror and dread.

Under these circumstances it was impossible for Quakers to avoid persecution had they wished to avoid it. But, on the contrary, they courted it. It was their business to reform the whole of Christendom, not to gather themselves into some quiet corner where they might worship unmolested. They were inspired by an aggressive missionary zeal which was apt to lead them where their company was not wanted, and so it happened in the case of Massachusetts.

Missionary zeal of the Quakers

The ideal of the Quakers was flatly antagonistic to that of the settlers of Massachusetts. The Christianity of the former was freed from Judaism as far as was possible; the Christianity of the latter was heavily encumbered with Judaism. The Quaker aimed at complete separation between church and state ; the government of Massachusetts was patterned after the ancient Jewish theocracy, in which church and state were identified. The Quaker was tolerant of differences in doctrine ; the Calvinist regarded such tolerance as a deadly sin. For these reasons the arrival of a few Quakers in Boston in 1656 was considered an act of invasion and treated as such. Under various penalties Quakers were forbidden to enter any of the New England colonies except Rhode Island. There they were welcomed, but that did not content them. The penalties against them were heaviest in Massachusetts, and thither they turned their chief attention. They came not to minister unto sound Rhode Island, but unto sick Massachusetts. The Puritan theocracy was their man of sin. They made up their minds to overthrow it, and they succeeded, because the party of the unenfranchised people in Boston were largely in sympathy with them. The furious scene in the council-room, when the venerable Endicott smote upon the table and threatened to go and end his days in England, marked the downfall of the theocratic ideal. Henceforth there was to be room for heretics in Massachusetts. The lesson has since been well improved, and all that now remains is to set up, on Boston Common, the scene of their martyrdom, a fitting monument to the heroes that won the victory.

The accession of Charles II. is commonly cited as the cause of this victory of the Quakers in Boston; but there can be no doubt that the chief cause was the disagreement between the people of Boston and their theocratic government, and the moment when it proved impossible to execute the sentence upon Wenlock Christison, the battle was virtually decided. As for Charles II., we shall see how his policy led him more and more to extend his favour to Quakers. At first their refusal to take the oath

Charles II. and the oath of allegiance

of allegiance cost them dear ; for many people, unable to understand their scruples, could not see in such contumacy anything but an evidence of disloyalty. Many were sent to Barbadoes and Jamaica, where they were sold into temporary slavery, like that of the white servants in Virginia. In 1662 they were forbidden to hold meetings, and their meeting-houses were closed by the police.

It is at about this time that William Penn may be said to have made his first appearance in history. He was born in London in 1644. His father, Sir William Penn, was a distinguished admiral in the navy of the Commonwealth, but afterward became a warm friend of Charles II. His mother was a Dutch lady, Margaret Jasper, daughter of a wealthy merchant of Rotterdam,— a fact which was probably of importance in view of Penn's future social relations and connections

Early years of William Penn

upon the continent of Europe. As a child Penn was educated at Chigwell, where dwelt the eccentric John Saltmarsh, whose book entitled " Sparkles of Glory " is one of the most remarkable productions of English mysticism, and in some places reads like a foreshadowing or prophecy of Penn's own ideas. It is not unlikely that Saltmarsh's book may have suggested to Penn the memorable experience which he had at the age of eleven. One day when alone in his chamber " he was suddenly surprised with an inward comfort; and, as he thought, an external glory in the room, which gave rise to religious emotions, during which he had the strongest conviction of the being of a God, and that the soul of man was capable of enjoying communication with Him. He believed also that the seal of Divinity had been put upon him at this moment, and that he had been awakened or called upon to a holy life." [1] From that time forth he felt that he had a mission in the world. After the Chigwell school, he studied with a private tutor on Tower Hill, until he was sixteen, when he saw the formal entry of Charles II. into the city across London Bridge. Admiral Penn was that year elected to Parliament, and William was matriculated at Christ Church, Oxford, where he remained two years. There he acquired a high reputation as a scholar and as an athlete, enthusiastic in field sports, a good oarsman, and a lover of Greek. Among the languages which he could speak fluently were Latin, Italian, French, German, and Dutch. At Oxford, along with sundry other students, he became converted to

[1] Stoughton's *Penn*, p. 8.

Quakerism, refused to wear surplices, forsook chapel worship, and got into trouble. There is a story that he was expelled from the college, but it is not well supported, and it seems more likely that his father took him away. He was then sent with some fashionable friends to Paris, in the hope of curing him of his Quaker notions. He was in his nineteenth year, tall, lithe, and strongly built, a picture of manly beauty, with great lustrous eyes under wide arching brows, a profusion of dark hair falling in curls upon his shoulders, a powerful chin, a refined and sensitive mouth. He seems to have been a skilful swordsman, for when attacked one evening on the street by a desperado who threatened his life, Penn overcame and disarmed the wretch without wounding him. He spent a year or more in hard study at the Huguenot college in Saumur, and then travelled for a year in Italy. After that he studied law at Lincoln's Inn, and presently visited Ireland, where he was thrown into prison for attending a Quaker meeting at Cork.

His conversion to Quakerism

Sir William Penn, who was a good churchman, was shocked and disgusted at the sort of reputation his son was earning, and we get glimpses of contention in the household. "You may *thee* and *thou* other folk as much as you like," quoth the angry father, "but don't you dare to *thee* and *thou* the king, or the Duke of

York, or me." [1] Young William did dare, however, even so far as to wear his hat in the royal
presence, which only amused the merry Trouble at
monarch. One day when William home
met him, the king took off his hat. "Why
dost thou remove thy hat, friend Charles?"
quoth the young man. "Because," said the
king, "wherever I am, it is customary for only
one to remain covered!" But the admiral did
not take it so pleasantly; he threatened to turn
his obstinate son out of doors without a shilling.
Lady Penn implored, and one of the family
friends, a nobleman of the court, insisted that
Sir William ought to be proud of a son of such
varied accomplishments and lofty character, in
spite of a few eccentricities of demeanour. It is
sad to relate that the father's threat was carried
out; but it was only for a time. Admiration for
dauntless courage and high principle at length
prevailed with the old naval hero, and he called
his son home again and ever after held him in
reverence.

In 1670 the admiral died, commending William with his last breath to the especial care of
the Duke of York. William was left in possession of an ample fortune, and devoted himself
to writing and preaching in defence and explanation of Quakerism. His learning and eloquence,

---

[1] For the use of these pronouns in the seventeenth century,
see below, p. 147.

with a certain sobriety of mind that qualified
his mysticism, made many converts; nor is it
unlikely that his high social position
and gallant bearing were helpful to
the cause in some quarters. It was
largely due to Penn that current opinion gradually ceased to confound the disciples of Fox
with the rabble of Antinomian fanatics with
which England was then familiar, and to put
them upon a plane of respectability, by the side
of Presbyterians and other Dissenters. Again
and again, while engaged in this work, Penn was
thrown into prison and kept there for months,
sometimes in the Tower, like a gentleman, but
once for six months in noisome Newgate, along
with common criminals. These penalties were
mostly for breaking the Conventicle Act. The
reports of the trials are often very interesting,
by reason of the visible admiration felt by the
honest judges for the brilliant prisoner. " I
vow, Mr. Penn," quoth Sir John Robinson
from the bench one day, " I vow, Mr. Penn, I
am sorry for you. You are an ingenious gentleman — all the world must allow you, and do
allow you, that; and you have a plentiful estate :
why should you render yourself unhappy by
associating with such a simple people?" Sometimes the prisoner's ingenuity and resourceful-
ness would baffle the prosecutor, and in despair
of other means of catching him the magistrate

would tender the oath of allegiance. But Penn's subtlety was matched by his boldness: once when the judge insulted him by a remark derogatory to his character, the reply came quickly and sharply, " I trample thy slander as dirt under my feet ! " And this <small>His courage</small> boldness was equalled by his steadfastness : once the Bishop of London sent word to him in the Tower, that he must either withdraw certain statements or die a prisoner. " Thou mayest tell him," said Penn to the messenger, " that my prison shall be my grave before I will budge a jot, for I owe obedience of my conscience to no mortal man."

During these years Penn kept publishing books and pamphlets, controversial or expository, wherein he argues and persuades with logic and with eloquence, and is not always meek ; sometimes the keen blade leaps from the scabbard and deals a mortal thrust. Mrs. Samuel Pepys read one of these treatises aloud to her husband, who calls it extremely well written and " a serious sort of book, not fit for every one to read." The titles of these books give an inkling of their savour : " Truth Exalted," " The Guide Mistaken," " A Seasonable Caveat against Popery," etc. The one which <small>Some of</small> Mr. Pepys would not recommend to <small>his writings</small> all readers was entitled " The Sandy Foundation Shaken," which was clearly open to the charge of Socinianism. Grave accusations of heresies were brought against Penn, to which he made reply in his " Innocency with her Open Face," some quotations from which will give us an impression of his style : —

" It may not be unreasonable to observe, that however industrious some (and those dissenters too) have been to represent me as a person disturbing the civil peace, I have not violated any truly fundamental law which relates to external propriety and good behaviour, and not to religious apprehensions; it being the constant principle of myself and friends to maintain good works and keep our consciences void of offence, paying active or passive obedience, suitable to If you will the meek example of our Lord Jesus not talk with me, I Christ. Nor would I have any ignomust write rant how forward I was by messages, letters, and visits, to have determined this debate in a sober and select assembly, notwithstanding the rude entertainment we had met with before ; but contrary to their own appointments our adversaries failed us, which necessitated me to that defence ;[1] and finding the truth so prest with

[1] A discussion in a Presbyterian meeting-house in London, between Penn with some friends and the Presbyterian minister, Thomas Vincent, had ended in an attempt to silence the Quakers by uproar. Penn persisted even after the lights were put out, but then yielded to Vincent's promise to meet him again in a fair and open discussion. It proved impossible,

slander, I cannot but say I saw my just call to her relief; but alas! how have those two or three extemporary sheets been tost, tumbled, and torn on all hands, yea, aggravated to a monstrous design, even the subversion of the Christian religion, than which there could be nothing more repugnant to my principle and purpose; wherefore how very intemperate have all my adversaries been in their revilings, slanders, and defamations! using the most opprobrious terms of seducer, heretic, blasphemer, deceiver, Socinian, Pelagian, Simon Magus, impiously robbing Christ of his divinity, for whom the vengeance of the great day is reserved, etc. Nor have these things been whispered, but in one book and pulpit after another have been thundered out against me, as if some bull had lately been arrived from Rome; and all this acted under the foul pretence of zeal and love to Jesus Christ, whose meek and gentle example always taught it for a principal mark of true Christianity to suffer the most outrageous injuries, but never to return any. . . . Tell me, I pray, did Luther, that grand reformer whom you so much reverence, justly demand from the emperor at the Diet of Worms . . . that none should sit upon his doctrines but

You call names at me instead of using argument

however, to make Vincent keep his promise, and so Penn had recourse to the press, and published his *The Sandy Foundation Shaken.* See Stoughton's *William Penn*, p. 57.

the scripture ; and in case they should be cast, that no other sentence should be passed upon him than what Gamaliel offered to the Jewish council, If it were not of God it would not stand ; and if you will not censure him who first arraigned the Christian world (so called) at the bar of his private judgment (that had so many hundred years soundly slept, without so much as giving one considerable shrug or turn during that tedious winter-night of dark apostasy), but justify his proceedings, can you so furiously assault others ?

If you do not blame Luther for asserting the right of private judgment, why blame me ?

" But above all you, who refuse conformity to others, and that have been writing these eight years for liberty of conscience, . . . what pregnant testimonies do you give of your unwillingness to grant that to others you so earnestly beg for yourselves ? Doth it not discover your injustice, and plainly express that only want of power hinders you to act ? But of all Protestants in general I demand, do you believe that persecution to be Christian in yourselves that you condemned for antichristian in the Papists ? You judged it a weakness in their religion, and is it a cogent argument in yours ? Nay, is it not the readiest way to enhance and propagate the reputation of what you would depress ? If you were displeased at their assum-

When you persecute others, you assume your own infallibility, as much as the Papists do

ing an infallibility, will you believe it impossible in yourselves to err? Have Whitaker, Reynolds, Laud, Owen, Baxter, Stillingfleet, Poole, etc., disarmed the Romanists of these inhuman weapons, that you might employ them against your inoffensive countrymen? Let the example and holy precepts of Christ dissuade you, who came not to destroy but save; and soberly reflect upon his equal law of doing as you would be done unto. . . . Have a care you are not upon one of Saul's errands to Damascus, and helping the mighty against God and his anointed; and rather choose by fair and moderate debates, not penalties ratified by imperial decrees, to determine religious differences. . . . But if you are resolved severity shall take its course, *But you cannot hurt us, for if God is with us, who can be against us?* in this our case can never change nor happiness abate; for no human edict can possibly deprive us of His glorious presence, who is able to make the dismallest prisons so many receptacles of pleasure, and whose heavenly fellowship doth unspeakably replenish our solitary souls with divine consolation." [1]

It is interesting to see how Penn's argument partly anticipates that of John Stuart Mill, in his famous " Essay on Liberty." The extent to which the sense of an ever present God replenished his soul with divine consolation is shown

[1] Penn's *Select Works*, London, 1825, i. 163-165.

in one of his most important works, " No
Cross, no Crown," written in the Tower of

No Cross, London in the year 1668. It is as
no Crown beautiful as its title, albeit we must
make allowance for the peculiar prolixity which
English writers of the seventeenth century seldom succeeded in avoiding. In spite of this
drawback the book abounds in the eloquence
that wins the soul : —

"This made the prophet David say, 'The
King's daughter is all glorious within, her clothing is of wrought gold.' What is the glory that
is within the true church, and that gold that
makes up that inward glory? Tell me, O super-
stitious man! is it thy stately temples, altars,
carpets, tables, tapestries; thy vestments, or-
gans, voices, candles, lamps, censers, plate, and
jewels, with the like furniture of thy worldly

Religion temples? No such matter ; they bear
thrives not
upon outward no proportion with the divine adorn-
show ment of the King of heaven's daughter, the blessed and redeemed church of Christ.
Miserable apostasy that it is ! and a wretched
supplement in the loss and absence of the apos-
tolic life, the spiritual glory of the primitive
church.

" But yet some of these admirers of external
pomp and glory in worship would be thought
lovers of the Cross, and to that end have made
to themselves many. But alas! what hopes can

there be of reconciling that to Christianity, that the nearer it comes to its resemblance, the farther off it is in reality ? . . . It is true, they have got a cross, but it seems to be in the room of the true one; and so mannerly, that it will do as they will have it that wear it; for instead of mortifying their wills by it, they make it and use it according to them; so that the cross is become their ensign that do nothing but what they list. Yet by that they would be thought his disciples, that never did his own will but the will of his heavenly Father.

It is but a false cross that comports with self-indulgence

"This is such a cross as flesh and blood can carry, for flesh and blood invented it; therefore not the cross of Christ that is to crucify flesh and blood. Thousands of them have no more virtue than a chip; poor empty shadows, not so much as images of the true one. Some carry them for charms about them, but never repel one evil with them. They sin with them upon their backs; and though they put them in their bosoms, their beloved lusts lie there too without the least disquiet. They are as dumb as Elijah's mock-gods; no life nor power in them (1 Kings xviii. 27). . . . Is it possible that such crosses should mend their makers? Surely not. . . .

Religion is not a fetich, but a discipline

"Nor is a recluse life (the boasted righteousness of some) much more commendable, or one

143

whit nearer to the nature of the true cross; for if it be not unlawful as other things are, it is unnatural, which true religion teaches not. The Christian convent and monastery are within, where the soul is encloistered from sin. And this religious house the true followers of Christ carry about with them, who exempt not them- Better resist temptation than flee from it selves from the conversation of the world, though they keep themselves from the evil of the world in their conversation. That is a lazy, rusty, unprofitable self-denial, burdensome to others to feed their idleness; religious bedlams, where people are kept up lest they should do mischief abroad. . . . No thanks if they commit not what they are not tempted to commit. What the eye views not, the heart craves not, as well as rues not. The cross of Christ is of another nature; it truly overcomes the world, and leads a life of purity in the face of its allurements. They that bear it are not thus chained up for fear they should bite, nor locked up lest they should be stole away; no, they receive power from Christ their captain, to resist the evil and do that which is good in the sight of God. . . . What a world should we have if everybody, for fear of transgressing, should mew himself up within four walls ! . . .

"Not that I would be thought to slight a true retirement; for I do not only acknowledge but admire solitude. Christ himself was

144

an example of it; he loved and chose to frequent mountains, gardens, seasides. They are requisite to the growth of piety; and I reverence the virtue that seeks and uses The wholesomeness of solitude it, wishing there were more of it in the world; but then it should be free, not constrained. What benefit to the mind to have it for a punishment, not for a pleasure? Nay, I have long thought it an error among all sorts that use not monastic lives, that they have no retreats for the afflicted, the tempted, the solitary, and the devout;[1] where they might undisturbedly wait upon God, pass through their religious exercises, and being thereby strengthened may with more power over their own spirits enter into the business of the world again; though the less the better, to be sure. For divine pleasures are to be found in a free solitude."[2]

From such sweet reflections we come now and then upon quaint arguments in justification of sundry peculiarities of the Friends, as for example their plainness of attire: "Were it possible that any one could bring us father Adam's girdle and mother Eve's apron, what laughing, what fleering, what mocking of their

[1] It was such a want that the noble and saintlike Nicholas Ferrar sought to satisfy in his Protestant monastery of Little Gidding. See my *Old Virginia and Her Neighbours*, i. 241.

[2] Penn's *Select Works*, i. 368–371.

homely fashion would there be! surely their
tailor would find but little custom, although we
read it was God himself that made them coats
of skins. . . . How many pieces of ribband,
and what feathers, lace-bands, and the like, did
Adam and Eve wear in Paradise or out of it?
What rich embroideries, silks, points, etc. had
Abel, Enoch, Noah, and good old Abraham?
Did Eve, Sarah, Susannah, Elizabeth, and the
Virgin Mary use to curl, powder, patch, paint,
wear false locks of strange colours,
rich points, trimmings, laced gowns,
embroidered petticoats, shoes with slipslaps
laced with silk or silver lace and ruffled like
pigeons' feet, with several yards of ribbands?
How many plays did Jesus Christ and the
apostles recreate themselves at? What poets,
romances, comedies, and the like did the apostles and saints use to pass away their time
withal? . . . But if I were asked, whence came
them [these follies]; I would quickly answer,
from the Gentiles that knew not God, . . . an
effeminate Sardanapalus, . . . a comical Aris-
tophanes, a prodigal Charaxus, a luxurious Aris-
tippus . . . [from] such women as the infa-
mous Clytemnestra, the painted Jezebel, the
lascivious Campaspe, the most immodest Post-
humia, the costly Corinthian Lais, the impudent
Flora, the wanton Egyptian Cleopatra, and most
insatiable Messalina; persons whose memories

The follies of fashion

146

have stunk through all ages and carry with them a perpetual rot. These and not the holy self-denying men and women in ancient times were devoted to the like recreations and vain delights." [1]

Or, as concerns the use of "thou" and "thee" for "you," the modern reader needs to be reminded of the English usage in Penn's time, which made the Quaker innovation seem especially heinous. The usage in English was like that in French to-day, and analogous to the German, Italian, and Spanish usage. The singular pronoun was reserved for solemn invocations to the Deity, or for familiar intercourse with the members of one's family, including the servants; for addressing parents, how- "Thee" ever (especially the father), or social and "thou" superiors or equals outside the circle of familiarity, the plural was necessary. The rule was much like that which governs the use of the Christian name to-day; you may call your wife, or sister, or brother, or children, or the housemaid, by the forename; but to address father or mother in that way is felt to be disrespectful, and to address a lady so, unless she is an intimate acquaintance, is an unwarrantable liberty. In the seventeenth century, to "thou" (French *tutoyer*) a lady was as rude as to call her Lizzie or Jane; to "thou" one's father was much like

[1] Penn's *Select Works*, i. 482.

147

addressing him as Tom or Jack. Probably few things did so much to make the Quakers shock people's sense of the proprieties as their use of the pronouns, which was in later days imitated by the Jacobins of the French Revolution. "There is another piece of our non-conformity to the world, that renders us [*i. e.* makes us seem] very clownish to the breeding of it, and that is, Thou for You, and that without difference or respect to persons; a thing that to some looks so rude, it cannot well go down without derision or wrath." Nevertheless, says Penn, we Friends have good reasons and high authorities on our side. "Luther, the great reformer, was so far from condemning our plain speech that in his 'Ludus' he sports himself with You to a single person as an incongruous and ridiculous speech, viz. *Magister, vos estis iratus?* 'Master, are You angry?' as absurd with him in Latin as 'My masters, art Thou angry?' is in English. Erasmus, a learned man and an exact critic in speech, not only derides it, but bestows a whole discourse upon rendering it absurd; plainly manifesting . . . that the original of this corruption was the corruption of flattery. Lipsius affirms of the ancient Romans, that the manner of greeting now in vogue was not in use among them. . . . Is it not as proper to say, 'Thou lovest,' to ten men, as to say, 'You love,' to one man? . . . Is it reasonable that

148

children should be whipt at school for putting
You for Thou, as having made false Latin; and
yet that we must be (though not whipt) re-
proached, and often abused, when we use the
contrary propriety of speech? . . . It cannot
be denied that the most famous poems, dedi-
cated to love or majesty, are written in this
style [*i. e.* with Thou]. Read of each in Chau-
cer, Spenser, Waller, Cowley, Dryden, etc.
Why then should it be so homely, ill bred, and
insufferable in us? This, I conceive, can never
be answered. . . . [The other style] was first
ascribed in way of flattery to proud popes and
emperors, imitating the heathen's vain homage
to their gods; . . . for which reason, You, only
to be used to many, became first spoken to one.
It seems the word Thou looked like
too lean and thin a respect; and therefore some, bigger than they should be,
would have a style suitable to their
own ambition. . . . It is a most ex-
travagant piece of pride in a mortal man to require or expect from his fellow-creature a more
civil speech . . . than he is wont to give the
immortal God his Creator, in all his worship to
him. . . . Say not, I am serious about slight
things; but beware you of levity and rashness
in serious things. . . . But I would not have
thee think it is a mere Thou or Title, simply
or nakedly in themselves, we boggle at, or that

The use of
"you" in
place of
"thou" is
undemo-
cratic

we would beget or set up any form inconsistent with severity or true civility ; . . . but the esteem and value the vain minds of men do put upon them constrains us to testify so steadily against them." [1]

Other things in Penn's career beside the free circulation of his heretical books occur to remind us that in the England of Charles II., in spite of grave shortcomings, we are in a free country. Attacks upon liberty are made in courts of justice, but are apt to fail of success. Such a damnable iniquity as the Dreyfus case, which has made every true lover of France put on mourning, shows us that the Paris of Zola still has lessons of vital importance to learn from the London of Congreve and Aphra Behn. In 1670 Penn was arraigned before the Lord Mayor's court for infringing the Conventicle Act and provoking a riot by speaking in Gracechurch Street to an unlawful assembly. He argued his own case, and proved much more than a match for the recorder. The twelve jurors failed to agree, and were sent out again and again after a scolding from the Court. At length they brought in the verdict, " Guilty of speaking in Gracechurch Street," but this was not enough. So they were locked up for the night " without meat, drink, fire, or tobacco,"

Memorable scene in the Lord Mayor's court, 1670

1 Penn's *Select Works*, i. 421–428.

and next morning the question was put to them, "Guilty, or not guilty?" The foreman replied, "Guilty of speaking in Gracechurch Street," and stopped, whereupon the Lord Mayor added, "to an unlawful assembly." "No, my lord," said the foreman, "we give no other verdict than we gave last night." So these brave men were scolded again, locked up again for several hours, and again brought into court, but their spirit was not quelled. "Is William Penn, the prisoner, guilty or not guilty?" asked the mayor. "Not guilty, my lord." Then the mayor, quite beside himself with rage, proceeded to fine each of the jurors in a sum equivalent to about $30, with jail until it should be paid. "What is all this for?" exclaimed Penn. "For contempt of court," quoth the Lord Mayor. But his was not the last word on the subject. The case was taken to the Court of Common Pleas, which summarily quashed the mayor's order and set free the sturdy jurors. Thus justice triumphed, and Penn straightway published his own account of the affair, in a pamphlet entitled, "The People's Ancient and Just Liberties Asserted." [1]

[1] Penn's *Select Works*, i. 179–223. At one point in the trial, the recorder, John Howell, exclaimed: "Till now I never understood the reason of the policy and prudence of the Spaniards in suffering the Inquisition among them. And

In 1672 Penn was married to Gulielma Ma-
ria, daughter of Sir William Springett, a noted
officer of the Parliamentary army who had lost
Penn's mar- his life in the Civil War. This lady
riage, and was celebrated for beauty, wit, and
charming
home accomplishments, and had withal a
handsome estate at Worminghurst, in Sussex,
overlooking the beautiful South Downs. There
all the things that make life delightful seemed
to be combined, — books and flowers, cultivated friends, the supreme restfulness of rural
England with its tempered sunshine, its gentle
showers, and the tonic fragrance of the salt
sea. In this blest retreat Penn spent his hap-
piest days, but he was often called upon to
leave it. One of his first visitors was his friend
George Fox, who had lately returned from a
journey through the American colonies, and
had much to tell. The time had arrived when
matters of business were to turn Penn's attention decisively toward America, but while these
matters of business were taking shape he visited Holland and travelled in the lower parts
of Germany with a party of friends, holding
His mission- meetings at all times and places, here
ary tour in and there meeting with rebuffs and
Germany insults, but finding many spirits to
whom his words were an inspiration and a sol-

certainly it will never be well with us, till something like the
Spanish inquisition be in England." *Id.* p. 194.

ace. There can be no doubt that this journey
had far-reaching results in afterward turning
the attention of Germany towards Penn's col-
onizing work in America. Penn afterward
published a diary of this missionary tour.[1] A
general outline of the route and a few of the
interesting scenes must suffice for the present
narrative.

Leaving his wife at the beautiful Sussex
home, Penn sailed for Rotterdam on a July
of 1677. Among his companions were
rge Fox, Robert Barclay, and George Keith,
at Rotterdam they held a great meeting
house of Benjamin Furly, with such
says Penn, that "the dead were raised
living comforted." With similar suc-
visited Leyden, Haarlem, and Am-
There the party left Fox behind,
accompanied them into Hanover.
ng with "the man of the inn" at
nd leaving with him "several good
ends, in the Low and High Dutch
ad and dispose of," the mission-
d next day to Her- Princess
phalia, where Eliza- Elizabeth
ncess Palatine, had her court.
eth, sister of Prince Rupert, cousin
II., and aunt to the German prince
ward became George I. of England,
contained in his *Select Works*, ii. 398–503.

was a woman of liberal and cultivated mind. It
may have been from her grandfather, James I.,
that she inherited her bookish proclivities. She
had received lessons in philosophy from the
immortal Descartes, who was reported to have
said that he " found none except her who thor
oughly understood his works." She had for
time given protection to Jean de Labadie, an
now she cordially welcomed Penn and his com
panions. After a pleasant day with the Pri
cess Elizabeth and her friend, Anna Ma
Countess of Hornes, the party were inv
to return next morning and continue
conference upon sacred themes. So " th
morning we were there between eig
nine; where Robert Barclay falling in
discourse with the princess, the coun
hold of the opportunity, and whispe

Penn withdraw, to get a meeti
preaches to more inferior servants of
the servants who would have been ba

presented themselves before the p
blessed be the Lord, he was n
us; but the same blessed pow
peared to visit them of high,
visit them of low degree; and
sweetly tendered and broken toge
tue went forth of Jesus that day, a
of our God was shed abroad among
sweet savour, for which their souls be

154

fore the Lord and confessed to our testimony.
Which did not a little please that noble young
woman, to find her own report of us, and her
great care of them, so effectually answered.
. . . I must not here forget that we found at
our inn, the first night at supper, a young
merchant, of a sweet and ingenuous   A merchant
temper, belonging to the city of Bre-   of Bremen
men, who took occasion from that night's discourse, the sixth day at dinner and supper, and
the seventh day also, to seek all opportunities
of conference with us; and, as we have reason to believe, he stayed twenty-four hours in
[Herwerden] on our account. . . . We asked
him, in case any of us should visit [Bremen],
if he would give us the opportunity of a meeting at his house; which he readily granted us.
So we gave him some books, etc. . . . It being
now three in the afternoon, we went to the princess's; where being come, after some little time,
the princess and countess put me in remembrance of a promise I made them in one of my
letters out of England, namely, that I would
give them an account (at some con-   Penn tells
venient time) of my first convince-   the ladies
                                       of his con-
ment, and of those tribulations and   version
consolations which I had met withal in this
way of the kingdom which God had brought
me to. After some pause I found myself very
free, and prepared in the Lord's love and fear

155

to comply with their request; and so, after some silence, began. But before I had half done it was supper time, and the princess would by no means let us go, we must sup with her; which importunity not being well able to avoid, we yielded to, and sat down with her to supper.

"Among the rest present at these opportunities, it must not be forgotten that there was a countess, sister to the countess, then come in to visit her, and a Frenchwoman of quality; the first behaving herself very decently and the last often deeply broken; and from a light and slighting carriage toward the very name of a Quaker, she became very intimately and respectfully kind and respectful to us. Supper being ended, we all returned to the princess's chamber; where making us all to sit down with her, she with both the countesses and the Frenchwoman pressed from me the continuance of my relation; . . . which, though late, I was not unwilling to oblige them with, because I knew not when the Lord would give me such an opportunity."

The ladies listened "with an earnest and tender attention," and afterwards a meeting was appointed for the next day, Sunday, at two o'clock, in Princess Elizabeth's palace; and so toward midnight the evening came to an end. The next day, at the inn dinner, "there were several strangers that came by the post-wagon, among whom there was a young man of Bremen, being a student at the college at Duysburgh, who informed us of a sober and seeking man of great note in the city of Duysburgh. To him we gave some books. . . . The second hour being at hand we went to the meeting; where were several as well of the town A meeting at as of the family. The meeting began the palace with a weighty exercise and travail in prayer, that the Lord would glorify his own name that day. And by his own power he made way to their consciences and sounded his wakening trumpet in their ears, that they might know that he was God, and that there is none like unto him. O, the day of the Lord livingly dawned upon us, and the searching life of Jesus was in the midst of us! O, the Word, that never faileth them that wait for it and abide in it, opened the way and unsealed the book of life. Yea, the quickening power and life of Jesus wrought and reached to them; and virtue from him, in whom dwelleth the Godhead bodily, went forth and blessedly distilled upon us his own heavenly life, sweeter than the pure frankincense; yea, than the sweet-smelling myrrh that cometh from a far country. . . . As soon as the meeting was done the princess came to me and took me by the hand (which she usually did to us all, coming and going) and went to speak to me of the sense she had of that power and presence of God that was amongst us, but was stopped. Emotion of the princess And turning herself to the window brake forth in an extraordinary fashion, crying out, ' I cannot speak to you; my heart is full;' clapping her hands upon her breast.

" It melted me into a deep and calm tenderness, in which I was moved to minister a few words softly to her, and after some time of silence she recovered herself, and as I was taking leave of her, she interrupted me thus : ' Will ye not come hither again ? Pray call here as ye return out of Germany.' I told her, we were in Penn takes leave the hand of the Lord, and being his, could not dispose of ourselves ; but the Lord had taken care that we should not forget her and those with her."[1]

From Herwerden our friends proceeded to Paderborn, "a dark popish town, and under the government of a bishop of that religion." Thence in floods of rain, with " only naked carts to ride in," to Hesse-Cassel, and thence to Frankfort and its neighbourhood Frankfort. At every place they made converts ; at Frankfort " a Lutheran minister was broken to pieces," " a doctor of physic was affected and confessed to the truth." These things happened in the parlour of a young maiden lady, who declared herself ready to go to prison, if need be, for har-

[1] Penn's *Select Works*, ii. 414–418.

which was only covered with an old ragged sheet. The company we had with us made twelve in number, which much straitened us. They were often if not always vain; yea, in their religious songs, which is the fashion of that country, especially by night. They call them Luther's songs, and sometimes psalms. We were forced often to reprove and testify against their hypocrisy, — to be full of all vain and often profane talk one hour, and sing psalms to God the next; we showed them the deceit and abomination of it. . . . All was very well; they bore what we said."

Fellow-travellers rebuked

From Wesel through the Netherlands the journey was brief, and at the end of October, after an absence of three months, Penn arrived at Worminghurst, and found wife, child, and family all well. " I had that evening a sweet meeting amongst them, in which God's blessed power made us truly glad together."

At home once more

A charming picture is this of the highly gifted young man, with his noble face, commanding presence, and magnetic demeanour, going about to win souls to a higher life. It was because they felt the divine authority in the nature of his utterances that his hearers were so "broken" and contrite. It was a renewal of Christ's teaching that religion is an affair of the inner soul and not of externals; and there can be little doubt that the Christian ideal has been, on the whole, more perfectly realized among the Quakers than with any other sect of Christians.

The importance of this journey in relation to the European peopling of the middle zone of the United States is obvious. It made Penn and his ideas familiarly known to many excellent men and women in Germany, persons of character and influence. At the time when he made the journey his American schemes were rapidly developing. We have now to observe the manner in which his attention was directed to the New World.

Historic significance of the journey

It will be remembered that in 1673 Lord Berkeley sold his half share in the province of New Jersey to a Quaker, John Fenwick, in trust for another Quaker, Edward Byllinge. Fenwick, who is described as a "litigious and troublesome person," soon got into a quarrel with Byllinge, and the affair was referred to William Penn as arbitrator. He adjudged one tenth of the Berkeley purchase to Friend Fenwick, along with a certain sum of money, and directed him to hand over the other nine tenths to Friend Byllinge. At first Fenwick was sorely dissatisfied with the award, and refused to abide by it, whereat he was gravely rebuked by Penn.

Penn becomes interested in West Jersey

162

Meanwhile Byllinge became insolvent. Presently Fenwick yielded, and made over nine tenths of the property to William Penn, Gawaine Laurie, and Nicholas Lucas, as trustees for the benefit of Byllinge's creditors. In 1675 Fenwick sailed for the Delaware River with a party of colonists, and landed at the mouth of a small stream which the Dutch had called by the unromantic name of Varkenskill, or " Hog's Creek," hard by the Swedish settlement of Elsingburgh. There he laid out a town and called it Salem. These proceedings aroused the ire of Andros, who demanded by what authority was Fenwick taking on airs of proprietorship within the Duke of York's dominions. Not getting a satisfactory reply, Andros summoned Fenwick to New York, and when he refused to come the summons was followed by an officer who seized the obstinate Quaker and carried him off to Fort James.

Salem founded by Fenwick

Meanwhile an important question was settled between the proprietors in England. The joint proprietorship of New Jersey between Carteret and Berkeley had passed almost unconsciously into two proprietorships of East and West Jersey in severalty ; and the boundary between the two had been declared to be a straight line running from Barnegat to Rankokus Creek. This was felt to be

The lines between East and West Jersey

163

an inequitable division, and in 1676 the matter was readjusted by what was known as the Quintipartite Deed, between Sir George Carteret on the one hand, and Penn, Laurie, Lucas, and Byllinge on the other. By this instrument it was agreed that the boundary between East and West Jersey should be a straight line running from Little Egg Harbour to the northernmost branch of the Delaware River in latitude 41° 40'.

In the summer of 1677 the good ship Kent, Gregory Marlow, master, dropped down the Thames with 230 passengers bound

Quakers go
to West
Jersey

for West Jersey, including a small board of commissioners for organizing a government for that province. As they were gliding down-stream, King Charles in his pleasure barge came alongside and asked whither they were bound. Hearing the name West Jersey, he asked if they were all Quakers, and gave them his royal blessing. On arriving at Sandy Hook the Kent dropped anchor while the commissioners went up to New York to pay their respects to Andros. The governor received them politely, but was particular to ask "if they had anything from the duke, his master? They replied, nothing particularly; but that he had conveyed that part of his country to Lord Berkeley, and he to Byllinge, etc., in which the government was as much conveyed

164

as the soil. The governor replied : 'All that will not clear me. If I should surrender without the duke's order, it is as much as my head is worth ; but if you had but a line or two from the duke, I should be as ready to surrender it to you as you would be to ask it.' Upon which the commissioners, instead of excusing their imprudence in not bringing such an order, began to insist upon their right and strenuously to assert their independency. But Andros, clapping his hand on his sword, told them that he should defend the government [of West Jersey] from them till he received orders from the duke to surrender it. He, however, softened and told them he would do what was in his power to make them easy till they could send home to get redress ; and in order thereto, would commissionate the same persons mentioned in the commission they produced. This they accepted, and undertook to act as magistrates under him till further orders came from England, and to proceed in relation to their land affairs according to the methods prescribed by the proprietors." [1]

Peremptory demeanour of Andros

This incident throws a strong sidelight upon the behaviour of Andros toward Philip Carteret. Neither personal friendship nor any other consideration could avail against his mastiff-like

[1] Smith's *History of Nova Cæsarea, or New Jersey*, Burlington, 1765, pp. 93, 94.

fidelity to his master. By their well-timed pliancy Penn's commissioners probably saved themselves from forcible detention in Fort James. After coming to terms with the governor of New York, the immigrants went on to the Delaware River and proceeded far up-
Founding of stream, above the Rankokus Creek,
Burlington as if it were part of their purpose to assert ownership of what had once belonged to East Jersey. Here they founded a village which they called Burlington, after the town in Yorkshire whence a goodly number of them came. Andros now, having sufficiently carried his point, released Fenwick.

A letter from one of the settlers, Thomas Hooton, to his wife in England, dated October 29, 1677, is full of interest: " My Dear, — I am this present at the town called Burlington, where our land is; it is ordered to be a town for the ten Yorkshire and ten London proprietors. I like the place well; our lot is the second
Hooton's next the water side. It's like to be
letter a healthful place and very pleasant to live in. I came hither yesterday with some friends that were going to New York. I am to be at Thomas Olive's house till I can provide better for myself. I intend to build a house and get some corn into the ground; and I know not how to write concerning thy coming or not coming hither. The place I like very well, and

166

believe that we may live here very well. But if it be not made free, I mean as to the customs and government, then it will not be so well, and may hinder many that have desires to come. But if those two things be cleared, thou may take thy opportunity of coming this [*i. e.* next?] summer."

The two things that thus needed clearing up were surely of supreme importance to the colonists. In sending them to New Jersey, Penn and his colleagues supposed they were founding a self-governing community. Penn had drawn up a constitution for it, providing that " no man was to have power over another man's conscience. A governing assembly was to be chosen by ballot; every man was eligible to vote, and to be voted for; each elected member was to receive a shilling a day as the servant of the people. Executive power was to be in the hands of ten commissioners appointed by the assembly; and justices and constables were to be elected by popular vote; and it is added, ' All, and every person in the province, shall by the help of the Lord and these fundamentals be free from oppression and slavery.'" Here we have democracy in quite modern shape, containing some of the features which are now found to be objectionable (such as an elective judiciary), as well as those which time and experience have

A democratic constitution

approved. A friendly message, commenting on the above provisions, exclaimed, "We lay a foundation for after ages to understand their liberty as Christians and as men, that they may not be brought into bondage but by their own consent, for we put the power in the people." [1] Our worthy Quakers did not foresee the day New phases when the people, lured by the bait of of tyranny high tariffs and the "spoils of office," would consent to be brought into bondage under petty tyrants as cheap and vile as ever cumbered the earth. They would have been sorely astonished if told that nowhere could be seen a more flagrant spectacle of such humiliating bondage than in the great commonwealth which bears Penn's name.

Now according to the claim which Andros asserted for the Duke of York, these Quakers were merely landowners in New Jersey under Andros the sovereign jurisdiction of New claims West York; their taxes were to be levied Jersey for the Duke not by their own representative asof York sembly, but by the despotic governor of New York; and at Newcastle on the Delaware there was a custom-house, where goods imported into West Jersey had to pay duties into the New York treasury. Under such circumstances, no wonder that some of the settlers felt dubious about staying and bringing over

[1] Stoughton's *William Penn*, p. 119.

their wives and children. Nevertheless, people kept on coming and agitating, and as the population grew the question was more and more warmly discussed.

In 1679 there was a strong anti-Catholic excitement in England, due largely to Titus Oates and his alleged detection of a Popish plot in the previous year. The horrors in Scotland and the defeat of Claverhouse by the Covenanters at Drumclog also produced a great effect; and amid it all the friends of the Habeas Corpus Act, led by the Earl of Shaftesbury, wrenched from the king his signature to that famous measure. The Duke of York, as a Romanist, was threatened with exclusion from the throne, and so strong was the feeling against him that he deemed it prudent for a time to leave the country. During his absence the West Jersey question was discussed. Penn argued that Berkeley's conveyance expressly included powers of government along with territorial possession, and that the Duke of York had no authority to levy duties on the

Penn's ingenious argument

colonists in West Jersey, or exclude them from their " English right of common assent to taxes ; " and then, skilfully alluding to " the duke's circumstances and the people's jealousies," it was suggested that since he had now an opportunity to free West Jersey with his own hand, " so will Englishmen here [in England]

169

know what to hope for, by the justice and kindness he shows to Englishmen there, and all men to see the just model of his government in New York to be the scheme and draft in little of his administration in Old England at large, if the crown should ever devolve upon his head."[1]

This argument was certainly defective in ignoring the legal facts attendant upon the loss and recovery of New Netherland in 1673–74, which should have made it plain that Penn and his friends could have no rights of sovereignty over West Jersey without an explicit release from the Duke of York.[2] Apparently their minds were not clear on this point; or perhaps they acted upon the maxim of worldly wisdom that it is just as well to begin by " claiming everything." The hope of Penn's subtle and weighty argument lay not so much in this preamble as in the suggestion of the duke's true interests. So the duke evidently understood it, Final release and in August, 1680, he executed a of the Jerseys deed whereby he released all his powers of sovereignty over West Jersey to Byllinge, Penn, and their colleagues. Two months later

[1] Brodhead's *History of the State of New York*, ii. 339 ; an excellent and scholarly work, though occasionally disfigured by a proneness to ascribe unworthy motives to New York's neighbours, whether in Massachusetts, or Connecticut, or Pennsylvania.

[2] See above, p. 42.

he released to the Carterets all his powers over
East Jersey, and due notification of these measures was sent to the peremptory Andros. Thus
were the Jerseys definitively set free from New
York.

In the course of these discussions Penn had
acquired a wide knowledge of American affairs,
and his mind was turned more and more to
thoughts of colonization. The new settlements
at Salem and Burlington were flourishing, and
in England there were thousands of industrious
and thrifty Quakers who would be likely to
flock to a new colony founded expressly in their
own behoof by their trusted leader. Penn's claim
Circumstances combined to favour against the
such a scheme. Penn inherited the Crown
claim to a debt of £16,000 due from the Crown
to his father, and there was no way in which
such a debt could more easily be paid than by
a grant of wild lands in America. Penn, as he
said of himself, was not destitute of " a moderate and seasonable regard " to worldly interests,
and he was shrewd enough to see that such an
American domain might prove to be better
property than the hard cash, even if he were
ever likely to get cash from the needy spend-
thrift who sat on the throne or the niggardly
brother who was expected to succeed him.
Uppermost in his mind, however, was the hope
of planting a free and self-governing commu-

nity wherein his own ideal of a civil polity might be realized. Irrespective of nationality, from the banks of the Rhine and Weser, or from those of the Thames and the Severn, he might draw people of various kinds and grades of free thinking, and deliver them from the The "holy vexations which pursued them in experiment" their old homes. The more he dwelt upon this scheme, the more it seemed to him "a holy experiment" which with God's help it was his duty to try. "The Lord is good to me," he wrote to a friend, "and the interest his truth has given me with his people may more than repay [this claim upon the crown]. For many are drawn forth to be concerned with me, and perhaps this way of satisfaction hath more the hand of God in it than a downright payment. . . . For the matters of liberty and privilege I purpose that which is extraordinary, and [to] leave myself and succession no power of doing mischief, that the will of one man may not hinder the good of a whole country."[1]

Penn's petition to the privy council asked for "a tract of land in America, lying north of Maryland, on the east bounded with Delaware River, on the west limited as Maryland, and northward to extend as far as plantable." The determining of these bounds was, as usual, attended with hard feelings and hard words. Lord Bal-

[1] Clarkson's *Life of Penn*, i. 288.

timore's charter fixed his northern boundary at the 40th parallel of latitude, which runs a little north of the site of Philadelphia. This latitude was marked by a fortress on the Susquehanna River, and when the Crown lawyers consulted with Baltimore's attorneys, they were told that all questions of encroachment would be avoided if the line were to be run just north of this fort, so as to leave Boundaries it on the Maryland side. Penn made no objection to this, but an inspection of maps soon showed that such a boundary would give his province inadequate access to the ocean. Of all the English colonies, his was the only one that had no seaboard, and he was eager to get an outlet at the head of Chesapeake Bay. His position as a royal favourite enabled him to push the whole line twenty miles to the south of the Susquehanna fort. But this fell short of attaining his object; so he persuaded the Duke of York to give him the land on the west shore of Delaware Bay which the Dutch had once taken from the Swedes. By further enlargement the area of this grant became that of the present state of Delaware, the whole of which was thus, in spite of vehement protest, carved out of the original Maryland.[1] Throughout the colonial period Delaware and Pennsylvania, though distinct provinces with separate legislative assem-

[1] See *Old Virginia and Her Neighbours*, ii. 168, 169.

The charter which made Penn lord proprietor of this goodly domain was drawn up by himself in imitation of the charter of Maryland, but differed from it in two very important particulars. Laws passed by the assembly of Maryland were valid as soon as confirmed by Lord Baltimore, and did not need even to be looked at by the king or his privy council; but the colonial enactments of Pennsylvania were re-

The charters of Pennsylvania and Maryland

quired to be sent to England for the royal approval. It was, moreover, expressly provided in the Maryland charter that the Crown should never impose any taxes within the limits of the province; and although nothing is said about the authority of Parliament in such matters, there is no doubt that the proviso was understood to mean that the right of taxing the colony was entirely disclaimed by the government in England. For the views of Charles I. were unquestionably identical with those of his father, who declared in 1624 that the government of colonies was the business of the king, and that Parliament

a hill or mountain in Wales and was generally called John Penmunnith, which in English is *John-on-the-Hilltop*. He removed from Wales into Ireland, where he acquired considerable property," and afterward removed to London. His Welsh nickname became abbreviated to John Penn, and in the new surroundings the old name Tudor was forgotten. See Watson's *Annals of Philadelphia*, i. 119. I relate the tradition for whatever it may be worth.

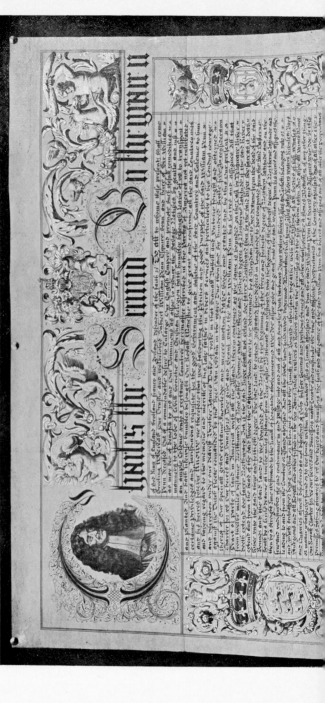

FACSIMILE OF THE PENNSYLVANIA CHARTER OF 1701

had nothing whatever to do with it.[1] But in the charter of Pennsylvania, half a century later than that of Maryland, the right of Parliament to levy taxes in the colony was expressly maintained. The younger colony was therefore less independent of the mother country than her elder sister, and the position of Penn was distinctly less regal than that of Baltimore.

This noticeable contrast marks the growth of the imperial and anti-feudal sentiment in England during those fifty years, the feeling that privileges like those accorded to the Calverts were too extensive to be enjoyed by subjects. It also marks the great decline in the royal power and the concomitant increase in the power and importance of Parliament. We see that august body putting forth claims to a voice in the imposition of American taxes, claims which the American colonies could never be brought to admit, but which were naturally resented and resisted with more alertness and decision by the older colonies than by the younger.

Significance of the contrast

The limitations in Penn's charter show also the influence of the conflict which had been going on for twenty years between Charles II. and the colony of Massachusetts. That stiff-necked Puritan commonwealth had coined money, set

Influence of the king's experience with Massachusetts

[1] See *Old Virginia and Her Neighbours,* i. 257.

the navigation acts at defiance, prohibited the Episcopal form of worship, snubbed the royal commissioners, and passed laws inconsistent with those of England. Hence in the Pennsylvania charter we see imperial claims more carefully guarded. Massachusetts, moreover, had neglected to appoint an agent or attorney to represent her interests at the English court, for, in the rebellious phrase of a later era, all she asked was to be let alone. Accordingly the Pennsylvania charter required that such an agent should be employed. The toleration of Episcopal forms of worship was also expressly provided for.

But in spite of these few limitations in the charter,[1] Penn was allowed the widest latitude in shaping the policy of his colony, and nothing could have been less like the principles of the Stuarts than the kind of civil government which Penn's humane and reasonable policy he forthwith proclaimed. Absolute freedom of conscience was guaranteed to everybody. It was declared, in language which to the seventeenth century seemed arrant political heresy, that governments exist for the sake of the people, and not the people for the sake of governments; and side by side with this came the equally novel doctrine that in legislating for the punishment of criminals, the

[1] These were probably added by Lord Chief Justice North, who revised the document.

reformation of the criminal is a worthier object than the wreaking of vengeance. The death penalty was to be inflicted only in cases of murder or high treason ; a notable departure from the customary legislation of those days. In Massachusetts, for example, there were fifteen capital crimes, including such offences as idolatry, witchcraft, blasphemy, adultery, bearing false witness, and cursing or smiting one's parents.[1] In such wise, with his humane and reasonable policy, did Penn seek to draw men to his new colony. To all who should come he offered land at forty shillings (equivalent to something between $40 and $50) for a hundred acres, subject to a quit-rent of one shilling a year.

In April, 1681, Penn sent his cousin, William Markham, to be deputy-governor of Pennsylvania, and with him a letter to the colonists already settled west of the Delaware River : " My Friends : I wish you all happiness, here and hereafter. These are to let you know that it hath pleased God, in his providence, to cast you within my lot and care. It is a business that, though I never undertook before, yet God has given me an understanding of my duty, and an honest mind to do it uprightly. I hope you will not be troubled at your change and the king's choice, for you are now fixed at the mercy of no governor that

His letter to the colonists

[1] *Colonial Laws of Massachusetts*, pp. 14–16.

179

comes to make his fortune great; you shall be governed by laws of your own making, and live a free, and, if you will, a sober and industrious people. I shall not usurp the right of any, or oppress his person. God has furnished me with a better resolution, and has given me his grace to keep it. In short, whatever sober and free men can reasonably desire for the security and improvement of their own happiness, I shall heartily comply with, and in five months I resolve, if it please God, to see you. In the meantime pray submit to the commands of my deputy, so far as they are consistent with the law, and pay him those dues (that formerly you paid to the order of the governor of New York) for my use and benefit, and so I beseech God to direct you in the way of righteousness, and therein prosper you and your children after you. I am your true friend, — William Penn." [1]

So great was the success of the " holy experiment" that in the course of the first year more than twenty ships sailed for the Delaware River,[2] carrying perhaps 3000 passengers. Penn did not come, as he had hoped, within five months of the date of his letter. Business connected with the new colony was driving him, and probably for the next year not a man in the three kingdoms worked harder

A Quaker exodus

---

[1] Hazard's *Annals of Pennsylvania*, p. 502.
[2] Proud's *History of Pennsylvania*, i. 216.

than he. It is worthy of note that at this time he was chosen a Fellow of the Royal Society. Devising a frame of government for his colony, making grants of land, sending out detailed instructions to his deputy, and keeping up a huge miscellaneous correspondence, consumed all his time. In the midst of it all he did not forget to preach. He went with Fox one day to a meeting (once more an " unlawful assemblage " in Gracechurch Street !), and Fox informs us that while Penn was speaking " a constable came in with his great staff, and bid him give over and come down ; but William Penn held on, declaring truth in the power of God." Late in the summer of 1682 he sailed for the New World, leaving his wife and children in England. He sailed from Deal, in the ship Welcome, with a hundred passengers, mostly Quakers. In the two months' voyage more than thirty of this company died of small-pox. Toward the end of October Penn landed at Newcastle, amid the welcoming shouts of Dutch and Swedish settlers in woodland garb, the men in leather breeches and jerkins, the women " in skin jackets and linsey petticoats." [1] Penn showed his deeds of enfeoffment, and two of the inhabitants performed livery of seisin by handing over to him water and soil, turf and twig. Thence he went on to Upland, where

Penn comes to the New World

[1] Watson's *Annals of Philadelphia,* i. 19.

there had been for some time a settlement. Turning to his friend and shipmate, Thomas Pearson, he said, " Providence has brought us here safe. Thou hast been the companion of my perils. What wilt thou that I shall call this place ? " " Call it Chester," replied Pearson, who had come from that most quaint and beautiful city of old England.[1] At this new Chester an assembly was held, which passed sixty-one statutes known as the Great Law of Pennsylvania. After visits to New York and Maryland, Penn sought the spot just above the confluence of the little Schuylkill and the great Delaware rivers, and there laid out the squarest and levelest city, no doubt, that our planet had ever seen.[2] The plan was like a checkerboard, and the first streets were named after the trees and shrubs, pine and spruce, chestnut and walnut, sassafras and cedar, that grew luxuriantly in the areas now covered with brick and mortar. The settlers at first came more rapidly than log huts could be built, so that many were fain to become troglodytes for a while in caves along the river's bank. Building went on briskly, and settlers

Chester

Founding of Philadelphia

[1] Smith's *History of Delaware County*, p. 139. This Pearson was maternal grandfather of the painter, Benjamin West. *Id.* p. 170.

[2] But not so level as it has since become. Many inequalities have been smoothed out.

kept coming, until by the end of 1683, this new Philadelphia, this City of Brotherly Love, contained 357 dwellings, many of them framed wooden houses, many of them stoutly built of bright red brick, and sometimes so uniform in aspect that a chalk-mark would seem needed to distinguish one from its neighbours, as in the Arabian tale of the Forty Thieves. The great city on the Delaware, like the great city on the Hudson, had its characteristic features strongly marked from the very outset.

Penn was charmed with his woodland. In a letter he exclaims, " O how sweet is the quiet of these parts, freed from the anxious and troublesome solicitations, hurries, and perplexities of woeful Europe ! " Again, he says, the land is like " the best vales of England watered by brooks; the air, sweet; the heavens, serene like the south of France; the seasons, mild and temperate ; vegetable productions abundant, chestnut, walnut, plums, muscatel grapes, wheat and other grain ; a variety of animals, elk, deer, squirrel, and turkeys weighing forty or fifty pounds, water-birds and fish of divers kinds, no want of horses; and flowers lovely for colour, greatness, figure, and variety. . . . The stories of our necessity [have been] either the fear of our friends or the scarecrows of our enemies; for the greatest hardship we have suffered hath been salt meat, which by

Penn's opinion of the country

fowl in winter and fish in summer, together with some poultry, lamb, mutton, veal, and plenty of venison, the best part of the year has been made very passable." [1] As regards the climate, however, the writer does not find it always mild
A fickle and temperate; in another letter he
climate says, "the weather often changeth without notice, and is constant almost in its inconstancy," — an excellent description of nearly all weather in the United States, except on the coast of California.

One of the most famous events of Penn's first visit to the New World was his treaty with a tribe of Delawares or Lenapé Indians under the elm-tree at Shackamaxon. Documentary evidence concerning this affair is extremely deficient, but there is little doubt that such a treaty was made,[2] probably in November, 1682, at Shackamaxon, under a great elm which was blown down in 1810. There is no doubt that the Indians from the first were greatly pleased with Penn's looks and manners. None can appreciate better than the red man that
The Shacka- union of royal dignity with affable
maxon grace which characterized the hand-
treaty some young cavalier. A lady who was present at a conference between Penn and the Indians,

[1] Clarkson's *Life of Penn*, i. 350, 402.
[2] *Memoirs of Pennsylvania Historical Society*, vol. iii. part 2, p. 143.

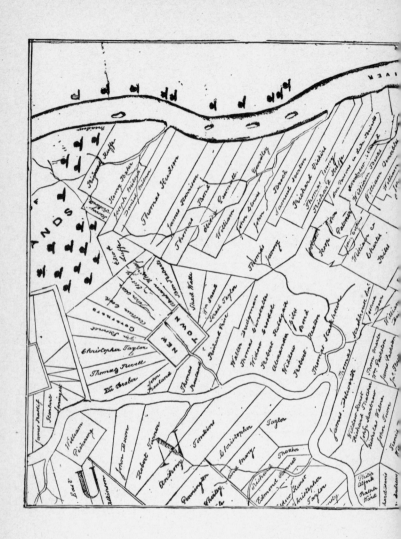

SECTION OF HOLME'S MAP OF PENNSYLVANIA, 1683

near Philadelphia, gave some detailed accounts
of it which were afterward used by the antiqua-
rian John Watson : " She said that the Indians,
as well as the whites, had severally prepared the
best entertainment the place and circumstances
could admit. William Penn made himself en-
deared to the Indians by his marked condescen-
sion and acquiescence in their wishes. He
walked with them, sat with them on the ground,
and ate with them of their roasted acorns and
hominy. At this they expressed their great delight, and soon began to show how they could
hop and jump; at which exhibition William
Penn, to cap the climax, sprang up Penn dances
and outdanced them all! We are not for the
prepared," continues the worthy Wat- Indians
son, " to credit such light gaiety in a sage Governor and religious Chief; but we have the posi-
tive assertion of a woman of truth, who said she
saw it. There may have been very wise policy
in the measure as an act of conciliation, worth
more than a regiment of sharpshooters. He was
then sufficiently young for any agility ; and we
remember that one of the old journalists among
the Friends incidentally speaks of him as having
naturally an excess of levity of spirit for a grave
minister." [1]

The testimony of the " woman of truth "
seems to me eminently credible, as the act was

[1] Watson's *Annals of Philadelphia*, i. 56.

plantation were bought from Canonicus by
Roger Williams; the island of Aquedneck was
Purchases
of land from
Indians duly paid for by Hutchinson and Cod-
dington; and Samuel Gorton obtained
Shawomet by fair purchase.[1]   The
first settlers of Boston found in that neighbourhood a solitary survivor of an Algonquin tribe
extirpated by the recent pestilence, and they
made a payment for the land to him. An Indian village at Beverly was afterward bought
from its tawny occupants for £6 6s. 8d., equivalent to about $158, which was more than
Minuit paid for Manhattan. In 1638 Davenport's company bought their New Haven lands
for " 12 coats of English cloth, 12 metal spoons,
12 hoes, 12 hatchets, 12 porringers, 24 knives,
and 4 cases of French knives and scissors; "
and in 1666 the pilgrims from the New Haven
republic paid for the site of Newark in "50
double hands of powder, 100 bars of lead;
of axes, coats, pistols, and hoes, 20 each; of
guns, kettles, and swords, 10 each; 4 blankets,
4 barrels of beer, 50 knives, 850 fathoms of
wampum, 2 anchors of liquor, and 3 trooper's
coats." So in 1610 Captain West bought the
site of Richmond, in Virginia, from The Pow-
hatan; in 1634 Leonard Calvert bought the
Algonquin village on St. Mary's River; and

[1] Arnold's *History of Rhode Island*, i. 70, 125 ; ii. 112.

in 1638 the Swedish settlers paid for their land on the Delaware.[1]

It appears, therefore, that the custom of paying the Indians a price for their lands was not peculiar to Quakers, or to Quakers and Dutch. On the contrary, the European settlers on the Atlantic seaboard of the United States seem all to have entertained similar ideas on this matter.

As for the proceedings at Shackamaxon, they seem certainly to have included the welding of a " chain of friendship," with the customary exchange of keepsakes and civilities. Whether any treaty of purchase was then made is uncertain. At all events, it can hardly have been completed until a later date, for in 1685, after Penn's return to England, the council concluded a negotiation with four chiefs — Shakkopoh, Sekane, Tangoras, and Malibore — for a large tract of land extending from the Delaware to the Susquehanna. The price paid was 44 lbs. of red lead, 30 pair of hawks' bells, 30 fathoms of duffels, 60 fathoms of " Strandwaters; "[2] of guns, kettles, shirts, combs, axes, knives, bars of lead, pounds of powder, pair of scissors, pair of stockings, glasses, awls, tobacco-boxes, 30 each ;

The price paid to four Delaware chiefs

[1] See Ellis, *The Red Man and the White Man*, p. 337 ; and my *Old Virginia and Her Neighbours*, i. 321.

[2] *Duffels* and *Strandwaters* were coarse kinds of cloth.

tionally safe position until its westward growth brought it within reach of the Algonquin tribes on the Ohio. These facts in nowise diminish the credit due to the Quaker policy, but they help us to a rational view of the Indian situation.

Penn had much reason to feel contented with the success of his noble experiment. Within three years from its founding Philadelphia had 2500 inhabitants, while in the whole province

Penn's return to England, 1684 there were more than 8000, — a growth as great as that of New Netherland in its first half century. Having made such an auspicious beginning, Penn heard news from England which made him think it desirable to return thither. He heard of Quaker meetings broken up by soldiers, and the worshippers sent to jail. His presence was needed. He sailed in August, 1684, and arrived at his home in Sussex early in October. He expected soon to return to America, but fifteen years were to elapse and strange vicissitudes to be encountered before he was able to do so.

XIII

DOWNFALL OF THE STUARTS

THE founding of Pennsylvania helped to accelerate the political revolution which had been preparing in New York ever since the first arrival of Andros. During the spring of 1680 many complaints against that energetic governor found their way across the ocean. Not only was fault found with his treatment of New Jersey, but it was said that he showed too much favour to Dutch shipping, and especially that he allowed Boston people to trade in furs with the Mohawks. These rumours led the duke to summon Andros to London in order to justify himself. The governor sailed in January, 1681, expecting to return so soon that he left Lady Andros in New York. He had little difficulty in satisfying the duke as to his official conduct, but during his absence serious troubles broke out in New York, which had been left in charge of Brockholls, the lieutenant-governor. The duke's customs' duties, which had been imposed in 1677 for three years, expired in November, 1680, and by some oversight Sir

Andros returns to England

195

Edmund neglected to renew them by special ordinance. After he had gone, divers merchants
refused to pay duties, and Brockholls
did not feel sure that he had sufficient
authority to renew them, a squeamish-
ness for which the duke was far from thanking
him. As soon as the merchants came to realize
the weakness of the situation in which Brockholls was placed, the discontent which had
smouldered during long years of autocratic rule
burst forth in an explosion that had momentous
consequences.

William Dyer, the duke's collector of customs
at the fort of New York, detained sundry goods
for non-payment of duties. He was promptly
indicted for high treason in taking upon himself "regal power and authority over the king's
subjects" by demanding the payment of taxes
that were not legally due. Brought to
trial before a special court, he began
by pleading "not guilty," but after a
while called in question the competency of the
court. The case was a somewhat novel exhibition of legal ingenuity, which puzzled the judges,
and it was decided to send Dyer over to England for trial. He was examined in London by
the king's legal advisers, who found that he had
"done nothing amiss," and presently he returned to New York to be "surveyor-general

of his Majesty's customs in the American Plantations."

The excitement over Dyer's case found vent in a clamorous demand for a legislative assembly. People wagged their heads as they asked whether the arbitrary rule of a lord-proprietor was any better than the arbitrary rule of a mercantile company. The old English and Dutch principle of " taxation only by consent " was loudly reiterated. At this juncture the duke's release of the Jerseys and the founding of Pennsylvania seemed to bring things to a crisis. Here, said the men of New York, in these new colonies, almost at their very door, no laws could be made and no taxes levied except by a colonial assembly of freemen. Why could not James Stuart conduct the *Demand for a representative assembly* business of government upon as liberal principles as his friends, Philip Carteret and William Penn? A petition was accordingly soon sent to the duke, in which the want of a representative assembly was declared an intolerable grievance. The document reached him at a favourable moment. He had been complaining that it was hard to raise a sufficient revenue in his province of New York, that his officers there were in difficulties and the air was full of complaints, so that he had half a mind to sell the country to anybody who would offer a fair price for it.

"What," cried William Penn, "sell New York! Don't think of such a thing. Just give it self-government and there will be no more trouble." James concluded to take the advice. Andros was made a gentleman of the king's chamber and presented with a long lease of the island of Alderney. In his place James sent a new governor to New York, with instructions to issue the writs for an election of representatives. With all his faults and in spite of his moroseness, this Stuart prince had many excellent men attached to him; and the new governor for Thomas New York was one of the best of Dongan them, Colonel Thomas Dongan, an Irishman of broad statesmanlike mind and all the personal magnetism that the Blarney stone is said to impart. His blithe humour veiled a deep earnestness of purpose, long experience with Frenchmen had fitted him to deal with the dangers that were threatening from Canada, and while he was a most devout Catholic none could surpass him in loyalty to Great Britain and its government.

The arrival of Governor Dongan in New York, with the news of his errand, was hailed with vociferous delight. The assembly was duly The first elected and held its first meeting in assembly, Fort James on the 17th of October, 1683 1683. Its composition forcibly reminds us of what places the Duke of York's pro-

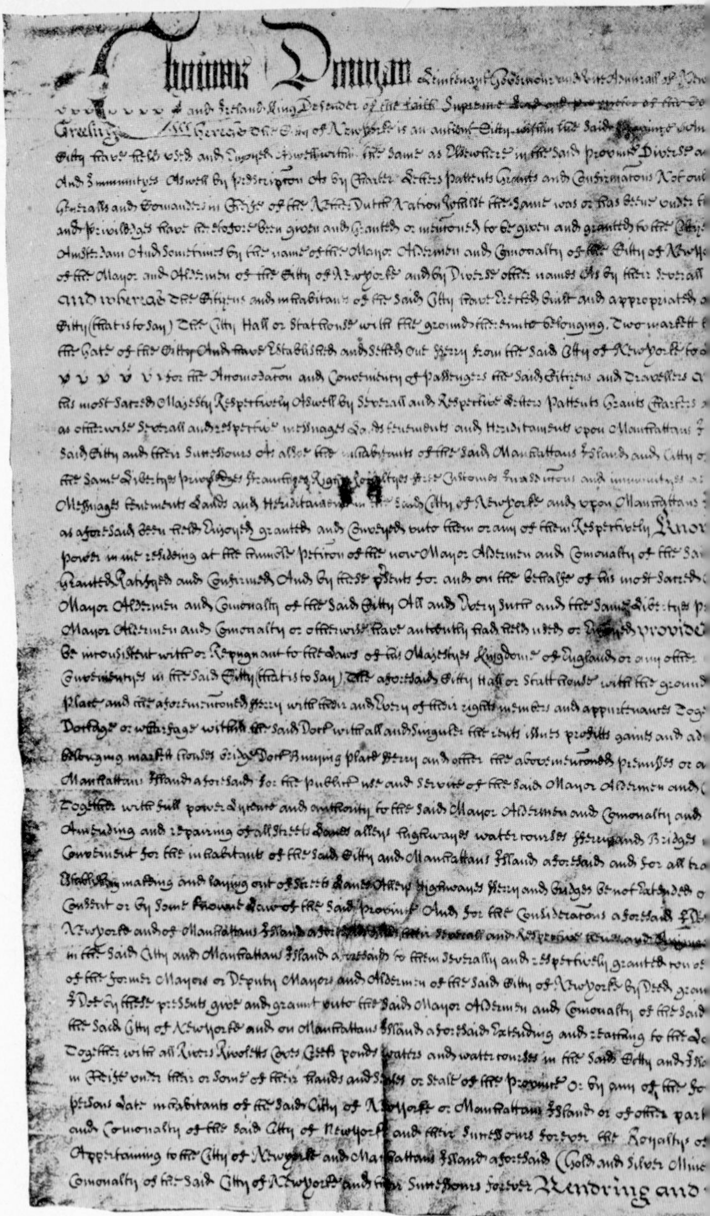

FACSIMILE OF FIRST SHEET

vince consisted. The places represented were Schenectady, Albany, Rensselaerwyck, Esopus, Harlem, New York, Staten Island, Long Island (under the name of Yorkshire in three districts called "ridings"), Martha's Vineyard and Nantucket, and distant Pemaquid. There were in all eighteen representatives.[1] Several wholesome laws were passed, and an admirable charter was drawn up and sent to England for the duke's approval. All this took some time, and before he had signed the charter an event occurred which wrought many changes. In February, 1685, a stroke of apoplexy carried off Charles II., and the duke became king. His proprietary domain of New York thus became a royal province, one among a group of colonies over which he now exercised similar and equal control, and his policy toward it was altered. He did not sign the charter, but let it lie in abeyance while he was turning over in his mind an alternative

---

[1] This assembly divided New York and its appendages into twelve counties, the names of some of which are curious : New York, Westchester, Dutchess (after the duke's new wife, Mary of Modena), Albany (Ulster, after the duke's Irish earldom), Orange (after William, the duke's Dutch son-in-law, destined to supplant him), Richmond (probably after Louise de Kéroualle's bastard), Kings, Queens, Suffolk (a good name for such a Puritan county), Dukes (including Martha's Vineyard and neighbouring islands), and Cornwall (comprising the Maine districts). See Brodhead's *History of the State of New York*, ii. 385, 386.

scheme the outcome of which we shall presently see.

Meanwhile the sagacious Dongan had his hands as full as they could hold of French and Indian diplomacy. Happily the determining feature of the situation was in his favour. We Iroquois have seen how the pivotal fact in early politics American history was the alliance between the Five Nations and the white men on the Hudson River, first Dutch, afterwards English. We have seen how they dealt with the Dutch, exchanged peltries for muskets, and then entered upon a mighty career of conquest. How they destroyed the French missions in the Huron country in 1649 is one of the most lurid chapters in history. By Governor Dongan's time they had reduced to a tributary condition nearly all the tribes east of the Mississippi and north of the Ohio and Potomac. They had lately wiped out of existence the formidable Susquehannocks, and now guaranteed the safety of Penn's new colony. We have seen how in 1675 they bestowed upon Andros the title of "Corlear," and promised to befriend the English as they had befriended the Dutch. Were they ready to go further, if need be, and attack Onontio himself, the Great White Father, in his strongholds upon the St. Lawrence? It was more than they had yet undertaken, and these dusky warriors of the Stone Age well knew the prowess of the soldiers of France. Dongan with a statesman's foresight knew that a deadly struggle between France and England for supremacy in this wilderness must soon begin, and his military eye saw that the centre of the fight must lie between the Hudson and the St. Lawrence. Either Louis XIV. must be checkmated in Canada or he would drive the English from New York. So Dongan's hands were full of Indian diplomacy as he sought to fan the fires of hatred in the Mohawk valley. His opponent, the Marquis Denonville, viceroy of Canada, was also an astute and keen-witted man, as one had need to be in such a position. No Russian game of finesse on the lower Danube was ever played with more wary hand than the game between those two old foxes. While their secret emissaries prowled and intrigued, their highnesses exchanged official letters, usually polite in form, but sometimes crusty, and always lively enough, despite the dust of these two hundred years. On one occasion the Frenchman lectures Dongan for allowing West India rum to be sent to the Long House. "Think you that religion will make any progress, while your traders supply the savages in abundance with the liquor which, as you ought to know, converts them into demons and their wigwams into counterparts of hell?" One seems to see the Irishman's

Some spicy letters

With these amiable instructions Frontenac was sent to Canada, but when he arrived, in October, 1689, he found things not as he had expected. It was indeed already known in France that the black war-cloud had burst over the colony, but the horrors of that summer had not yet been told. In all directions the ruins of smoking villages bore witness to the fright-

The Iroquois defeat the plan

ful ravages of the Iroquois. The environs of Montreal were a scene of mournful desolation, the town itself had barely escaped capture, and the inhabitants, who had looked out upon friends roasted and devoured before the very gates, were sick with terror. It became necessary for Frontenac to send a force at once to Lake Ontario, where the French had abandoned Fort Frontenac after an unsuccessful attempt to destroy it, so that the Iroquois had forthwith occupied it and got hold of more muskets and ammunition than the red man's boldest fancy had ever dreamed of. The fur-trade from the upper lakes had been cut off for two years, and so great had been the destruction of property that a military expedition down the Hudson was utterly out of the question.

Thus it was that the scheme of Louis XIV. against New York collapsed at the outset, and thus it soon sank into oblivion, so that we are liable to forget how much we owe to those

dreadful Iroquois. Meanwhile in these six years
how had it fared with the knightly Irishman
and his fair province? James, as we Plan of
have seen, had undertaken to grant James II.
constitutional government to New for uniting
all the north-
York, and was about ready to sign a ern colonies
charter, when suddenly he became king and
changed his mind. This change of purpose had
a military reason. In order to oppose a more
solid front to Canada, James wished to unite
all his northern colonies under a single military
governor. Circumstances seemed to favour him.
Massachusetts, the most populous and powerful of the colonies, had sustained a bitter quarrel with Charles II. during the whole of that
king's reign, until just before his death he had
succeeded in getting a chancery decree annulling
the charter of Massachusetts. In 1686 James II.
sent Sir Edmund Andros to Boston Sir Edmund
to assume the government over all Andros viceroy of New
New England. Poor little Plymouth England
had never had a charter, and those of Connecticut and Rhode Island might be summarily
seized. As for New York, the king revoked
his half-granted charter and annexed that province to New England. New Jersey soon met
the same fate, and legal proceedings were begun
against the charter of Maryland. Apparently
nothing was safe except the sturdy infant col-

with the spirit of rebellion. The flames burst
forth when on the 5th of November (Guy
Fawkes's day !) the Prince of Orange landed in
Devonshire. Before Christmas the last Stuart
king had fled beyond sea, leaving a vacant
throne.

It was of course a moment of engrossing business for the great Dutch prince, and he took the
Dr. Mather occasion to prepare a short letter for
detains King
William's the American colonies enjoining upon
letter them to retain all King James's arrangements undisturbed for the present until
leisure should be found for revising them. Dr.
Mather did not wish to have any such instructions sent to Boston, for he saw in them the
possibility that Andros might hold over until
it would be awkward to get rid of him without
interfering with some plan of William III. By
skilful pleading with the new king, in which
he was aided by Sir William Phips, the wily
Mather succeeded in delaying the departure of
the letter. This was in February, 1689, and
it was not until late in March that the flight
of James II. and the success of the Prince of
Orange became known in Massachusetts. The
Overthrow glowing embers of rebellion were
of Andros quickly fanned into a blaze. On the
18th of April armed yeomanry began pouring
into Boston in response to the signal on Beacon
Hill, and Sir Edmund saw that his hour had

come. He tried to escape to the Rose frigate in the harbour, in the hope of finding a refuge in New York, but his Puritan foes had no mind to let him off so easily. He was seized and securely lodged in jail, and several of his agents and abettors were also imprisoned, among them Chief Justice Dudley, who had lately had the impudence to tell the people of New England that the only liberty left them was that of not being sold for slaves.

Massachusetts then at once restored her old government as it was before her charter was annulled, and she caused this to be announced in England, explaining that it was done provisionally until the new king's pleasure should be known. Obviously the improvement in her position through Dr. Mather's astuteness was great. No one could interpret her rebellion as aimed at any other sovereign than the dethroned James. Instantly the other New England colonies followed suit. Plymouth, Rhode Island, and Connecticut quietly resumed their old governments. James's consolidated New England thus fell to pieces.

The old governments restored in New England

There were people in New York upon whom these events were not for a moment lost. The lieutenant-governor, Francis Nicholson, was in an awkward position. If Andros had come away in the Rose frigate to New York, where he could direct affairs from Fort James, all would have been simple enough. If he had been killed there would have been no difficulty, for Nicholson would have become acting-governor. But as Andros was only locked up, Nicholson did not know just in what light to regard himself or just how much authority to assume. He belonged to that large class of commonplace men who are afraid of assuming responsibility. So he tried to get messages to Andros in his Boston jail, but found very little counsel or comfort in that way.

Nicholson's government in New York was supported by three members of the council. They were Dutch citizens of the highest social position : Frederick Philipse, the richest man in the province, Stephanus van Cortlandt, mayor of New York, and Nicholas Bayard, colonel of the city regiment of train-bands. The other members of the council were scattered, some of them as far away as Pemaquid. These three were the only ones present in the city. On the 26th of April they heard of the imprisonment Rumours of war of Andros, and the very next day they heard that Louis XIV. had declared war against Great Britain and the Netherlands. This report was premature, for war was not declared until May 7, but the very air was full of premonitions of that bloody struggle which was to last for eight years.

Small blame to Nicholson and his three coun-
cillors if the grim tidings disturbed them!
Small blame to the mass of worthy citizens
if something like a panic was created! There
were many Huguenot refugees in the city;
they had been coming for several years, and
especially for the last four years since the king
had revoked the Edict of Nantes; and they
had been received with warm welcome. They
knew, as everybody knew, that Louis XIV.
had a very long arm. There never was a time
when an attack by France seemed more formidable than in 1689. The king had not yet
been cast down from his pinnacle of military
glory, and the spirit of Catholic propagandism
had been taking fuller and fuller possession of
him. We now know what his truculent purpose was with regard to New York. Frontenac
was just starting to execute it. Of course the
burghers of New York did not know of those
secret instructions to Frontenac, but they understood perfectly the danger of the situation. As
for the frightful blow with which the Iroquois
baffled the scheme of Louis XIV. (which for
the sake of clearness we have mentioned by
anticipation), it did not come till the summer
of 1689, and still further time was needed to
disclose its effects. In the spring of that year
it was still in the future.

It was not at all strange, then, that the elements of an anti-Catholic panic were rife in New York. Other things contributed to destroy

Causes of the anti-Catholic panic confidence and make men distrustful of one another. In spite of all pretences of liberality, it had always been the design of James II. to force the Catholic faith upon the American colonies; so he afterwards told Pope Innocent XI.[1] People were not wrong, then, in suspecting him. The two regiments of regular troops which Andros had brought to America were made up of Irish Catholics, and one had been commanded by Nicholson, who was now in command of New York. Nicholson was really an Episcopalian, but it was rumoured that he had knelt at the Mass once on Hounslow Heath in presence of King James, and many people believed him to be a Papist in disguise.

At the first news of war Nicholson directed the city train-bands to take turns in guarding Fort James, and a watch was placed upon Coney Island to look out for French ships. The money collected as revenue was placed within the fort for safety, and the new receipts after May-day were to be applied to building new fortifications. At this juncture a cargo of wine arrived from Europe, consigned to a well-known wine-merchant, Jacob Leisler. The duty was about a hundred pounds sterling, and

[1] Brodhead, *History of the State of New York*, ii. 531.

Leisler refused to pay it, taking the ground that Matthew Plowman, collector of the port, was a Roman Catholic, and that since King James's flight no duly quali- fied government existed in New York.

Jacob Leisler refuses to pay duties

This Jacob Leisler was a German of humble origin, born at Frankfort-on-the-Main. In earlier days he had been a soldier in the pay of the West India Company, and had come to New Amsterdam a few years before its capture by the English. A residence of thirty years had made him one of the most

Character of Leisler

prosperous and conspicuous citizens. Through his marriage with Elsie Tymens, a niece of Anneke Jans, he had become connected with the aristocracy, but was not cordially welcomed among such people. One can imagine that Van Cortlandt and Bayard might not feel proud of such a connection, and that occasions would be afforded for Leisler to cherish resentment. Indeed, there had been a bitter quarrel, with one or two lawsuits between Leisler and these two gentlemen, so that their families were not on speaking terms. Leisler was a man of integrity, noted for fair and honourable dealing in matters of business. We hear, too, that he was kind-hearted and generous with money. But he was evidently of coarse fibre, ignorant, stubborn, and vain, — just the man to be seized and dominated by a fixed idea. His letters

of William III. by saving for him his province of New York despite the diabolical plots of Catholic officials and the Dutch aristocrats who supported them ; for although such men as Bayard and Van Cortlandt were thorough Protestants and deacons in the Dutch Reformed Church, they were none the less to Leisler's distorted fancy a " crew of Papistical renegades."

It is clear that the feelings which found vent in Leisler's conduct had long been gathering in this little community. His refusal to pay his tax was followed by other refusals. Nicholson's act in sheltering the public revenues within the fort was interpreted as part of a deep-laid plan for using them against the people. All through the month of May agitated whispers ran about the town ; a French fleet was coming, and traitors in power were ready to welcome it. Popular imagination filled the woods on Staten Island with emissaries of Louis XIV., and it was said that Nicholson had gone over there by night to consult with them. Dongan was down at Navesink, getting his armed brigantine ready to take him back to England ; in that golden age of pirates it was necessary for ships to go armed ; that innocent vessel was supposed to be intended for a part in the plot.

At last on May 30 Nicholson got into an

altercation with an insubordinate lieutenant in
Captain De Peyster's train-band. "Who commands this fort, you or I?" shouted the angry
governor. Probably the lieutenant made some
reference to the city being in danger, which
caused Nicholson to retort, "I would
rather see the city on fire than take
the impudence of such fellows as you," *Nicholson's rash exclamation*
or words to that effect. What he really said
may have been quite different in purport, but
at all events fire was mentioned, and that was
fire enough to kindle insurrection. The rash
remark was overheard, it was said that the governor had threatened to burn the town, and
next morning the streets were in an uproar.
Leisler himself was captain of one of the train-
bands. His company, led by Joost Stoll, the
sergeant, marched to Fort James, shouting,
"They have betrayed us, and are going to murder us." The lieutenant whom Nicholson had
upbraided let them into the fort, and
presently Leisler arrived there and
took command. That afternoon while *Leisler takes command of the fort*
Nicholson and his three councilmen were in the
City Hall discussing the situation, Captain Lod-
wyck, at the head of his company, entered the
chamber and demanded the keys of the fort.
There was no help for it, so the keys were given
him.

Two days of uncertainty followed, while Leis-

popular support as to venture to defy it on grounds of his own. King William was evidently ignorant of the situation. He never would willingly have entrusted responsible command to these "popishly affected, lying dogs," not he. These rogues must be put down, and the king must be told why. The very next day Leisler turned the city government out of doors, and two or three gentlemen were roughly handled by the soldiers, but Bayard escaped and made his way to Albany. Leisler called a convention, and a committee of safety was organized which appointed him commander-in-chief over the whole province.

Leisler appointed commander-in-chief

While these things were going on, Nicholson was in mid-ocean on his way to England. The king, in ignorance of what had occurred, addressed a letter to him with words of advice and counsel; the letter was not addressed to Nicholson by name, but to " Our lieutenant-governor and commander-in-chief of our province of New York in America." After sundry vicissitudes this letter reached New York early in December and was received by Leisler, who understood it to be addressed to himself.[1]

The king's letter

[1] The circumstances under which Leisler obtained the letter should be noted. The bearer of the king's despatches, John Riggs, expected to deliver it to the three councilmen, but in passing through Boston he was told that he ought to deliver

His vanity was tickled to the bursting point. He had sent his friend, Joost Stoll, keeper of a dram-shop, and rather a laughable sort of envoy, to explain matters to the king; and now, doubtless, this was the response! So Leisler at once assumed the title of Lieutenant-Governor, appointed a council, and took his seat next Sun-

Leisler assumes the title of lieutenant-governor

it to Leisler, who was actually in command at New York. To Riggs, coming from England, this was puzzling, for he was sure that there was nothing in the packet intended for any such person as Leisler. When Riggs arrived in New York late at night, he met Philipse and Bayard at the latter's house, and they sent for Van Cortlandt, who was out of town. On Van Cortlandt's arrival next morning, Riggs would have delivered the packet to the three councilmen in presence of each other. But early in the morning Leisler sent a party of soldiers who arrested Riggs and took him to Fort William. Van Cortlandt and Philipse, hearing of this, followed him thither, and an altercation ensued, in which Leisler called them rogues and papistical dogs who had nothing to do with government. He showed Riggs his commission from the council of safety, and prevailed upon him to deliver the packet to himself. He gave Riggs a written receipt for the packet.

No doubt Leisler, as a " crank " with his brain dominated by a narrow group of morbid fixed ideas, believed that King William, the Protestant, could not possibly have intended his letters to be received by three ex-officials of King James, the Catholic. His subsequent logic, on opening the letter to Nicholson and understanding it to be addressed to himself, was crank logic. Leisler seems to have felt that others might dispute his conclusion, for he never allowed the contents of the letter to be made public.

of knowledge and capacity, and sent him up the river with three sloops to tame the frowardness of Albany. His persuasive tongue won a number of adherents and succeeded in sowing some seeds of dissension, but Livingston and Schuyler were too much for him, and his mission was unsuccessful.

This was in November, 1689, and Frontenac had arrived in Canada. As we have seen, the Iroquois had been there before him, and his grand scheme for conquering New York dwindled ignominiously into the sending of three scalping parties to destroy the most exposed frontier settlements of the Dutch and English. It was necessary to make some show of strength in order to retrieve in the minds of the Indians the somewhat shaken military reputation of the The French French. The Algonquin allies must war parties be encouraged and the Iroquois foes confounded, and there was nothing, of course, that the red men appreciated more highly than a wholesale massacre. The distances to be traversed were long and difficult, and this made it all the easier to surprise the remote villages that sometimes forgot to be watchful against the diabolism that lurked in the forest. The first of the three scalping parties was sent to the Hudson River, the second into New Hampshire, the third into Maine.

The first party consisted of 114 French Cana-

dians skilled in all manner of woodcraft, and 96
Christian Indians ; their leaders were French
noblemen, among them the famous LeMoyne
d'Iberville, founder of Louisiana. The march
of seventeen days was attended with terrible
hardships. It was an alternation of thawing and
freezing. On one day they were struggling
against a blinding snowstorm, on another they
were half drowned in the mud and slush of
treacherous swamps, on another their ears and
toes were frozen in the icy wind. Their coats
and blankets were torn to shreds in the stubborn
underbrush, and their stock of food, dragged
on sleds, was not enough, so that they had to
be put on starving rations. They could not
have encountered more hardships if they had
been a party of scientific explorers, and they
fought their way through it all with the tenacity
and the ferocious zeal of crusaders. Their original plan was to strike at Albany, but as the
limit of human endurance was approaching before they could accomplish the distance, they
turned upon Schenectady, some fif- The situation
teen miles nearer. This little Dutch at Schenec-
village was the extreme frontier out-   tady
post of the New York colony. Its population
numbered about 150 souls. It was surrounded
by a palisade and defended by a blockhouse in
which there were eight or ten Connecticut militia. The Leisler affair had bred civil dudgeon

would feel like refusing help from any quarter, Milborne and his men were admitted into the town, and Leisler's authority was virtually recognized.

When in April, however, he issued writs for the election of an assembly, his weakness was

Election of representatives

revealed. Imperative need of the sinews of war drove him to this step. Many people refused to pay taxes, and it was necessary to call an assembly of representatives of the people. But some towns refused to choose representatives on the ground that Leisler was usurping authority. This tone was taken especially by the Puritan towns on Long Island, which wished to be joined to Connecticut and always welcomed a chance to annoy the government at New York, whatever it might be.

Leisler's next step was a memorable event in American history. He called for a Congress of

The first American Congress, May, 1690

American colonies to concert measures of attack upon Canada ; and this Congress, the first of a series which was by and by to end in the great Continental Congress, assembled in New York on the first of May, 1690. None of the southern colonies took part in it. The Carolinas were in their early infancy ; Virginia was too remote to feel keenly interested. The task of invading Canada was shared between New York, Massachusetts, Plymouth, Connecticut, and Maryland. There were to be 855 men from these colonies,[1] and the Iroquois sachems promised to add 1800 warriors. As finally carried out, a part of the expedition, under Sir William Phipps, of Massachusetts, sailed up the St. Lawrence and laid siege to Quebec; while the rest of the allied forces, under Fitz John Winthrop, of Connecticut, proceeded from Albany toward Montreal. But these amateur generals were no match for Frontenac, and when they turned their faces southward it was with wiser heads but sadder hearts than when they started. Boston preachers, with bated breath, spoke of "this awful frown of God." Leisler stormed and raved, and saw disguised Papists everywhere, as usual. The affair ended in bitter recriminations, and Massachusetts was driven to issue paper money, which plagued her till Thomas Hutchinson got her out of the scrape in 1749.

Unsuccessful attempt to invade Canada

What a picturesque creature was Frontenac! We can seem to see him now, aristocrat and courtier to the ends of his fingers, with his gleaming black eyes, the frost of seventy win-

---

[1] The several contingents were, New York 400, Massachusetts 160, Plymouth 60, Connecticut 135, Maryland 100 — total, 855 men. The New York contingent was disproportionately large ; on the other hand, Massachusetts furnished most of the naval force.

ters on his brow, and the sardonic smile on his lips, as he presides over a grim council of sa-chems; we see him as he suddenly daubs vermilion on his cheeks and seizes a tomahawk, and leads off the war-dance, screaming like a cougar and inflaming to madness those warriors of the Stone Age. Here it need only be said that after checkmating Leisler he devoted himself to clearing off scores with the Iroquois, and in 1696, in his seventy-eighth year, after one of the most remarkable forest campaigns on record, he dealt the Long House a blow from which it never quite recovered. Again we may reflect how fortunate it was for New York that the Iroquois were there to serve as a buffer against this redoubtable foe.

Frontenac attacks the Long House

To go back to the May of 1690, the month of the Colonial Congress, — it saw Leisler's doom approaching. His friend Joost Stoll brought him evil tidings from London. The king had not so much as deigned to look at that grotesque ambassador. Not a scrap of notice or attention could he get from anybody. But the king had shown favour to Nicholson by making him lieutenant-governor of Virginia. Still worse, he had appointed Colonel Henry Sloughter to be governor of New York, and Major Richard Ingoldsby to be lieutenant-governor. New

Appoint-ment of Henry Sloughter

York was to have a free government with representative assemblies. One of the councilmen was to be Joseph Dudley, the founder of New England Toryism, who had been chief aid and abettor of Andros in Boston. And worst of all, among the old members of the council now reappointed were Philipse and Van Cortlandt and Bayard. As for Jacob Leisler, his existence had not been so much as recognized. There was a terrible sound to this news. Leisler's violence had not spared these members of the council. He had accused them of conspiracy against him. He had seized Bayard and the attorney-general, William Nicolls, and kept them for months in prison and in irons, suffering doleful misery. Now these " Papist rogues," as his distempered fancy called them, were high in the great Protestant king's favour, while Jacob Leisler, most devoted of his Protestant servants, was ominously ignored ! I think we may safely suppose that such facts were too much for that poor distorted mind to take in. How could such things be ? Stoll must have been deceived ; he was a sturdy old toper and must have got things muddled. His news was simply incredible.

Only on the supposition that Leisler's mind was half dazed can we explain his subsequent conduct, which finally reached the heights of madness. Months were yet to pass before the catastrophe, for various affairs delayed the new governor and his party. Meanwhile Leisler Leisler loses grew more and more tyrannical, until popularity petitions against him were sent to London, the dominies came in and rebuked him in the name of the Lord, old women taunted and defied him on the street, and the mob threw stones at him and called him "Dog driver," "Deacon Jailor," "Little Cromwell," "General Hog," and other choice epithets. The great democrat had fallen from grace. It was said that the wedding in January, 1691, when his young daughter Mary was married to his staunch friend Milborne, was more like a funeral than a wedding.

It seems proper here to make some mention of a historical novel, "The Begum's Daughter," by the late Edwin Lassetter Bynner, which Two histor- is based upon the events of Leisler's ical novels time. Though it does not rise to the very high level of the same author's "Agnes Surriage," it is an extremely creditable piece of work. As a study in history, it reflects a trifle too closely, perhaps, the bitter feelings of the aristocrats, but after making a slight allowance for this, "The Begum's Daughter" gives us a truthful picture of the time, and is worth reading by all who are interested in American history.[1]

[1] Another story, *In Leisler's Times*, written by Mr. El-

It was sorely against her will that Mary Leisler consented to become the bride of Jacob Milborne. It was generally believed that she entertained a very decided preference for Abraham Gouverneur, one of two young Huguenot brothers, whose family has played an important part in American history. Against poor Mary's submissiveness to her father's despotic and violent will, Mr. Bynner has furnished us with an impressive contrast in the character which he attributes to her younger sister, Hester. The element of domestic conflict needed in the story is supplied by having Hester betrothed to the handsome and gallant son of Van Cortlandt, while her father is determined that she shall marry Barent Rynders, the sensible but ungainly son of a blacksmith. Hester's will is as strong as her father's, and in spite of his blustering threats, although nearly benumbed with terror, she shows herself as unyielding as adamant. But after the great catastrophe, when her aristocratic lover imprudently identifies himself with the scorn and hatred felt by his family for her unfortunate father's memory, the high-spirited girl instantly and irrevocably dismisses him. The

The marriages of Leisler's daughters

bridge Brooks for young readers, but interesting also to older readers, shows a decided leaning of sympathies in the opposite direction, and undoubtedly takes more liberties with the records.

grave warnings to take heed what he was doing and stop before it should be too late.

All such friendly entreaties were lost upon the infatuated Leisler. On March 17, quite losing his patience, he sent word to Ingoldsby to disband his forces, and gave him two hours to reply. Not getting a satisfactory answer, he fired upon the king's troops, and a few were killed and wounded. And now occurred an incident of evil omen indeed. Leisler had ordered a militia garrison in the Vly blockhouse at the Water Gate to fire upon a party of Ingoldsby's troops in the Slip; but at this juncture the men threw down their arms, abandoned the blockhouse, and dispersed to their homes!

Leisler fires upon the king's troops

Nothing was done next day, but the next thereafter at nightfall the Archangel frigate arrived at the Narrows. Word was sent down to Sloughter to make all haste. He came up the harbour in a boat, went straight into the City Hall, and read aloud his commission as royal governor. After taking the oath of office he sent Ingoldsby to demand the instant surrender of Fort William, but with almost incredible fatuity Leisler insisted upon retaining it until a written order from the king addressed to him, Jacob Leisler, by name should be shown him. Evidently the poor man's mind was dazed. That in view of all that had hap-

Arrival of Governor Sloughter

236

pened the king should utterly ignore his faithful Protestant "lieutenant-governor" Leisler was a fact too strange for him to grasp. From a soul thus stiffened and benumbed no rational conduct was to be expected. Toward midnight a second demand was made, and then Leisler sent the diplomatic Milborne to explain that it was against the rules to surrender the fort in the night. Sloughter's only reply was to make a sign to the guards, who forthwith seized Milborne and dragged him off to jail.

Arrest of Milborne

In the morning Leisler sent a conciliatory letter to the governor, disclaiming any wish to withhold the fort from him, but asking further explanation on certain points. Sloughter took no notice of the letter, but sent Ingoldsby to order the garrison of Fort William to ground arms and march out, promising full and free pardon to all concerned in the late proceedings except Leisler and his council. The men instantly obeyed, and the forlorn usurper was left alone. In a few moments Bayard and Nicolls, pale and haggard with ill usage, were set free from their dungeon, and Leisler was cast into it, with the same chain upon his leg that Bayard had worn for more than a year.

Arrest of Leisler

On March 30 the prisoners were brought before a court over which Dudley presided.

for which we are condemned, is to declare as our last words, before that God whom we hope before long to see, that our sole aim and object in the conduct of the government was to maintain the interest of our sovereign Lord and Lady and the reformed Protestant churches of these parts."

Concerning Leisler's essential integrity of purpose there can be little doubt. His methods were arbitrary and many of his acts tyrannical, and the bitter hatred felt for him had doubtless adequate cause. It has been the fashion with some writers [1] to treat him as a mere demagogue actuated by no other motive than vulgar ambition. But this theory does not explain his conduct. Insane as was his persistence after Ingoldsby's arrival, it is not reasonable to suppose that during the two years of his rule over New York he can ever have deliberately intended to resist King William and bring about a revolution. Nor can it for a moment be allowed, as has sometimes been insinuated, that the anti-Catholic panic was either got up by Leisler or used by him as a blind for concealing his real intentions. There can be no doubt, as we have already seen, that there was plenty of apparent ground for the panic, or that Leisler's impulse in assuming the government was thoroughly honest. Un-

Leisler's honesty of purpose

---

[1] Brodhead, for example, can see no good in Leisler.

questionably he believed himself, in holding New York against Papist conspirators, to be doing a great and needed service to his Protestant king; and when he found himself simply ignored and set aside without a word, his mind was confronted with a fact too deep for him to fathom. There is something very pathetic in his utter inability to grasp the fact that there was nowhere a missive from the king addressed to him by name.

Had things gone as Leisler hoped and expected, the aristocratic party and the friends of Andros and Tories like Dudley, and all who had accepted honours or office from James II., would have been snubbed by the new king, while his own prompt action in saving New York would have been cordially re- His motives
cognized by making him governor or at least a member of the council, and thus the cause of democracy would be furthered and helped. Thenceforth the name of Leisler would be inseparably associated with the firm establishment of representative government and the first triumph of democracy in the province of New York. In this dream Leisler was mistaken because he totally misconceived so many essential facts in the case, but the kind of ambition which it discloses is not a vulgar kind or such as to make it proper to stamp him with the name of demagogue. Even as it is, even in spite of his

blunders and his failure, in spite of the violence and fanaticism which stain his record, Leisler stands as one of the early representatives of ideas since recognized as wholesome and statesmanlike. Moreover, the name of the man who called together the first Congress of American colonies must always be pronounced with respect.

As for the execution of Leisler and Milborne, it was of course entirely legal. They had caused a wanton loss of life while resisting the king's commissioned officers, and there was no court of that day, as there is no court of the

The execution was ill-advised

present day, which would not regard such an offence as properly punishable with death. Nevertheless it was afterwards generally admitted that the execution was a mistake. It made martyrs of the two victims. Increase Mather declared that they were "barbarously murdered," and there were many in New York who said the same. Four years afterward Parliament reversed the attainder against Leisler and Milborne, and their estates were restored to their families. But the legacy of hatred remained, and the spirit of dissension so earnestly deprecated in Leisler's dying speech, far from being buried in oblivion with his ashes, renewed its life from year to year, and it was long before it ceased to vex men's minds.

XIV

THE CITADEL OF AMERICA

W HETHER from a commercial or a
military point of view, the Dutch
and Quaker colonies occupied the
most commanding position in North America.
It is that part of the continent which
sends streams flowing in divergent
courses into the Gulf of St. Lawrence,
the Atlantic Ocean, and the Gulf of
Mexico. Through deep chasms in the Alle-
ghanies, which run irregularly across it, those
superb rivers, the Hudson, Delaware, and Susquehanna, flow into the Atlantic ; while the
Mohawk, coming from the west, serves to join
the valley of the Hudson with the Great Lakes ;
and in like manner the lovely Juniata, rushing
down to join the Susquehanna, has its head-
waters not far from the spot where the currents
of the Allegheny and Monongahela unite to
form the Ohio. With such pathways in every
direction, whether for peace or for war, the New
Netherland (curious misnomer for a region so
mountainous) commanded the continent ; and
could the Dutch settlement at Manhattan have

Commanding position of the Dutch and Quaker colonies

been adequately supported, it might have threatened or prevented the ascendency of England in the New World. It was partly owing to this advantage of position that the League of the Iroquois was enabled to domineer over the greater part of the country between the Atlantic and the Mississippi; and through the divergent river valleys and across the chain of mighty fresh-water seas those ferocious but long-headed barbarians in their bark canoes established those lines of trade which modern civilization, with its steamboat and railway, has simply adopted and improved. For a century after its conquest by the English, New York, with the western mountains of Pennsylvania, served as a military bulwark for New England and for the southern colonies. The hardest fighting done in the War of Independence was the struggle for the possession of this vantage-ground; and in the second war with England the brilliant victories of Perry and Macdonough maintained on Lakes Erie and Champlain the sanctity of the citadel of America.

It was not, however, until the great immigration of Presbyterians from Ireland and the cross-

The war with France ing of Lake Erie by the French that the Pennsylvania frontier acquired its military significance. At the period with which we are dealing in the present volume, the vital point to be defended in the citadel was the stretch of lakes and woodlands between Albany and Montreal. The upper Connecticut valley and the Maine frontier also presented opportunities to a watchful enemy. The danger was sufficiently constant to be an important factor in the policy of all the northern colonies ; in New York it was often the dominant factor. Of the twenty-five years which intervened between the accession of William and Mary and the death of Anne, nineteen were years of deadly warfare between French and English, in the New World as well as the Old. Then, after a lull of thirty years, interrupted by a few local outbreaks like that of Norridgewock in 1724, we come to the final contests in which out of twenty-one years sixteen are years of war. The burden, at first borne chiefly by New York and New England, comes at last to bear upon all the colonies ; but first and last New York takes the brunt of it. The strife which had begun with the diplomacy of Andros and Dongan, and which had broken out in bloodshed in the time of Leisler, was thenceforth forever present to the minds of those who sat in council at Fort William or in the City Hall on the island of Manhattan. Until the final overthrow of New France, the development of New York was powerfully influenced by the circumstances which made it the citadel of America.

The accession of William and Mary, which

precipitated this warfare with the French, marked in other ways an era in New York, as it did in other colonies, and notably in Maryland, Plymouth, and Massachusetts. It transformed Maryland into a royal province, and although the proprietary government was by and by to be restored, yet the days of the old semi-indepen-

Accession of William and Mary

dent palatinate were gone never to return.[1] It abolished the separate existence of Plymouth, and it changed the half-rebellious theocratic republic of Massachusetts into a royal province. New York also became a royal province after the fashion of Massachusetts, but the change was in the reverse direction. The days of the autocrats were over. Self-government gained much in New York, as it lost much in Massachusetts, from the accession of William and Mary. Hereafter New York was to be governed through a representative assembly.

The first thing which Colonel Sloughter did after the arrest of Leisler was to issue writs for the election of such an assembly ; and the day on which it met in a tavern on Pearl Street, the

A representative assembly, 1691

9th of April, 1691, marks the beginning of continuous constitutional government in New York. James Graham, of the famous Grahams of Montrose, was chosen speaker of the assembly, in which the

[1] See *Old Virginia and Her Neighbours*, ii. 197, 198.

party opposed to Leisler had an overwhelming majority. This assembly declared its enthusiastic loyalty to William and Mary, while it ascribed its own existence, not to royal generosity, but to the inherent right of freemen to be governed only through their own representatives. Resolutions were passed, condemning the acts of Leisler. A grant was made for public expenditures, but only for a period of two years. The wave of anti-Catholic feeling attendant upon the mighty war between William of Orange and Louis XIV. was revealed in an act prohibiting " Romish forms of worship " in New York. At the same time the king was requested to annex Connecticut, the Jerseys, and Pennsylvania, with Delaware, to the province of New York, which would thus comprise the whole of the original New Netherland, and somewhat more.

In midsummer of that year the worthless Sloughter died so suddenly that suspicions of poison were aroused, but the particular suspicions were proved to be groundless, and a more probable explanation was to be found in delirium tremens. Major Ingoldsby then acted as governor until the arrival of Colonel Benjamin Fletcher in August, 1692. Fletcher was a man of large stature, *Arrival of Benjamin Fletcher* fair, florid, and choleric, with plenty of energy and a pompous demeanour. One of the conspicuous sights of the little city was his handsome chariot, drawn by six gayly caparisoned steeds and carrying Mrs. Fletcher and her daughters decked in the latest and most gorgeous European finery. He was devoted to the Church of England and to missionary enterprise; as a soldier he was so prompt and vigorous that the Mohawks named him "Great Swift Arrow." Withal it was commonly whispered that he was a consummate adept in the art of feathering his own nest, making both religion and warfare redound to the increase of the credit side of his ledger.

One of Fletcher's first acts was to go to Albany and take council of Peter Schuyler, its mayor. This gentleman, grand-uncle of Philip Schuyler, the eminent general of the War of Independence, was a person of extraordinary qualities. His skill in dealing with red men was equal to that of Frontenac, and the situation called for all such skill that could be had. The danger lay in the possibility that French diplomacy might succeed in detaching the Iroquois from their English alliance. Their loyalty to the alliance was of course based much more upon hatred of Onontio than upon love for Corlear, and could they be brought to fear the French as enemies more than they respected the English as protectors, that loyalty was liable to be weakened. The

Peter Schuyler

positively denied. I must tell you that it seems very unmannerly. There never was an amendment yet decided by the council but what you rejected; it is a sign of stubborn ill-temper. . . . You ought to let the council do their part. They are in the nature of the House of Lords, or upper house. But you seem to take the whole power into your own hands and set up for everything. You have had a very long session to little purpose, and have been a great charge to the country. Ten shillings a day is a large allowance and you punctually exact it. You have been always forward enough to put down the fees of other ministers in the government ; why did you not think it expedient to correct your own to a more moderate allowance ? " [1]

Even when it came to voting supplies for the defence of the colony against actual invasion, Fletcher found his assembly very intractable. But when he tried to exact authority outside of the colony it was still worse. The difficulty of securing that concerted military action which the Mohawk chiefs recommended had led James II. to try to unite the northern colonies under the single rule of Sir Edmund Andros, unhampered by any representative assemblies. To meet the

[1] *Journal of the Legislative Council*, i. 47, 48. Compare Governor Spotswood's remarks in dissolving his assembly, in *Old Virginia and Her Neighbours*, ii. 433.

same difficulty, William III. authorized Fletcher to take control of the militia of Connecticut and the Jerseys. In 1693 the king revoked the proprietary grant of Pennsylvania and Delaware to William Penn,[1] and handed over the administration of those two colonies to Fletcher as royal governor. Fletcher accordingly spent a few weeks in Philadelphia, where he found the good Quakers so mildly but inexorably intractable that he was fain to write to the king excusing himself from the charge of this additional burden. He left Pennsylvania as he found it, and the next year Penn prevailed upon the king to reinstate him in his proprietary rights.

Fletcher in Philadelphia

In Connecticut Fletcher had no better success. He visited Hartford in October, 1693, while the assembly was in session, and demanded that the military forces of the colony should be placed at his disposal, at the same time promising to retain Governor Treat in the immediate command over them as his lieutenant. These proposals were flatly refused, and the angry Fletcher wrote to the secretary of state in London : " The laws of England have no force in this colony. . . . They set up for a free state." There is a tradition that one bright afternoon the train-bands of Hartford were drawn up before the place where the as-

Fletcher at Hartford

[1] See below, p. 355.

253

an absolute necessity. Either Parliament must
be that head, or the colonies must enter into a
Federal Union ; no third course was practicable.
It was the conflict with France that taught this
lesson, and therefore the calling of a Continental Congress at New York in 1690 by Jacob
Leisler was an event of great interest and significance. Of the same order of importance was
the Plan of Union presented by William Penn
to the Lords of Trade in 1697. In order to
accomplish by rational and constitutional means
the ends which William III. was seeking when
by a mere order in council he invested the governor of New York with arbitrary control over
Penn's plan for a Federal Union neighbouring colonies, Penn recommended a Federal Union. As the
earliest suggestion of so great a step
in constructive statesmanship, his plan must
always be interesting. It provided for a Congress of two deputies from each colony to meet
once a year, and to have for chairman or president a king's commissioner especially appointed
for the purpose. The place of meeting might
be New York, as conveniently central, and also
because the province was a military frontier and
under a royal governor. For further conven-
ience this governor might be the king's commissioner, " after the manner of Scotland," and
also commander-in-chief of the forces. The
business of the Congress should be " to hear

and adjust all matters of complaint or difference between province and province. As, 1, where persons quit their own province and go to another, that they may avoid their just debts though they be able to pay them ; 2, where offenders fly justice . . .; 3, to prevent or cure injuries in point of commerce; 4, to consider of ways and means to support the union and safety of these provinces against the public enemies. In which Congress the quotas of men and charges will be much easier and more equally set than it is possible for any establishment made here [*i. e.* in England] to do ; for the provinces, knowing their own condition and one another's, can debate that matter with more freedom and satisfaction and better adjust and balance their affairs in all respects for their common safety."[1]

Such was the first simple outline of the scheme which was further developed in Franklin's Plan, in 1754, and again in the Articles of Confederation, until maturity was reached in our present Federal Constitution. When we fully understand that it was the failure to adopt such wise schemes as those of Penn and Franklin that ultimately led to the Stamp Act,[2] we shall be

[1] Preston, *Documents Illustrative of American History*, p. 147.

[2] This is too large a subject to receive full treatment in the present volume. My next work in the present series will be

York, who coveted their wares, knew also that their ships were apt to be formidable, and so treated them usually with politeness. Sometimes the pirate captain was a man of polished address and entertaining speech, who could make himself acceptable at dinner tables and in good society. One of them, we are told, before venturing ashore, was careful to send some silks and cashmeres, with a trifle or so in the shape of costly gems, to Mrs. Fletcher and her stylish daughters. For a dozen years or more the streets of New York might have reminded one of Teheran or Bassora, with their shops displaying rugs of Anatolia or Daghestan, tables of carved teakwood, vases of hammered brass and silver, Bagdad portières, fans of ivory or sandalwood, soft shawls of myriad gorgeous hues and white crape daintily embroidered, along with exquisite ornaments of ruby, pearl, and emerald. In the little town which had been wont to eke out its slender currency with wampum, strange pieces of gold and silver now passed freely from hand to hand ; Greek byzants, Arabian dinars, and mohurs from Hindustan, along with Spanish doubloons and the louis d'or of France. A familiar sight in taverns was the swaggering blade attired in blue coat trimmed with gold lace and pearl buttons, white knee-breeches and embroidered hose, with jewelled dagger in his belt,[1] paying scot for all who would listen to his outlandish yarns, and tipping everybody from the pot-boy, as it was whispered, even to the worshipful governor.

The East India companies, English and Dutch, complained of this state of things, and all merchants who felt interested in the navigation laws added their complaints. But the warships of William of Orange were so fully occupied in the waters about France [2] that the Indian Ocean was inadequately guarded. Under these circumstances a scheme was formed which was highly characteristic of the age, and which introduces us to the most famous name, perhaps, in all the annals of piracy.

Whether Captain William Kidd ever really deserved such a gruesome renown is, however, more or less questionable. He was William certainly no ruffian, but an educated Kidd mariner who for the greater part of his life was esteemed a model of integrity. He was probably the son of a Presbyterian minister at Greenock, in Scotland. In his marriage certificate, in 1691, he is styled "gentleman." At that time he had considerable wealth and lived

[1] See the description of Thomas Tew, in Todd, *op. cit.* p. 175.

[2] Captain Mahan has treated this war in a masterly manner, in his *Influence of Sea Power upon History*, chap. iv.

in a pleasant home on Liberty Street. In earlier days he seems to have been a navigator in various parts of the world. In 1695 King William was discussing with Richard Coote, Earl of Bellomont, and other members of his council, the most feasible means of suppressing piracy, and it was decided to make it a private undertaking. A swift frigate should be sent to the East Indies, under a captain of tried courage and probity, the sea robbers should be vanquished and brought to justice, and their spoil should defray expenses and leave a handsome profit. Robert Livingston and William Kidd happened to be in London, and Livingston recommended Kidd to Lord Bellomont as the very man for the enterprise. These three, with several members of the council, entered into partnership, and subscribed £6000. Kidd received letters-of-marque authorizing him to capture French vessels, and a special commission instructing him to arrest all pirates wheresoever found, and bring them to trial. After reserving a royalty of 10 per cent. for the king, the proceeds of the cruise were to be divided among the partners. Kidd was to render a strict account of all prizes to Lord Bellomont, and Livingston became his surety.[1] A thirty-six-gun frigate, the Adventure,

His commission for arresting pirates

---

[1] Kidd's name often appears in tradition as Robert Kidd, and is sometimes so given in books that should know better.

was duly equipped, and in May, 1696, Kidd sailed from Plymouth, with a crew of eighty men. In New York he picked up about ninety more, and in February, 1697, set sail for Madagascar. The civilized world saw nothing more of him for more than two years.

In the mean time the Leislerites brought about the recall of Governor Fletcher. Two of them — Leisler's son Jacob, and Abraham Gouverneur, who was presently to marry the widowed Mary Milborne — were very busy in London. They secured the restoration of Leisler's estates and the rehabilitation of his memory so far as that could be done by an act of Parliament. Lord Bellomont, who was one of the king's most trusted advisers, declared that the execution of Leisler and Milborne was a judicial murder. *Charges against Fletcher* He was a nobleman of generous and lofty character and entertained sundry democratic notions, so that he soon became a favourite with the Leislerians. They accused Fletcher of complicity with the pirates, or, at the very least of accepting from them bribes or hush-money. It is difficult to tell how far these charges were founded on fact. *He is superseded by Lord Bellomont* Fletcher always resented them, and they were

I have sometimes wondered if this might have been a confusion arising from some vague memory of his connection with Robert Livingston.

not irrefragably proved; but such charges are apt to be hard to prove, even when true. At all events, they led to the recall of Fletcher and the appointment of Bellomont to be governor of New York, with explicit instructions to move heaven and earth for the suppression of piracy. This appointment was made before Kidd sailed, but various causes delayed Bellomont so that he did not arrive in New York until April, 1698.

In order to effect as much concentration as possible without creating disturbance, Bellomont was appointed royal governor of Massachusetts and New Hampshire, as well as New York. His graceful and courteous manners made him generally popular, but his administration was not a tranquil one. As Fletcher quarrelled with the Leislerians, Bellomont kept himself in hot water with the aristocrats. He began by issuing a writ of restitution to put the families of Leisler More party and Milborne in possession of their strife estates, and turmoil at once ensued, for many pieces of this property had passed into the hands of innocent purchasers who were now despoiled. He tried to enforce the navigation laws and to confiscate ships and cargoes for non-payment of custom-house dues. This brought on a quarrel with the merchants and with the collector of the port, whom he cashiered for remissness in enforcing the laws. As the Leis-

Richard Coote, Earl of Bellomont

lerites had accused Governor Fletcher of receiving stolen goods from the pirates, so Bellomont in turn charged some of the members of his aristocratic council with similar practices. Mrs. Bayard one evening wore an extraordinary diamond, which rumour said had been given to her husband as hush-money by some scoundrel who had robbed and murdered an Eastern princess. It was also reported that Gabriel Minvielle had under his bed a big chest full of gold dinars, which, could they have spoken, would have told just as foul a tale. And as for Philipse, why did his son go down to the Narrows in a pinnace, to meet some merchantmen just come from Madagascar?

Bellomont was the more inclined to believe such rumours because of his ingrained prejudices against rich men. He was inclined to regard great wealth as incompatible with perfect honesty. The immense landed estates of the patroons and their feudal privileges disgusted him. He lost no opportunity of attacking land grants in which any flaw could be suspected, and he even proposed a bill which should make it illegal for any person in the province to hold more than one thousand acres.

Bellomont's levelling tendencies

With these levelling tendencies, which accorded well with his Leislerian sympathies, Bellomont was only too ready to believe ill of

Bayard and his friends. He accused them of complicity with pirates and removed Bayard, with four other gentlemen, from his council. In their place he appointed able and well-known Leislerians. Much commotion was thus excited throughout the province, and the next election of representatives was fiercely contested. Never Election before in America had an election day of 1699 consumed so much grog or broken so many pates. The aristocracy suffered a crushing defeat at the polls, and the government thus became Leislerian in all its branches.

This result created something like a panic among the merchants and great landowners, and a report was circulated that the Leislerians were intending to obtain compensation for all the damages which they had suffered since the beginning of the troubles. The king felt it necessary to warn Bellomont against such a policy, which would tend to drive some of the best citizens away from New York. Bellomont replied that he was not so foolish as to countenance such measures. But the complaints against him multiplied, and were presently complicated by a quarrel with the dominies. In the midst of these dissensions came the rumour that William Strange Kidd, the pirate-catcher, from whom rumours nothing had been heard for two years, about Kidd had himself turned pirate! This was a dire mortification for the governor.

The friends of the displaced councilmen could now wag their heads and cry, " Aha ! just see what sort of agents and tools this Earl of Bellomont, so prudish in all such matters, employs !" We can fancy that the need for attending to the affairs of Massachusetts and New Hampshire afforded the governor some relief from this stifling atmosphere of contention and distrust. We can also see that it will be likely to go hard with Captain Kidd if ever he falls into the hands of honest Richard of Bellomont.

Bellomont goes to Boston

Nevertheless it happened, curiously enough, that scarcely had the governor been a month in Boston when a message addressed to him by that mariner disclosed his presence in Narragansett Bay. The message informed Bellomont that he was in a sloop with £10,000 worth of goods on board, and was entirely innocent of the acts of piracy which lying rumour had laid to his charge. Let us briefly note some of the events in this career of innocence.

A message from Kidd

After a tedious voyage of nine months from New York, during which the stores were nearly exhausted and the crew threatened with famine, Kidd arrived off Madagascar in the autumn of 1697. He had encountered neither pirates nor French vessels on the way, and now at the island he found no prey ; all the pirates were

not used pistol nor dagger, but only struck the offender with a bucket, and on the worst construction was guilty only of manslaughter. The prosecution did not break down this de-

His trial and execution

fence, and one cannot read the report of the trial without feeling that the verdict of guilty was predetermined. Kidd was hanged in May, 1701. In spite of the unfairness of the trial, he had probably done enough to deserve his sentence; but his preeminent notoriety is clearly due to other causes than preëminence in crime.

Lord Bellomont's stay in Boston was little more than a year, and his acquaintance with New Hampshire was limited to a fortnight. He was much liked in Boston for his personal qualities and his opposition to the Toryism represented by the friends of Joseph Dudley. For his own part he liked the people of Boston, but as a liberal-minded Episcopalian

Death of Bellomont

he confessed he could not see how so much learning could coexist with so much fanaticism as in some of the Puritan clergymen and professors. In the summer of 1700 he returned to New York. He had long been troubled with gout, and in the following winter died very suddenly.[1]

His death was the signal for an explosion

[1] His mortal remains now rest in St. Paul's churchyard. See Mrs. Lamb's *History of the City of New York*, ii. 446.

which had long been preparing. It soon appeared that some of the reports which had been circulated as to the designs of the Leislerians were well founded. That party had a majority both in the assembly and in the council, and now that Bellomont's restraining hand was removed, they brought in a bill to enable the Leisler family to institute lawsuits for damages which they alleged they had sustained at the hands of the aristocracy during the change from the House of Stuart to the House of Orange. They also brought outrageous charges against prominent members of the aristocratic party. They accused Robert Livingston of defalcation in his accounts, and petitioned the king to remove him from his office of secretary of Indian affairs; they made a similar charge against the late Stephanus van Cortlandt, and brought suits against his widow. In view of the anticipated passage of their Leisler Act for damages, they invited all the injured persons to bring in an inventory of their losses, and some astounding estimates followed, as when a rusty sword and dilapidated gun, which Governor Sloughter had seized, were valued at £40 (say nearly $800).

This last step was unwise, for it seemed to herald a carnival of spoliation and created intense alarm. There was a rumour that Viscount Cornbury had been appointed governor, to succeed

other and soften the animosities between the Leislerites and the aristocracy by uniting them to some extent in opposition to himself. He thus introduced fresh grievances, but some of these were of a kind conducive to growth in constitutional liberty. He obtained from the Assembly a grant of £1500 for fortifying the

A treasurer for the Assembly

Narrows against French fleets, and was very wroth at the suggestion that the Assembly should appoint a treasurer to handle the money. What! did they distrust his integrity? So the business was left to his integrity and three years slipped by, until one fine afternoon a French warship sailed in through the Narrows, and great was the commotion. The batteries had not been built; what had been done with the £1500? Cornbury protested that he had never seen the money, but the Assembly knew better. There was a sound, wholesome discussion, in the course of which the doctrine was plainly stated that the rights of a colonial assembly were precisely the same as those of the House of Commons. The matter was referred to the queen in council, and it is an interesting fact that the Assembly was sustained against the governor. Henceforth it appointed a treasurer and saw that his accounts were properly audited.

It was not only with the New York Assembly that Cornbury had contentions, for he was also

278

governor of New Jersey. Since the overthrow of
Andros, the history of the two provinces of East
and West Jersey had been a plexus
of difficulties which need not here
concern us, until in 1702 all the proprietors agreed in surrendering their
proprietary rights of sovereignty to
Queen Anne. Their ownership of their landed
estates was not disturbed by this surrender.
The two provinces were united into one, and
thenceforward until 1738 New Jersey was an
appendage to New York, in much the same
way that Delaware was an appendage to Pennsylvania. There was the same governor, but the
assemblies were distinct and independent. This
preserved the local life, and prevented New
Jersey from being merged in New York, and
Delaware from being merged in Pennsylvania.
Any such absorption would have been a calamity, for what the civilized world most needs is
variety and individual colour in social development, and the more that local independencies
can be preserved, in so far as such preservation is compatible with general tranquillity, the
better.

Governor Cornbury's first demand upon the
New Jersey Assembly was for a yearly salary of
£2000, to be granted for twenty years. When
we bear in mind that this sum represented nearly
$40,000 in our present currency, we shall ap-

The gov-
ernorship of
New Jersey
united with
that of New
York

St. Lawrence several ships were wrecked upon
ledges of rock, with the loss of more than 1000
lives. Then with preposterous logic a council
of war decided that the mighty river was im-
practicable for such vessels as theirs, and so the
fleet returned to England. The disaster was reported to Nicholson in time to prevent his im-
perilling his army. The affair ended in recriminations, and presently the treaty of Utrecht
allowed New France another half century of
life.

Amid these incidents of war the business of
legislation was encumbered with the usual difficulties. The council, though by no means a tool
in the governor's hands, was very apt to agree
with his views of constitutional questions. The Assembly, on the other
hand, was almost certain to differ
from the governor on questions relat-
ing to revenue, if on no others. In most of the
colonies military exigencies made a greater demand upon the exchequer than people could
comfortably meet. Hence the governor's requests did not usually meet with prompt or
adequate response, and operations were apt to
languish. There is no doubt that despotic
Onontio could mobilize his forces much more
speedily than constitution-hemmed Corlear. It
was half a century of this sort of experience that
led to the Stamp Act.

Difficulty of raising money for military purposes

Under these circumstances the constitutional position and functions of the council gave rise to important discussions. The council maintained that it was properly an upper house, like the House of Lords, Constitutional discussions and this was generally the governor's opinion; but the Assembly insisted that the council was merely an advisory board. Especially jealous was the Assembly of any pretension on the part of the council to initiate or amend money bills. Then there was the burning question of the governor's salary, which the Assembly usually insisted upon granting only for a year at a time, in order to keep a check-rein upon the governor. Sometimes an earnest patriot, like Hunter, bent upon getting things done, would furnish the money from his own pocket. From some of Hunter's letters to Dean Swift we catch glimpses of his feeling about the people's representatives: " This is the finest air to live upon in the universe ; and if our trees and birds could speak, and our assemblymen be silent, the finest conversation also. The soil bears all things, but not for me. According to the custom of the country, the sachems are the poorest of the people. . . . I thought in coming to this government I should have hot meals and cool drinks, and recreate my body in Holland sheets upon beds of down; whereas I am doing penance as if I were a hermit. . . . I am used like a dog, after having done all that is in the power of man to deserve better treatment."

Notwithstanding such expressions of feeling, and in spite of many altercations with the Assembly, Governor Hunter was greatly liked and admired, and there was much sorrow when private business called him back to England in 1719. His friend and successor William Burnet, who came next year, was another upright and able governor. He was a son of Gilbert Burnet, Bishop of Salisbury, the famous historian, and was himself a man of learning and accomplishments, with much practical sagacity and rare personal charm. One of his first measures, however, was for a time extremely unpopular. There was far too much intercourse between the French and the warriors of the Long House. It was an excellent instance of the shrewdness with which Onontio made trade and religion support each other. Jesuit priests had made converts to Christianity even among their arch-enemies the Mohawks, and with these converts they formed a colony at Caughnawaga, a place on the right bank of the St. Lawrence, a short distance above Montreal. These Caughnawaga Indians soon became a source of danger to New York. The most prolific source of the furs which made so large a part of the wealth of the province was the country about the Great Lakes, inhabited

William Burnet

by Ottawas, Sacs and Foxes, Pottawatomies and other Algonquin tribes, besides Dakotahs. These were commonly called the " Far Indians." Now since the English commercial policy, however narrow, was far more liberal than that of Louis XV., the best supply of goods for the Indians was in New York and Albany, not in Montreal. Knives and guns, powder and blankets, were apt to be plenty and cheap among the English, while scarce and dear among the French. Accordingly the Caughnawagas soon became the middlemen in a brisk and lucrative trade. By way of the St. Lawrence and Lake Champlain they brought furs from the Great Lakes to Albany and exchanged them there for tools and weapons, blankets and beads, which they forthwith carried to Montreal and sold to the French traders. It was often in this way only that the Frenchmen obtained the wares which they needed for getting furs from the " Far Indians." [1]

The Caughnawagas and their trade

Now this trade through the Caughnawagas was profitable to merchants in New York and Albany, as well as in Montreal. But every Caughnawaga was a Jesuit spy whose presence upon English soil was a possible source of danger. Moreover, the use of the St. Lawrence route played into the hands of the enemy by diverting trade from the safer

Its dangers

[1] See Parkman, *A Half-Century of Conflict*, i. 15.

two docks. Up near the present foot of Chambers Street was a garden for popular resort, with a new bowling green or skittles ground. Most of the open country between Cortlandt Street and the village of Sappokanikan or Greenwich, an area of more than sixty acres, was then known as the King's Farm. It was the land which the blooming widow Anneke Jans had brought to Dominie Bogardus, and it was long known as the Dominie's Bowery. In 1664 it was confirmed by Governor Nicolls to Anneke Jans and her heirs. In 1671 five of the heirs sold the farm to Governor Lovelace, and in 1674 the Duke of York confiscated it, so that it was the Duke's Farm until 1685, when with James's accession to the throne it became the King's Farm. In Governor Fletcher's time Trinity Church was founded, and in 1705 Queen Anne granted this farm to the church. It happened that one of the sons of Anneke Jans had not joined in the sale to Lovelace, and the heirs of this son claimed that his failure to join invalidated the sale. At first the property was not of great value, but with the growth of the city its value increased enormously, and suits in ejectment were brought against Trinity Church by heirs who coveted the property. Between 1750 and 1847 not less than sixteen or seventeen such suits were brought, with a persistency which seemed to

The farm
of Anneke
Jans

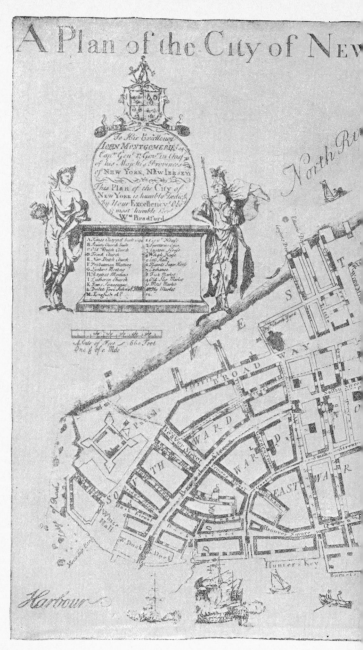

JAMES LYNE'S PLAN OF NEW

ORK from an actual Survey

Made by James Lyne

Col: Rob: Lurting MAYOR

W A R D

Kings Farm

Rop Walk

COMMON

THE

W A R D

Kip Street

High Road to Boston

William Street

WARD

RIE'S

Beekmans Swamp

MONT GOME

Chappel Street

CITY: W. BRADFORD, CIRCA 1731

learn no lessons from defeat. In 1847 Vice-chancellor Sanford decided that, after waiving all other points, the church had acquired a valid title by prescription, and all the adverse claims were vitiated by lapse of time.

Above the Freshwater Pond in 1740 there had been little change since 1680, except that there were a few more country houses along the Bowery Lane. While we note the slow rate of growth in the city, we must also bear in mind the limited extent of the province. Its 50,000 inhabitants lived on Long Island and the banks of the Hudson, all save some 2000 Germans who had come in Governor Hunter's time, and had pushed up the Mohawk valley beyond Schenectady, making settlements at German Flats, Palatine Bridge, and Stone Arabia. Far beyond these and quite alone in the wilderness stood the fortified trading-post of Oswego. The territory of the Six Nations, stretching northerly toward the Adirondacks, southerly into the Susquehanna valley, and westward to Lake Erie, was of course claimed by Corlear as protector and overlord; but for the present he had as little control over it as the Grand Turk has over Tripoli. It is important to remember, if we would do justice to the pivotal part played by New York in early American history, that so late as 1776, with a population of 170,000, she ranked only seventh among the thirteen states, while her geographical limits had scarcely changed since 1720. The supreme greatness of New York dates from a period subsequent to the Revolution, and in its origin was closely connected with the westward migration from New England, the settlement of the northwestern states, and the opening of the Erie Canal. In the colonial period the agriculture of New York was considerable, and a great deal of wheat was exported ; but the fur-trade was always the controlling interest, and was often the source of immense wealth. Nevertheless, inasmuch as New York was preëminently the frontier colony against the French, and as it was made the scene of military operations to a much greater extent than any other colony, it was always necessary to keep up an army. Besides the British regular forces, which were stationed on Manhattan Island, there was a colonial regular army of 2500, and there were more than 15,000 trained militia. These circumstances, as well as the actual frequency of wars between 1690 and 1760, entailed ruinous expense and oppressive taxation, and interfered seriously with the normal growth of the colony.

Some causes of slowness in growth Such a state of things had been to some extent foreseen and dreaded by Andros and Dongan, as it was deplored by the later governors who had to contend with it. One of the worst ills was the chronic affliction of a depreciated paper currency. By the end of the French wars New York had a public debt of £300,000, and the taxation, including direct levies upon real and personal property as well as duties on imports, was an acute annoyance.

It was probably due to the prevalence of warfare that the power of the assembly was somewhat less and the arbitrariness of the governor somewhat greater than in the other colonies. After seventy years of arbitrary rule, representative assemblies and incessant warfare began at just the same time in the Citadel of America, with Governor Fletcher. The most important part of the constitutional progress achieved by the assemblies came within the interval of peace between the Treaty of Utrecht and the War of the Austrian Succession. Usually the headquarters of the commanding general were in the city of New York, and various courtly visitors were attracted by the army. More than elsewhere the royal governor had somewhat the air of a sovereign holding court, and the political atmosphere about him was thick and heavy with Toryism. The officials generally were demonstrative in their loyalty, keeping the king's birthday with festivities and speeches. Under such auspices a powerful Tory party was developed in New York, and in the War of Inde-

Comparative weakness of the assembly

pendence it was made to seem all the more powerful in that the Tory Johnsons controlled the Whigs and military policy of the Long House. Tories Nevertheless the Whig party in New York was also very strong and vigorous, nor was it by any means confined to the lower grades of society. Among the leaders of the Revolutionary party were the Schuylers and Livingstons, Van Rensselaers, Van Cortlandts, Morrises, Alexanders, Clintons, and Jays. It is a common mistake to overrate the strength of New York Toryism. The truth is that both parties were very powerful in their leaders, while beneath there was a surging mass of people with uncertain proclivities, some strongly Whig, some strongly Tory, some independent, some stolidly indifferent to everything outside of private business. The result was seen in excitement and disorder at elections, and occasional violent vicissitudes in party supremacy. In Massachusetts or Virginia you could usually foretell the action of the assembly upon an important question, there was so much homogeneity of thought among the members of those purely English communities. But in New York the effects of the few independent Great value thinkers and of the stolid mass were of New York things with which it was difficult to as a "doubt-ful state" reckon quantitatively. Similar characteristics have distinguished the state of New

York down to the present day. The politics of some communities are so swayed by the inert mass of ingrained prejudice that independent thinking finds it nearly impossible to reverse the customary verdict. You know beforehand that in these days the vote of Vermont will be Republican and that of Alabama will be Democratic, no matter what are the principles and issues at stake ; but in New York an immense majority on one side may be followed the next year by an equally overwhelming majority on the other side. This uncertainty, combined with the great magnitude of its vote, almost enough of itself to determine a national election, has made New York a factor of inestimable value in American history. It has made that state one of the chief safeguards of the republic, and for it we have largely to thank the spirit of cosmopolitanism which has characterized it ever since the days of Peter Minuit. That cosmopolitan spirit, weakening the grasp of local prejudices, leaves the public mind responsive to the needs and exigencies of the time. One of the worst calamities that could happen in our time would be the conversion of New York into a " sure " state ; one of the greatest benefits would be the change of Pennsylvania into a perennially " doubtful " state.

Returning to our old Knickerbocker community, we may note that the old antagonism between the Leislerians and the aristocrats was not parallel to the opposition between Whigs and Tories. Some features of Leislerism were reproduced in the democratic views of Jefferson's extremest followers in the days of the French Revolution. Among our Revolutionary leaders there was aristocracy enough in temper and views, as exemplified in Washington, Schuyler, Jay, Trumbull, and Hancock. Especially in New York we may note the conspicuousness of well-born and accomplished leaders as hardly less notable than in Virginia. This fact was an outcome of the social conditions established early in the colonial period.

The old aristocracy

The tone of colonial New York was always aristocratic. Neither Maryland nor Virginia furnished a much stronger contrast to that peculiar type of New England democracy which was exemplified perhaps most completely in Connecticut. In the latter colony, with its lowest stratum of society far above the peasant type, there were few if any great landed estates or accumulations of wealth in any form. Yet nowhere else in America were so large a proportion of the people in easy circumstances ; nowhere was there more comfort and refinement " to the square mile." The relation of landlord and tenant was seldom met with in Connecticut. Education

The Connecticut type of democracy

308

was universal, and the country squire was a much more cultivated person than his contemporary in England, as the country minister was more learned. Self-government by town-meeting was ubiquitous, public debts were very unusual, taxation was light, governors as well as assemblies were chosen by the people, and the commonwealth was for all practical purposes as independent of Great Britain as it is to-day. Connecticut in the eighteenth century was preëminently the home of unpretentious and refined democracy, a " land of steady habits," but with perhaps a little more monotony and provinciality than its neighbours on either side.

In New York, on the other hand, there was a considerable stratum of peasantry, among the Germans and Dutch at least, and in the city there was something of a " populace " of rough water-side characters, discontented artisans, and idlers in tap-rooms. In New York, as in Boston, it was this sort of populace that now and then relieved the tedium of existence by mobs and riots. Yet neither New York nor Boston could be called an unruly town. Between the peasantry and the patroons, as between the populace and the merchant princes, the social interval was very wide. Of the lowest and poorest classes it must be said that there were extremely few paupers or beggars. But at the other extreme of society immense fortunes were accumulated; and there was a distinct consciousness of a gulf between high and low which gave to Leislerism certain features that in Connecticut would have been impossible. The relation of landlord and tenant was extremely common. The great manors of the Cortlandts and Van Rensselaers and Livingstons extended over many square miles and were cultivated by a vast number of tenants. Each of these manors had a representative in The manors and their tenantry the assembly; their lords held court-baron and court-leet, very much as in Maryland,[1] and could even in some instances inflict capital punishment. On rent-days, twice a year, the tenants came flocking to the manor-house and, after paying their rent in coin or produce, were entertained by the landlord with a barbecue and plentiful draughts of 'Sopus ale.[2] These vast estates were held together by primogeniture, usually somewhat qualified by small legacies to the younger sons and the daughters. The prevalence of this manorial system was often cited, and no doubt correctly, as one reason for the slow increase of population in New York; a small farmer would prefer to be a landowner in New Jersey

[1] See *Old Virginia and Her Neighbours,* ii. 169–172.
[2] At Esopus and elsewhere the water of the Hudson has always made a light ale of fine body and extremely delicate flavour.

or Pennsylvania, rather than the tenant of a manor on the Hudson. Most of the manorial privileges were swept away during the War of Independence, and the patroons lost their position of political superiority.

As an example of a rural mansion may be cited that of the Schuylers at the Flats, near Albany, as described by Mrs. Grant of Laggan, in her charming "Memoirs of an American Lady." The estate ran along two miles of the western bank of the Hudson, bordered with drooping elm-trees of enormous girth. "On the right you saw the river in all its beauty, there above a mile broad. On the opposite side the view was bounded by steep hills, covered with lofty pines, from which a waterfall descended. . . . Opposite to the grounds lay an island, above a mile in length and about a quarter in breadth, which also belonged to the colonel; exquisitely beautiful it was, and though the haunt I most delighted in, it is not in my power to describe it. . . . Southward, on the confines of an interminable wild, rose two gently sloping eminences, about half a mile from the shore. From each of these a large brook descended, bending through the plain, and having their course marked by the shades of primeval trees and shrubs left there to shelter the cattle when the ground was cleared. On these eminences,

Description of the Schuyler manor

311

in the near neighbourhood and full view of the mansion at the Flats, were two large and well-built dwellings, inhabited by Colonel Schuyler's two younger sons, Peter and Jeremiah. To the eldest was allotted the place inhabited by his father, which, from its lower situation and level surface, was called the Flats. . . . They had also a large house in Albany, which they occupied occasionally."

The mansion at the Flats "was a large brick house of two or rather three stories (for there were excellent attics), besides a sunk story, finished with the exactest neatness. The lower floor had two spacious rooms, with large light closets ; on the first there were three rooms, and in the upper one four. Through the middle of the house was a very wide passage, with opposite front and back doors, which in summer admitted a stream of air peculiarly grateful to the languid senses. It was furnished with chairs and pictures like a summer parlour. Here the family usually sat in hot weather, when there were no ceremonious strangers. . . . The mirrors, the paintings, the china, but above all the state bed, were considered as the family Teraphim, secretly worshipped and only exhibited on very rare occasions. . . . The rooms were shut up to keep the flies, which in that country are an absolute nuisance, from spoiling the furniture. Another motive was that they

The Schuyler mansion

312

might be pleasantly cool when opened for company. This house had also two appendages common to all those belonging to persons in easy circumstances there. One was a large portico at the door, with a few steps leading up to it, and floored like a room; it was open at the sides, and had seats all around. Above was either a slight wooden roof, painted like an awning, or a covering of lattice-work, over which a transplanted wild vine spread its luxuriant leaves and numerous clusters. These, though small and rather too acid till sweetened by the frost, had a beautiful appearance. What gave an air of liberty and safety to these rustic porticoes, which always produced in my mind a sensation of pleasure that I know not how to define, was the number of little birds domesticated there. For their accommodation there was a small shelf built round, where they nestled, safe from the touch of slaves and children, who were taught to regard them as the good genii of the place, not to be disturbed with impunity."

The protection which these little birds bestowed " was of more importance than any inhabitant of Britain can imagine. . . . The insect population is numerous beyond be- American insects lief. . . . These minute aerial foes [1] are more harassing than the terrible inhabitants

[1] A London newspaper of 1710 thus speaks of the mosquito : " The New York people are greatly troubled with a

to a great height in the midst, and sloped down till it came within ten feet of the ground, when The barn the walls commenced; which, like the whole of this vast fabric, were formed of wood. It was raised three feet from the ground by beams resting on stone; and on these beams was laid a massive oak floor. Before the door was a large sill, sloping downwards, of the same materials. About twelve feet in breadth, on each side of this capacious building, were divided off for cattle; on one side ran a manger, at the above-mentioned distance from the wall, the whole length of the building, with a rack above it; on the others were stalls for the other cattle. . . . The cattle and horses stood with their hinder parts to the wall, and their heads projecting towards the threshing floor. There was a prodigious large box or open chest in one side built up, for holding the corn after it was thrashed; and the roof, which was very lofty and spacious, was supported by large cross-beams; from one to the other of these was stretched a great number of long poles, so as to form a sort of open loft, on which the whole rich crop was laid up. The floor of those parts of the barn, which answered the purposes of a stable and cow-house, was made of thick slab deals, laid loosely over the supporting beams. And the mode of cleaning those places was by turning the boards and per-

mitting the dung and litter to fall into the receptacles left open below for the purpose. . . .
In the front of this vast edifice there were
prodigious folding doors, and two others that
opened behind." [1]

Mrs. Grant's description of Albany is too
much to our present purpose to be omitted :
" One very wide and long street lay parallel to
the river, the intermediate space between it and
the shore being occupied by gardens. A small,
steep hill rose above the centre of the   The town
town, on which stood a fort, intended   of Albany
(but very ill-adapted) for the defence of the place
and of the neighbouring country. From the
foot of this hill another street was built, sloping
pretty rapidly down till it joined the one before
mentioned. . . . This street was still wider than
the other ; it was only paved on each side, the
middle being occupied by public edifices. These
consisted of a market-place, a guard-house, a
town hall, and the English and Dutch churches.
The English church, belonging to the Episcopal
persuasion and in the diocese of the Bishop of
London, stood at the foot of the hill, at the
upper end of the street. The Dutch church was
situated at the bottom of the descent where the
street terminated. Two irregular streets, not so
broad but equally long, ran parallel to those,

[1] *Memoirs of an American Lady*, i. 142, 143, 147, 164–
168, 171–173, 176–178.

hut. I think he retired to Canada at last; but I remember being ready to worship him for the sanctity with which my imagination invested him, and being cruelly disappointed because I was not permitted to visit him." [1]

In the middle of the eighteenth century Albany was much more distinctively Dutch than the city of New York, which was so cosmopolitan. In general Dutch habits held their own with much more conservatism in towns like Esopus, or Schenectady, or Flatbush, than in the centre of travel and traffic. With some Flatbush details we may complete our sketch of the Dutch country house. Ordinarily it had not three stories, like the Schuyler mansion, but was a low and rambling affair, covering much territory but needing few stairs. It was usually built of brick. In the earlier times the front roof swept down without break from ridgepole to eaves and beyond, so as to cover a veranda, while the much longer back roof sometimes came within eight feet of the ground. Sometimes in the front were dormer windows. About the middle of the eighteenth century the hipped roof with dormer windows came into vogue. From tin spouts at the end of the gutters the clear rain water fell into tubs or casks. It was not unusual to have a projecting beam from

A Flatbush country house

[1] *Memoirs of an American Lady*, i. 44–49.

the gable end of the spacious garret, so that heavy articles might be hoisted into it with tackle, as is often seen in Holland to this day.[1] The shutters were usually of solid wood, with a crescent-shaped aperture near the top, and held back when open by a piece of iron shaped like the letter S. Instead of the huge central chimney of New England houses, there were usually two broad and stately chimneys, one at each gable end. The Dutch front door was almost always divided into an upper and a lower half, so that when the lower half was shut the upper half served the purposes of an open window. The upper half when shut was usually lighted with a large pair of glass bulls'- eyes. Quaint knockers and spoon-shaped latches of iron or polished

The stoop

brass were the outfit of the door. The spacious "stoop" outside, with its long seats cosily facing each other, was a very important adjunct to the house. In summer time it fulfilled the functions of family sitting-room and reception-room ; neighbours gathered there and talked politics and gossip amid the fragrance of tobacco smoke.

In the interiors of these Dutch houses the

---

[1] I am indebted for many details to Mrs. Vanderbilt's *Social History of Flatbush*, New York, 1881, an excellent and scholarly work; but the absence of an index to such a book is an unpardonable sin.

heavy oak beams which supported the upper floor often projected below the ceiling of the room underneath, a pleasing architectural feature. In the humbler houses a plain protecting board, known as a "chair rail," ran around the plaster walls about three feet above the floor; but panelled wainscots were not very uncommon, and sometimes a wainscoting of tiles might be seen. The jamb of the enormous fireplace was usually faced with blue or pink tiles, upon which were often represented scenes from the Bible. In winter time the fireside played a part similar to that of the stoop in warm weather. The one in the dining-room was likely to be the place of chief resort. Its dancing flames lighted up the china and silver in the cupboard opposite, and the moon's face on the tall clock in the corner, and afforded enough illumination for a game of backgammon or dominoes on the cherry dining-table, though many worthy Dutch families esteemed such diversions, even to the noble chess, as fit only for alehouse parlours. The same flickering light, eked out perhaps by a couple of dip candles, sufficed for grandma with her knitting, beside the chintz-curtained window in her low rush-seated chair with bright red cushion. Other chairs in the room were of mahogany, high-backed, with claw feet, their broad seats covered with brocade. Often, how-

The dining-room

ever, the chairs were of painted wood and rush-work, and the table of deal, and the family living-room the ample kitchen. In the latter case there was usually a separate back kitchen for the servants, who were likely to be negro slaves.

The deep dark cellar, with its coolish and even temperature, was for much more than half the year a storage-place for provisions. The farmers of New York raised upon their own farms the greater part of the food which they consumed, and even in the city, where orchards, kitchen-gardens, and hen-coops were not yet uncommon, there was no such The cellar complete dependence upon markets as in our time. A large part of the autumn work was the preparation of the stores that were to be put away in the spacious cellar. The packing of butter in firkins and pickled pork in barrels, the smoking of hams and bacon, the corning of beef rounds and briskets, the chopping of sausage-meat and head-cheese, the trying of lard, the careful and dainty salting of mackerel and other fish, — made it a busy time for all the household. In the cellar might be found all these good things, with kegs of soused pigs' feet, stone jars of pickles, barrels of red and green apples, bins heaped high with potatoes, parsnips, and turnips; along with barrels of vinegar, cider, and ale, and canty brown jugs of rum. In the houses of the wealthier sort there was also plenty of wine, either of the claret family or some kind of sack, which was a generic name covering sherries, Canaries, and Madeiras. For your new-fangled hot-house notions of "teeto-talism" would have been quite unintelligible to the farmer or burgher of those healthy days of abundant and breezy activity out-of-doors. In the Dutch cupboard or on the sideboard always stood the gleaming decanter of cut glass or the square high-shouldered magnum with its aromatic schnapps.[1]

Here's your good health, and your family's!

[1] In connection with the subject of eating and drinking it may be interesting to cite the caterer's bill for the banquet given by the corporation of New York to Lord Cornbury, upon his arrival as governor, in 1704 : —

1704. THE MAYOR, ALDERMEN, ETC., *Dr.*

		£	s.	d.
Dec. 19	To a piece of beef and cabbage .	0	7	6
	To a dish of tripe and cowheel	0	6	0
	To a leg of pork and turnips .	0	8	3
	To 2 puddings . . .	0	14	6
	To a surloyn of beef .	0	13	6
	To a turkey and onions . .	0	9	0
	To a leg mutton and pickles .	0	6	0
	To a dish chickens . .	0	10	6
	To minced pyes . . .	1	4	0
	To fruit, cheese, bread, etc. .	0	7	6
	To butter for sauce . .	0	7	9
	To hire of 2 negroes to assist .	0	6	0
	To dressing dinner, etc. . .	1	4	0
	To 31 bottles wine . .	3	2	0
	To beer and syder . .	0	12	0
		10	18	6

This is cited from Todd's *City of New York*, p. 224.

In the bedrooms, or sometimes in an entry way, you would come here and there upon a long deep chest of cherry or oak, filled *Chests and* with rolls of homespun linen, or with *secretaries* blankets and coverlets. A different kind of foresight was then needed from that of the present day, when all manner of shops are so accessible. Large quantities of linen were spun and woven into pieces, from which table-cloths, sheets, and garments could be cut when wanted. A bride's trousseau was not ordered all at once from fashionable modistes and milliners, but was taken from the family stores of silks and cambrics and laces that years had accumulated. Chests were therefore indispensable, and tall cases of drawers were very common. A very beautiful piece of furniture was the secretary or covered writing-desk, with drawers below ; it was usually made of mahogany adorned with polished brass, and it was apt to contain secret drawers or pigeon-holes, where gold, coins, or jewels, or valuable papers could be hidden.

The bedstead was almost always the kingly "fourposter," with its feather-beds resting upon a straw mattress supported by tight cords. It was draped with white dimity curtains and coverlet, or, perhaps, instead of dimity a kind of chintz was used, with vines and birds and flowers in bright colours. The *Beds* legs of the bedstead were so long that there was

325

plenty of room beneath for the low children's bed which was kept there during the day and trundled out at bedtime. In the days before Satan had invented hot-air furnaces and steam radiators, it was apt to be cold in the bedroom on winter nights. Sometimes water froze in the ewer; and at such times, in spite of Sergeant Buzfuz, there were those who did trouble themselves about the brass warming-pan, filled with glowing embers, which was thrust here and there between the linen sheets to take off the chill.[1]

[1] For further information concerning the contents of the house, I cite from an appraisement in 1792 the following list, in which the pound sterling has approximately its present value : —

	£	s.	d.
25 pewter plates, 1s. each . . .	1	5	0
37 earthen plates	0	10	0
9 pewter dishes, 4s. each . . .	1	16	0
8 earthen dishes, 2s. 6d. each .	1	0	0
2 waffle-irons, 6s. each . . .	0	12	0
1 musket	0	16	0
1 saddle and bridle	3	0	0
10 keelers (wooden milk-tubs) . .	1	0	0
6 spinning wheels, 12s. each . .	3	12	0
1 pair kitchen andirons . . .	0	8	0
2 bookcases, 1s. 6d. each . .	0	3	0
1 bed, bedstead, and curtains .	10	0	0
1 dining-table	16	0	0
1 looking-glass	1	10	0
15 Windsor chairs, 6s. each . .	4	10	0
12 rush-bottom chairs, 2s. each .	1	4	0

KNICKERBOCKER SOCIETY

In general, so far as concerned the homestead with its equipments, the style of living in colonial New York was one of much comfort with little display. But when we come to the subject of dress, the case was somewhat different. In all parts of the world, and in all ages down to the present, display has

Dress

	£	s.	d.
4 mahogany chairs, 8s. each	1	12	0
8 old chairs, 6d. each	0	4	0
1 mahogany dining-table	4	0	0
1 writing-desk	0	10	0
1 cupboard	0	16	0
1 large chest	0	16	0
1 looking-glass	1	0	0
1 large Dutch cupboard	4	0	0
1 bed, bedstead, and curtains	15	0	0
1 wild-cherry dining-table	1	0	0
1 looking-glass	1	5	0
1 eight-day clock	14	0	0
1 looking-glass	5	0	0
1 desk and bookcase	20	0	0
1 mahogany tea-table	2	0	0
1 bed, bedstead, and curtains	10	0	0
1 Dutch Bible	2	0	0
1 English dictionary	1	0	0
1 parcel of books	7	0	0
6 sets of china cups and saucers	3	0	0
27 Delft plates	0	13	6
1 silver tankard	15	0	0
1 silver sugar-cup	14	0	0
1 silver milk-pot	4	0	0
13 silver table-spoons	13	0	0

This is cited from Mrs. Vanderbilt's *Social History of Flatbush*, pp. 81, 82.

been the primary motive in dress, and considerations of comfort have been distinctly secon-
dary. Of late years marked improvement has
been shown, and possibly in the endeavour to
subordinate display, too little heed has been
given to æsthetic requirements. Early in the
eighteenth century the streets of New York
were gorgeous with costumes. One eminent cit-
izen is described as clad in a long-skirted coat
and knee-breeches of cinnamon cloth trimmed
with silver lace; the coat is lined with sky-blue
silk, the hose are of dove-coloured silk, and the
shoes have large silver buckles. Over his enormous wig, elaborately curled and scented with
ambergris, he wears a wide-brimmed hat of black
felt with a band of gold lace; through the opening of his red satin waistcoat finely bestrewn
with threads of gold peep the dainty ruffles of
the white Holland shirt; and at his left side,
fastened with a bright scarlet sword-knot, hangs
a diamond-hilted sword. And as for the ladies,
with blue-and-gold atlas gowns "laced over
very tight stays," showing glimpses of black
velvet petticoat trimmed with silver, and not
falling so low as to hide the crimson stockings
and fine Morocco shoes,[1] we should soon lose
ourselves if we were to try to describe more
closely the dress-stuffs of the time, with their
weird names,—"chilloes, betelees, deribands,

[1] Todd, *The City of New York,* pp. 207, 208, 230.

tapsiels, surbettees, sannoes, gilongs, mulmuls, and cushlashes," — that were familiar enough over the shop counters in the days when New York was so near to the Indian Ocean.

One fancies that something of the same undefinable but potent charm for which New York is to-day so eminent among the world's great bustling cities must already have characterized it when its roof-trees sheltered but ten thousand souls. Whether it be in the journals of visitors, or in private correspondence, we always get the impression of a lively and cheerful town, where people like to come, and from which they are sorry to go away. In the old days, indeed, there was a restful sense of leisure which the rapid pace of modern life has ruthlessly destroyed. For architecture, for other fine arts in their various forms, for learning, for intellectual stimulus of whatsoever sort, the New York of Burnet's time could not be compared with its mother-city, Amsterdam, to say nothing of such centres of civilization as Venice, or Florence, or Paris; but there was about the little city an air of dignity and refinement which scholars and men of the world found attractive. In 1668 Governor Lovelace wrote, in a letter to Charles II., " I find some of these people have the breeding of courts, and I cannot conceive how such is acquired." The explanation was simple enough; the manners of an

Cheerfulness of New York

329

1600 volumes, was established in 1729, in a room in the City Hall on Wall Street. It was known as the Corporation Library until 1754, when it was merged in the New York Society Library, founded in that year. In the Dutch period there were some good schools, but these declined under English rule. In 1757 the historian William Smith exclaimed : " What a contrast in everything respecting the cultivation of science between this and the colonies first settled by the English. . . . Our schools are of the lowest order ; the instructors want instruction ; . . . and the evidences of bad taste, both as to thought and language, are visible in all our proceedings, public and private." [1] This William Smith, son of the accomplished lawyer in the Zenger case, was himself one of the few literary men of the province, the author of a " History of New York to the Year 1732," which is sturdy and racy, but so full of partisan bitterness that Smith himself admits it " deserves not the name of a history." As literature, however, it has decided merits. The only other literary name which needs to be mentioned before the Stamp Act period is that of Cadwallader Colden, son of a Scottish parson in Berwickshire. He was born in 1687 and educated at the University of Edinburgh, after

Reading and literature

William Smith

Cadwallader Colden

[1] Smith's *History of New York*, i. 328, ii. 379.

which he studied medicine and began the practice of it in Philadelphia. In 1718 Governor Hunter made him surveyor-general of the province of New York. The next year Colden bought a fine estate in Orange County, some 3000 acres, and built a house on it. There he lived for many years in rural quiet, devoting himself to the physical sciences and to history, and keeping up a correspondence with the most eminent scholars and philosophers of Europe. At the time of the Stamp Act he was lieutenant-governor of New York, acting as governor. The work by which he is best known is his " History of the Five Nations."

No outline of the Knickerbocker social life can pass without mention the lower strata of society, the servile classes. These were the same in kind as in Virginia, indented white servants and negro slaves. I have discussed them so elaborately in that connection that I need not here repeat myself.[1] In New York, as in Virginia, the indented white servants were either, 1, convicts shipped from Great White servants Britain, to get rid of them; 2, poor men and women kidnapped and sold into servitude; or, 3, redemptioners, who paid their passage by servile labour after arriving in this country. As the great landed estates of New

---

[1] See *Old Virginia and Her Neighbours*, ii. 205–236.

ters. They were prohibited from gathering in groups of more than four, and they were forbidden to carry guns, swords, or clubs, under penalty of ten lashes at the whipping-post. One curious act provided that no slave could go about the streets after nightfall anywhere south of the Collect without a lighted lantern, "so as the light thereof may be plainly seen."[1]

In 1712, during Governor Hunter's administration, there was an attempt at a slave insurrection. A party of negroes, armed with guns, The negro knives, and hatchets, assembled one plot of 1712 evening, in an orchard near Maiden Lane, and set fire to an outhouse. At sight of the flames people came running to the spot, and as fast as they came were shot or slashed. Nine had been killed and six wounded when a squad of soldiers came upon the scene and captured the murderers. Many negroes were arrested, and twenty-one were executed in ways intended to strike terror. One was broken on the wheel, and several were burned alive at the stake, while the rest were hanged.[2]

The recollection of this affair may have had something to do with the virulence of the panic that was brought on in 1741 by what has been called the "Great Negro Plot." This was a melancholy instance of panic and delusion, not

[1] Morgan, *Slavery in New York*, p. 13.
[2] *Colonial Documents*, v. 341, 346, 356, 367, 371, 525.

wholly unmingled with fraud, and has often been likened to the witchcraft delusion at Salem Village in 1692. It might also be compared with Titus Oates's miserable "Popish Plot," inasmuch as it was a symptom of a wave of fierce anti-Catholic excitement. To the generally mild and tolerant policy of New York we have now and then had occasion to note some exceptions. At the close of the seventeenth century, when the Counter-Reformation was still showing such formidable strength in the giant war between Louis XIV. and William III., the dread of Catholics showed itself again and again in the legislative acts of Protestant countries. For example, in 1700 it was enacted in New York that any Popish priest discovered within the province after the first day of November of that year should be seized and imprisoned for life ; and for every such person who should escape and be found at large, the penalty should be the gallows. Any person convicted of aiding or concealing such priest should be set in the pillory for three days and give bonds at the discretion of the court.[1] This

The " Great Negro Plot " of 1741

Dread of Catholic priests

---

[1] *Colonial Laws of New York*, i. 428. About the same time the law was passed in Rhode Island, debarring Catholics from the franchise; see Arnold's *History of Rhode Island*, ii. 490–494. In Massachusetts a Romish priest was liable to imprisonment for life.

ney took fire, but no harm was done. Then a fire broke out in a storehouse, which was traced to the careless dropping of ashes from a tobacco pipe. Three days afterward the hay in a cow-stable was found burning; there was an alarm, and the fire was put out, but people had scarcely left the scene, when flames were described shooting up in a loft over a kitchen where negroes were known to lodge. " The next morning coals were found under a haystack near a coach-house on Broadway. The following day a fire burst forth from the house of Sergeant Burns opposite the fort ; and a few hours later, the roof of Mr. Hilton's house near the Fly Market was discovered on fire, and, on the same afternoon, Colonel Frederick Philipse's storehouse was all ablaze." [1]

Alarms of fire

From such alarming incidents there was nothing at all strange in the rapid genesis of a fierce and bloodthirsty panic. On April 11 the common council offered £100 reward, with a full pardon, to any conspirator who should tell what he knew about a plot for burning the city. This offer elicited a " confession " from Mary Burton, who swore that, in meetings at Hughson's Tavern, certain negroes had matured such an incendiary plot, as the first step in a revolution which was to make

The alleged conspiracy

[1] Mrs. Lamb's *History of the City of New York,* ii. 582.

340

Hughson *king* and a darky named Cæsar *governor*. She further averred that Colonel Philipse's Cuffy used to say that " some people had too much and others too little, but the time was coming when Master Philipse would have less and Cuff more." The only white people present at these meetings besides herself were Hughson and his wife and a loose woman named Carey. After a while, however, she " confessed " that a poor school-teacher, John Ury, who was known to be a Catholic, had taken part in the affair. The result of these disclosures was a reign of terror which lasted until September. In the course of it, Hughson and his wife, the teacher Ury, and the woman Wholesale Carey were hanged, and twenty other executions white persons were imprisoned. One hundred and fifty-four negroes were arrested, of whom fourteen were burned alive at the stake, and eighteen were hanged. Throughout the affair Mary Burton seems to have played the part which at Salem was shared among the " afflicted children," and just as at Salem, when the panic was clearly waning, the end was hastened by her aiming the accusations too high and striking at persons of consequence. The wretched girl received £100, the wages of her perjury. But after the terror was over, it began to be doubted, and has ever since been doubted, whether the

341

lics and the Quakers. Yet circumstances were such in Penn's time that this radical hostility did not prevent the existence, for a moment, of something like a tacit alliance between the two; and the same cruel king, who broke the legs and crushed the thumbs of his Scottish Presbyterian subjects with all the zest of an inquisitor, was glad to seize an occasion for setting free the Quakers who crowded the jails of England. This was because Quakers and Catholics differed so far, though in opposite directions, from the opinions generally held by the English people that they were alike condemned by everybody. Even the warmest advocates of toleration were wont to make an exception in the case of Catholics and Quakers, who for different reasons were regarded as hardly within the pale of Christianity. Hence Quakers and Catholics had, for the moment, an interest in common, as opposed to the intermediate Christian sects, and hence, both as duke and afterward as king, the Catholic James found it worth his while to befriend the chief of the Quakers. It was a singular alliance, that between the man for whom such words as pity and clemency were meaningless terms, and the man whose faith in the ethical teachings of Jesus was so genuine that he was eager to see them embodied in civil legislation and made the corner-stone of a new Christian state. It is strange to think of the

344

champion of truthfulness and toleration as a
Jacobite, leagued in political bonds of sympathy
with a family whose very name has come to be
almost a synonym for bigotry and falsehood. It
is this singular alliance which once _{Macaulay's}
kindled the wrath of the prejudiced _{hasty charges}
and impetuous Macaulay, and led him to bring
some foul charges against Penn's integrity.

Of Macaulay's charges, the only one that
needs mention[1] is that which relates to the affair
of the Maids of Taunton. When the _{The Maids}
handsome Duke of Monmouth was _{of Taunton}
making his silly attempt to dethrone James II.,
and on a bright June day of the year 1685 rode
into Taunton with much bustle and parade, he
was met in the market-place by a procession
of school-girls, from ten or twelve to sixteen
years, all in their prettiest summer gowns.
They gave him a royal standard richly embroidered, and the good schoolmistress gave him a
Bible, and all felt, no doubt, that they had done
what was right. A few weeks later, when Mon-

[1] They were conclusively refuted by W. E. Forster, in his
preface to a new edition of Clarkson's *Life of Penn*, London,
1850 ; and by Hepworth Dixon, in his *Life of Penn*, London,
1851 ; and others. After Macaulay had replied to his critics,
the matter was again taken up and treated with consummate
ability, by John Paget, in his *New Examen*, London, 1861.
Mr. Paget's evidence and arguments are absolutely conclusive,
and leave Macaulay in a very sorry plight.

for him, that intervened between the accession of James and the accession of Anne. As for the king, Penn always maintained that, with all his faults, he was not so black as people painted him ; and this we may readily admit. A man who had and retained such friends as Nicolls and Dongan could not have been entirely devoid of redeeming traits. But there was one side of James's character to which Penn was not sufficiently awake. Unlike other Stuarts in many respects, James was as false as any of the race, but his treacherousness was more or less concealed under an appearance of honest and awkward dulness. One would not look for Machiavelism in such a dense atmosphere. Nevertheless, James was able to impress Penn with the belief that in extending royal favour to Quakers he had the interests of religious liberty at heart, and, so long as Penn was thus hoodwinked, his demeanour towards the king was liable to be such as to excite the suspicion of patriots, who realized how dangerous that personage really was. When the great Quaker came to be known as a royal favourite, and scores of people crowded his doorsteps, in order to obtain through him royal aid for their schemes, he was at once placed in a position that could hardly fail to be misunderstood.

Penn was not awake to James's treacherous qualities

The difficulty of his position was well illustrated in the famous case of the Seven Bishops. It should be distinctly understood that in 1687 England was in serious danger, and that the interests of civil and religious liberty were gravely imperilled. All over Europe the Counter-Reformation had made alarming progress; and the ground gained by the peace of Westphalia, in 1648, seemed for the moment lost again. The most recent great event was the revocation of the Edict of Nantes, and Louis XIV. seemed as formidable as in later days Napoleon at Tilsit. Under these circumstances the intense anti-Catholic excitement in England was natural; it was one of the forms assumed by the instinct of self-preservation. The new king of England intended to destroy Protestantism, and civil liberty with it, wherever he could. To achieve his ends he relied ultimately upon military force to be summoned from Ireland, and aid to be extended by the king of France, as well as upon the development of a strong party loyal to himself in England. For this latter purpose he offered favours to Dissenters, hoping to secure their support until the time when he should feel strong enough to desert and betray them. Hence his attempt, under the hypocritical pretence of liberality in matters of religion, to annul the various test acts which, in the course of his brother's reign, had been passed against Presbyterians, Indepen-

The affair of the Seven Bishops

ment, but when a king undertook to override
such vile laws, he could not find it in his heart
to oppose him. Thus did Penn find himself, in
this national crisis, quite out of sympathy with
the national feeling. The natural results followed. He was called " William the Jesuit,"
an emissary in the pay of Rome ; he was accused

Absurd
notions about
Penn

of saying mass at Whitehall ; he was
supposed to have prompted the king
to his Declaration of Indulgence ; and
even the high-handed arrest of the seven bishops was laid at his door, although he earnestly
disapproved of it. No aspersion was too black
to be cast upon him.[1] He suffered all the more
injustice because of the noble courage with which
he declared his opinions, then as always. When
William III. arrived, and it became fashionable
to vilify or deride the exiled James, Penn's beautiful fidelity to his old guardian was unimpaired,
and he had always his good word to say for the
fallen prince.

It followed from all this that many persons
believed our good Quaker to be implicated in

Penn sus-
pected of
complicity
with the
Jacobites

Jacobite plots, and in the year 1691
he felt that prudence required him to
live very quietly in obscure lodgings
in the city of London. For an innocent man it seemed better thus than to seek

[1] Clarkson's *Life of Penn*, ii. 11.

safety abroad,[1] and Penn was sure that he could satisfy William III. of his innocence of any complicity with Jacobite intrigues. For more than two years he continued to live thus in retirement, writing a number of admirable books and pamphlets, one of which, entitled "Fruits of Solitude," is in some respects the most charming of his works. During this period an incident occurred which deserves mention for its intrinsic interest in coupling Penn's name with that of John Locke. In 1685, during Monmouth's insurrection, the great philosopher Penn and was in Holland. His patron, Lord Locke Shaftesbury, had once supported Monmouth's claim to the succession, and there were das-

---

[1] Macaulay, indeed, makes him escape to France in the autumn of 1691, but his only authority is the Diary of the book-collector Narcissus Luttrell, as worthless a mess of rubbish as was ever printed. On the other hand, Paget has proved that Penn was in London during the whole of his "retirement."

Macaulay goes on : "Scarcely had he again begun to harangue in public about the unlawfulness of war, when he sent a message earnestly exhorting James to make an immediate descent on England with 30,000 men." (*History of England*, vi. 32.) The memorandum on which this charge is based is, as Macaulay tells us, "among the Nairne MSS. and was translated by Macpherson," whereat the reader is no doubt duly overawed. Macaulay ought to have added that the writer of the memorandum was one Captain Williamson, a hired spy of low character, whose unsupported statements are of no value.

for some time as "Keithian Quakers." It was not long, however, before Keith passed over to Episcopacy. After a visit to England he came back to America in 1700 as the first missionary of the Society for Promoting Christian Knowledge, and travelled about the country making converts and organizing new Episcopal churches. Most of the Keithian Quakers likewise went back into the Church of England.

The loss of his province, the defection of his old friend, and the knowledge that some of his fellow-Quakers suspected him of sympathy with Jesuits, were blows which it taxed all of Penn's buoyant strength to bear. Added to those calamities came the loss of his wife, in February, 1694. But soon after, in the midst of the valley of the shadow of death, there came voices of comfort. Renewed expressions of love and trust on the part of his brethren were followed, in August, 1694, by an order in council restoring to Penn the proprietary government of his woodland in the New World. Again we find him travelling and preaching in England and Ireland: in 1696 he is married to Hannah Callowhill, a "devout and comely maiden" of Bristol; and in 1699, with this new wife and his grown-up children, William and Letitia, he comes once more across the wave to visit his woodland.

The king restores Penn's government

356

When Penn arrived in Philadelphia, the city had scarcely recovered from the panic into which it had been thrown by a deadly visita- His return to Phila- delphia tion of yellow fever. But, in spite of the pale, scared faces, the evidences of prosperity abounded on every side. There were more than 700 houses in the city, indicating a population of not less than 4000 souls. There were some spacious and well-built brick warehouses, and two Friends' meeting-houses, as well as an Episcopal church. Here and there were gardens brilliant with roses, lilies, and carnations. Penn now dwelt for a while in the famous " Slate-roof House," at the corner of Second Street and Norris Alley, which was pulled down in 1867. But he much preferred a country home, called Pennsbury, in Bucks County, northeast of the little city. There in 1682 he had begun building a fine house, which cost him £7000. An inventory of the furniture mentions plush couches, embroidered chairs, curtains of camlet and satin, and in the drawing-room such a carpet as was seldom seen outside of a palace. The silver and china were of the finest, and Penn's orders to his steward show that asceticism formed no part His home and habits of his theory of life. Not vain display, but refined and bountiful comfort, was his ideal. He could appreciate a toothsome haunch of venison, and tells how " the old priest at Philadelphia had rare shads." With such a companion he would sit till a late hour discussing learned questions over a stoup of good ale or wine.[1] He was much interested, like Washington, in the details of domestic affairs; and the devout maiden of Bristol, whose executive ability was marked and manifold, proved a most competent housewife.

Between his rural mansion and Philadelphia, the Lord Proprietor used either to ride his horse by the river's bank or to go on the river in a six-oared barge, of which he was very fond. "Above all dead things," he wrote to his steward, "take care of my barge." Once, on a stormy day, as he was fighting the waves with it, the governor of New Jersey overhauled him, His ready wit and expressed surprise that he should thus venture out against such a wind and tide. Quick and pithy was the reply: " I have been sailing against wind and tide all my life."

In the government of his New World province he encountered other adverse winds and tides than those of the Delaware River. From the outset, there was a human element of strife in the City of Brotherly Love. There was, first, the question as to how much or how little democracy might best comport with the pro-

[1] See Swift's letter to Stella, September 30, 1710, in his *Works*, ed. Scott, ii. 37.

prietary rule. Penn was, for his age, an advanced democrat; yet he never ceased to regard himself as a kind of patriarch who knew Democratic questions much better what was good for his little sylvan community than the people themselves. In this assumption he was very likely correct; but it is one of the essential features of thoroughgoing democracy that those who do not know what is best should have a much greater part in governing than those who do know, since they are much the more numerous. In the minds of many people democracy rests upon the colossal untruth that "one man is as good as another,"[1] so that a large number are more likely to be right than a small number. In reality democracy rests upon the ubiquitous fact that all men are directly interested in securing good government, while its successes have often been due to its practical recognition of the truth that some men are born to lead and others to follow. The fact that William Penn was a born leader was too obvious to be questioned, and between him and his people there was not much contention. But with his deputies, when he was absent in Eng-

[1] The only sense in which this can at all be said to be true is the Irishman's : "Why, Patrick," exclaims the landlord, whose mind is dallying with Bentonian ideas, "is n't one man as good as another?" "Faith, he is, your honour, and a d—d sight better!"

359

land, the case was different. Constitutional questions at once came to the foreground, and one of the first was that which concerned the shares to be taken by the assembly and the council in the work of legislation. It was Penn's original intention to give the sole power of originating laws to the council, while all laws required confirmation by the assembly. But this scheme was never realized. By 1693 all power of law-making was absorbed by the assembly, while the council became a mere board of advisers to the governor; and thenceforth for a hundred years the government of Pennsylvania was practically unicameral.

Along with such questions there were disagreements between the "province" and the "territories," or between Pennsylvania and Delaware, which resulted permanently in separate legislatures for the two. There were also troubles between Quakers and non-Quakers, especially the members of the Church of England. Some increment of confusion and bitterness came from Keith's apostasy. Meanwhile the quit-rents failed to be collected, and each dissatisfied party was inclined to accuse its antagonists of surreptitious dealings with the ubiquitous pirates.

Penn approached the situation in a most amiable spirit. " Friends," said he, " if in the

360

constitution by charter there be anything that jars, alter it." The revised charter _{The revised} of 1701 comprised but nine articles. _{charter}

The first grants liberty of conscience to all who " confess and acknowledge Almighty God," which, on a strict interpretation, would have admitted Mussulmans and Jews, and would have excluded such persons as Denis Diderot or the late Mr. Bradlaugh. At the same time, the right to hold executive or legislative offices was restricted to persons " who profess to believe in Jesus Christ," a provision which ought hardly to have barred out Unitarians, but was sometimes used for that purpose.

The second article " requires an assembly to be chosen yearly by the freemen, to consist of four persons or more from each county. This assembly has full powers to choose its officers, to judge of the qualifications of its own members, to adjourn itself, to prepare bills and make laws, impeach criminals and redress grievances, ' with all other powers and privileges of an assembly, according to the rights of free-born subjects of England.'

" The third requires the freemen to elect two or three people for each position of sheriff or coroner or other court officers, and the governor to choose among them; or, if the governor fails to select, the first named shall serve.

purposes? Different opinions were expressed. Some worthy Friends, who abhorred warfare as much as any, nevertheless did not feel bound to sit still and let the enemy cut their throats. Others deemed it right to adhere to their principles and trust in Providence for the result. So for four days "there was an unpleasant parley," which ended in a postponement of the vote, while sundry resolutions were adopted, vague and ambiguous enough for any modern political platform. Warned by such symptoms, Penn was careful to leave in the province deputy-governors who were not averse to fighting in self-defence.

Could Quakers fight in self-defence?

In the Christmas time of 1701, Penn arrived once more in England; before Easter the great king had passed away, and by Whitsuntide the gigantic war of the Spanish Succession had begun. Queen Anne was inclined to befriend Penn for her father's sake, and there was no further serious risk of his losing his province. Of his military deputies, however, one contrived, through excess of zeal, to make much trouble. The appointment of this man, John Evans, was one of a number of instances which seem to show that Penn was liable to err in his judgments of character. He was apt to be too generous in his estimates of men. Evans was a youth of five

Penn's return to England

The deputy-governor, John Evans

364

and twenty or so, with some scholar-like traits which attracted Penn's admiration, but he soon showed himself unworthy of trust. There was not much danger of an attack upon the little Quaker commonwealth on the Delaware River; that community did not extend westward enough, nor did the French-Algonquin conflagration, against which New York and New England were fighting, as yet extend westward enough; the Five Nations, an insuperable barrier, stood between. But Evans, who was not a Quaker, believed in going forth to smite the hosts of Amalek, and to help the cause of England wherever it was imperilled. His call for troops met with no response, whereupon he resorted to an almost incredibly shameful and puerile trick. On a bright spring day in 1706, while His folly the good people of Philadelphia were holding their annual fair, a courier came spurring into the town with consternation depicted upon his face, and announced that a dozen French warships were coming up the river. The governor straightway sprang upon his horse and cantered about the streets, waving a drawn sword and calling people to arms. At this sudden alarm, which was simply a brazen falsehood, some people threw their silver spoons and goblets into their wells for hiding, some ran out to the woods, some crowded into boats and

Proprietor. The antics of this graceless boy nearly broke his father's heart.

These troubles were presently followed by a dire calamity. For steward of his province Penn had appointed one Philip Ford, who turned out to be a scoundrel. It was a fresh illustration of Penn's weakest point, an occasional slowness in recognizing the bad side of human nature. With all the worldly wisdom of which he had so much, Penn now and then showed a streak of guilelessness that reminds one of Tom Pinch. This trait helps us to understand his belief in the honesty of James II. The wretched Ford died in 1706, leaving a very murky set of accounts, and a widow and son as unscrupulous as himself. In these days Penn, in spite of his wealth, often found himself in need of ready money. Large sums were sunk in his holy experiment; his dissolute son had debts amounting to £10,000; and his daughter's husband, William Aubrey, a mean-spirited creature, extorted money from him. At one time Penn borrowed money of Ford, and mortgaged his province of Pennsylvania as security; when he repaid the loan, he neglected to get back from Ford the bond and mortgage. So after Ford's death his widow and son brought against Penn a trumped-up claim for £14,000, and petitioned Queen Anne to hand over to them the proprietorship of Pennsylvania. The

Philip Ford

base attempt failed, but not until it had led to Penn's incarceration for nine months in the Fleet prison.

By 1712 Penn was on the point of selling for £12,000 his proprietary government to the Crown, while retaining the landed estates which he owned in Pennsylvania. But in the course of that year a paralytic stroke nearly put an end to his power of doing business. He lingered for six years, with memory failing until he could scarcely recognize his nearest friends. The contemplated surrender of the proprietary government was never made ; but after divers questions had been decided by the courts, it passed to the founder's three surviving sons by his second wife. Of these the eldest, John Penn, called " the American " because he was born in Philadelphia in 1700, died in England in 1746 without issue. The second brother, Thomas Penn, died in England in 1775, leaving two sons, John and Granville, both of whom attained distinction. The third brother, Richard Penn, died in England in 1771, leaving two sons, John and Richard, who were successively lieutenant-governors of Pennsylvania. When the proprietary government came to an end in 1776, it was in the possession of these heirs of Thomas and Richard. For seven years after the founder's death, while his three sons were still young, the interests of

Penn's illness and death

the proprietorship were managed with great ability by his widow.

One of the most important personages in the Quaker commonwealth was James Logan, the friend of the founder and representative of his ideas. This remarkable man, a native of Ulster, was descended from the Scotch Logans of Restabrig who lost their estates for connection with the mysterious Gowrie conspiracy.

James Logan

James was an infant prodigy; at the age of twelve his attainments in Greek, Latin, and Hebrew had attracted much notice, and he afterward attained distinction in modern languages, mathematics, physics, and natural history. Penn brought him to Philadelphia on his second coming, in 1699, and for the next forty years he was always in some high position, — secretary of the province, member of the council, judge of common pleas, chief justice, mayor of Philadelphia, and, in 1736–38, acting governor of Pennsylvania. Like his friend Penn, he knew how to win and keep the confidence of the red men, and it was in honour of him that the chieftain Tagahjutè received the name of Logan, long to be remembered for the tale of woe which cast such unjust aspersions upon the fame of Captain Michael Cresap.[1] The singular variety of his genius is shown by the fact that his friend Linnæus, in compliment to his

[1] See my *American Revolution,* ii. 119.

botanical attainments, named after him a natural order of herbs and shrubs, the Loganiaceæ, containing some thirty genera in 350 species, of which *strychnos nux vomica* is one of the best known. He published Latin essays on reproduction in plants, and on the aberration of light; translated Cato's " Disticha " and Cicero's " De Senectute ; " and bequeathed to the city his library of 2000 volumes, comprising all the Latin classics, and more than a hundred folios in Greek, with the original edition of Ptolemy's " Almagest " and Timon's commentary, " from my learned friend Fabricius, who published fourteen volumes of his ' Bibliotheca Græca ' in quarto, in which, after he had finished his account of Ptolemy, on my inquiring from him at Hamburg how I should find it, having long sought for it in vain in England, he sent it to me out of his own library, telling me it was so scarce that neither price nor prayers could purchase it."

A very different figure was that of the stout Welshman, David Lloyd, whom Penn sent over in 1686 to be attorney-general of the province. At various times Lloyd was member of the assembly and of the council, David Lloyd judge of admiralty, and chief justice of the commonwealth. Without any pretence to such profound and varied attainments as Logan's he was a learned jurist and had an extensive knowledge of Welsh history and philology. In politics Lloyd represented the popular party, while Logan stood for the proprietary interests and prerogatives of the Penns, and the strife between them was often intense and bitter. The general character of Pennsylvania politics early in the eighteenth century we have already indicated; the details are so closely implicated with the struggle against France that they will be best treated in my future volumes which are to deal with that mighty conflict. Lloyd was contentious, and his methods were sometimes objectionable, but they surely helped to carry out Penn's democratic ideas to their logical conclusions.[1]

The associations connected with such men as Logan and Penn served at once to give something of a literary atmosphere to Philadelphia, which was greatly heightened after the return of Benjamin Franklin from London in 1726. The founding of the Philadelphia Library in 1731, of the American Philosophical Society in 1743, and of the University of Pennsylvania in 1749–55, were evidences of the rapid development of the Quaker commonwealth in scholarship and in literary tastes. In these respects Philadelphia was in contrast with New York, and by the middle of the eighteenth century her reputation for culture

[1] Cf. Sharpless, *A Quaker Experiment in Government*, p. 97.

was second only to that of Boston and Cambridge. The immense contributions made by Franklin to the higher life of Philadelphia are a striking commentary upon the excellence of Penn's unflinching insistence upon "soul liberty." Franklin, though born in Boston, was hardly a product of the Puritan theocracy. His parents, who did not quit their ancient home in Northamptonshire until a few years before his birth, were Puritans of a liberal type who had but lately left the Church of England. The atmosphere of Boston was too stifling for the youthful Benjamin, who was born with the temperament of a free-thinker, and soon began to hear himself called an "infidel." There can be no doubt that this circumstance was potent in turning the young man's attention to the more liberal Dutch and Quaker commonwealths,[1] and thus his footsteps were led to Pennsylvania, which could furnish more work for printers than New York. Thus Boston's loss was Philadelphia's gain.

In spite of their liberalism, the Quakers attached far less importance to education than

[1] "I was rather inclined to leave Boston when I reflected that I had already made myself a little obnoxious to the governing party, . . . and farther, that my indiscreet disputations about religion began to make me pointed at with horror by good people as an infidel or atheist." Franklin's *Autobiography*, ed. Bigelow, 1868, p. 106.

the Puritans of New England. The majority of their preachers and instructors were men of

Attitude of Quakers toward learning

high moral tone and spiritual insight with scant learning, like George Fox himself. Fox used to say that " God stood in no need of human learning," and that " Oxford and Cambridge could not make a minister." Quakers, in studying the Bible, depended upon their Inner Light rather than that critical interpretation of texts to which the orthodox Puritans attached so much importance. A knowledge of Hebrew, therefore, was not highly valued; and as for Greek and Latin literature, it was the unsanctified work of pagans, while the poets of France and Italy dealt with worldly and frivolous themes. In these respects we must remember that Penn was as far from being a typical Quaker as Milton, with his pervading artistic sense, his love of music and the theatre, and his long curling hair, was from being a typical Puritan. George Fox and John Cotton are respectively the typical men. The latter, who spent twelve hours a day in study and said, " I love to sweeten my mouth with a piece of Calvin before I go to sleep," could write and speak fluently in Greek, Latin, and Hebrew, besides carrying a ponderous burden of philological, metaphysical, and theological erudition. Among the Puritan divines of New England, real scholarship was commonly found, and

374

it was sometimes of a high order; and this was because sound scholarship was supposed to be conducive to soundness in doctrines. This explains the founding of Harvard College in the wilderness in 1636.

To the Quaker, whose mind was directly illuminated by light from above, this elaborate equipment was mere rubbish. It was therefore not strange that in colonial times the higher education in Pennsylvania owed little to the Quakers. They were nevertheless careful, as people of practical sense, to teach their children "the three R's," and it was unusual to find a member of the community who could not write and cipher. The first school in Philadelphia was opened in 1683, when the town was scarcely a year old. In that humble establishment the master, Enoch Flower, taught reading for four shillings per quarter; for six shillings the pupil could add writing, and for eight shillings arithmetic likewise, to his initial accomplishment. In 1689 the Society of Friends set up their public school, which was chartered by Penn in 1711. *The first schools*

The impulse toward literary culture, given from the outset by Penn and his friends, was visible in the early establishment of a printing-press, the first one south of New England, by William Bradford, in 1685. *The Bradfords* In 1690 the same Bradford set up a paper-mill

on the bank of the Schuylkill. After his removal to New York in 1693,[1] his son Andrew
kept up the press, with a considerable bookstore,
and in 1719 issued the first newspaper in the
middle colonies. In 1735 he was finely established as a bookseller at the sign of the Bible
in Second Street, whence he afterward moved
to South Front Street, and in 1741 began to
publish "The American Magazine." In the
following year Andrew's nephew, William Bradford, started the "Pennsylvania Journal," which
was continued under that name until 1801, when
it became "The True American." It was in
Andrew Bradford's office that Franklin in 1723
found work as a compositor. The standard English books of the period could be found on the
shelves of Philadelphia booksellers, and the demand for works like Robertson's "Charles V."
and Blackstone's "Commentaries" became so
great that they were reprinted. Among Penn-
sylvanians who attained distinction for scientific
or literary achievement were the astronomer
David Rittenhouse, the botanists John Bartram
and his son William, the self-taught mathema-
tician Thomas Godfrey, one of the inventors
of Hadley's so-called quadrant,[1] and his son

[1] See above, p. 290.

[2] This useful instrument, which is more properly called a
sextant, was invented by Thomas Godfrey and also by John
Hadley. The Royal Society decided that both were en-

376

Thomas, author of the first American dramatic work, " The Prince of Parthia." This tragedy, rapid and strong in action, and digni- fied if somewhat monotonous and con- ventional in its language,[1] suggests that, had not the author been cut off at the early

The first American drama

titled to the credit of the invention, and awarded to each a prize of $200.

[1] On a stormy night two arch-conspirators thus parley together : —

VARDANES. Why rage the elements ? They are not cursed
Like me ! Evanthe frowns not angry on them;
The wind may play upon her beauteous bosom,
Nor fear her chiding ; light can bless her sense,
And in the floating mirror she beholds
Those beauties which can fetter all mankind.

LYSIAS. My lord, forget her ; tear her from your breast.
Who, like the Phœnix, gazes on the sun,
And strives to soar up to the glorious blaze,
Should never leave ambition's brightest object,
To turn and view the beauties of a flower.

VARDANES. O Lysias, chide no more, for I have done.
Yes, I 'll forget the proud disdainful beauty.
Hence with vain love! ambition now alone
Shall guide my actions. Since mankind delights
To give me pain, I 'll study mischief too,
And shake the earth, e'en like this raging tempest.

LYSIAS. A night like this, so dreadful to behold,
Since my remembrance' birth I never saw.

VARDANES. E'en such a night, dreadful as this, they say,
My teeming mother gave me to the world.
Whence by those sages who, in knowledge rich,
Can pry into futurity and tell
What distant ages will produce of wonder,
My days were deemed to be a hurricane.

LYSIAS. Then, haste to raise the tempest.
My soul disdains this one eternal round,
Where each succeeding day is like the former.
Trust me, my noble prince, here is a heart

but in greater part Irish and German "re-demptioners" who sold themselves into temporary servitude to defray the cost of their ocean voyage. In the eighteenth century, probably more such redemptioners came to Pennsylvania than to any of the other colonies. They were in general kindly treated. The regular term of service was four years, with five days additional for every day of truancy. They could not be sold out of the province without their consent freely given in open court, or before a justice of the peace ; and good behaviour entitled them at the end of their service to a suit of clothes and a set of farm tools. These white freedmen often became useful and respectable members of society.

From the first there were negro slaves in Pennsylvania, used mostly for household service, but seldom as field-hands except in Delaware. But the Quaker conscience was aroused on the subject of slavery at a time when other

Quaker op-position to slavery

Christians could see nothing wrong in it. The Memorial of 1688, in which the German Friends of Germantown protested against " the buying and keeping of negroes," is still in existence. During the next half-century the assembly laboured assiduously to check the importation of slaves by imposing prohibitory duties on such traffic. Some years before 1776 slaves had ceased to be brought into Pennsylvania. In 1758 the Yearly Meeting enjoined all Friends to set free their slaves, "making a Christian provision for them." Many complied, but a few held out until "in 1776 a declaration of independence for all slaves held by Friends was decreed, and monthly meetings were directed, after proper effort, to exclude from membership all Quakers who refused to comply."[1] Long before the Revolution the practice of manumission had been sufficiently frequent to create a much larger class of free blacks than could be found in any of the other colonies.

The Quaker spirit in dealing with pauperism and crime was equally admirable, although with regard to capital punishment it proved impossible to realize the ideal of Penn and confine the death penalty to cases of murder and treason. The list of capital offences grew to fourteen, including highway robbery, horse-stealing, and counterfeiting. In 1731 Catherine Bevan was burned alive at Newcastle for the murder of her husband. It was intended to strangle her before the fire could reach her, but a sudden outburst of flame severed the rope and drove away the executioner, so that she died in torment. For larceny, fornication, and assault, the usual penalties were pillory and whipping-post. It was said

Crimes and punishments

[1] Sharpless, *A Quaker Experiment*, pp. 31–33.

381

next after Virginia and Massachusetts in popu-
lousness. The chief elements in this rapid increase were two great streams of immigration —
the Palatinate German and Scotch-Irish streams
— which were drawn thither in consequence
of Penn's ideas. One of the most interesting
aspects in which to consider Pennsylvania is
as the chief centre of diffusion of the people
who became afterward the pioneers of the democratic West. In our next and concluding chapter, something must be said concerning this
matter.

XVII

THE MIGRATIONS OF SECTS

THE colonies of New York and Pennsylvania were not only more heterogeneous in population than any of the others, but they were the principal centres of distribution of the non-English population from the seaboard to the Alleghany Mountains. In the New England colonies, during the seventeenth century, the non-English element might most succinctly be described by saying that there was no such element; in the eighteenth century it was extremely small, though not without importance. Virginia and Maryland also were at first purely English, but the tidewater region, in the eighteenth century, received some foreign accessions and the Appalachian region far more. Among the oldest colonies, therefore, New York was the only one which had any considerable foreign population, and there it formed a large majority of the whole. Of the younger colonies the two Carolinas had a large foreign element among the dwellers on the seaboard, and still larger in the back country. But all

Centres of distribution of the non-English population

this mountain population, in the Carolinas as well as in Virginia and Maryland, entered the country by way of Pennsylvania; and this migration was so great, both in its physical dimensions and in the political and social effects which it has wrought, that Pennsylvania acquires especial interest as the temporary tarrying-place and distributing centre for so much that we now call characteristically American.

Of the different classes of non-English immigrants during the colonial times, while all were represented in the city of New York, the Jews and the French Protestants settled chiefly on the seaboard, and on the other hand the Germans and the so-called Scotch-Irish found their way in great numbers to what was then the western frontier. We must devote a few words to each of these classes.

The city of New York has always been the principal home of the Jews in the United States, and it was in connection with the Dutch enterprise in founding New Netherland that they were first brought here. It was from various quarters, but mainly from the Spanish peninsula The Jews that they had come to Holland. In in Spain all the history of this wonderful people there is no more brilliant chapter than that of their career in Spain under the Mohammedan dynasties between the tenth and fourteenth centuries. In point of civilization, in the days

386

when Philip Augustus and lion-hearted Richard
went together on their crusade, such cities as
Toledo and Cordova were as far in advance of
London and Paris as London and Paris are now
in advance of Toledo and Cordova, and in this
Spanish preëminence the Jews played a foremost part. Such men as Ibn Gebirol and Mai-
monides were the great teachers of their time,
and influences wafted across the Pyrenees had
much to do with the Albigensian culture in
southern France. As the Christians in Spain
slowly conquered and drove back the Mussulmans, the persecution of Jews began and steadily
increased in virulence, until the year 1492,
which witnessed the surrender of Granada and
downfall of the last Moorish kingdom, saw also
the abominable edict which drove from their
homes and their native land 200,000 honest and
industrious Spanish citizens of Hebrew race and
faith. In that eventful year, when an inscrutable
Providence put into the hands of Spain the rich
prize of America, did she enter upon that course
of wholesale persecution which proved her to
be unworthy of such opportunities and incapable
of using them. The cost of Columbus's second
voyage was partly defrayed with stolen money,
the property of Jews who had been dragged on
shipboard and carried over to Morocco. Meanwhile several industries received a death-blow,
and in particular many cities were left without

Company's orders. In that hope they were not disappointed. The Company replied to Stuyvesant that his request " was inconsistent with reason and justice," and the States General followed this up with the act of July 15, 1555, " expressly permitting the Jews to trade to New Netherland, and to reside there, on the simple condition that they should support their own poor." [1] This condition has been well fulfilled, for such a kind of person as a Jewish pauper has seldom been seen.

The incidents here recounted were the beginnings of thrifty and valuable Jewish settlements in New York and Rhode Island. After the English conquest of New Netherland, the Duke of York was led, as we have seen, by considerations of expediency, to continue the liberal policy of the Dutch. The instructions to Governor Andros, on his first coming, were to give full toleration to persons " of what religion soever," but perhaps the failure to exclude Jews may have been due to oversight; for this clause was omitted from the instructions to Governor Dongan, and when in 1685 the Jewish residents in New Amsterdam petitioned for leave to build a synagogue, he referred the petition to the mayor and common council, who refused to grant it, on the ground that toleration of public worship extended only to sects professing faith in Christ.

[1] Daly, *op. cit.* 10.

But Dongan, himself an Irish Catholic, was a man of extremely liberal views. Next year, whether at his own instance or not, a fresh set of instructions was sent him, in which the omitted clause was restored. Probably Dongan took advantage of this to grant the Jews' petition, for neither Andros, who came back as his successor, nor Leisler, was at all likely to take such a step; and we know that in 1691 the Jews had a place for public worship. In 1695 there were twenty families, or probably about one hundred souls, in the city, and their little synagogue stood on the south side of the present Beaver Street, midway between Broadway and Broad Street. In 1712 an English clergyman informs us that one can learn Hebrew in New York as easily as in Europe, because of divers ingenious and learned men of that nation that dwell there. In 1748 the Swedish traveller, Peter Kalm, tells of the fine shops, the large country estates, and the richly freighted ships belonging to the Jews whom he visited in New York. At that time they possessed all civil rights and privileges in common with the other inhabitants, except that of voting for members of the legislature. In 1737 this point was decided by the New York assembly itself in a contested election case. The decision was that, since Jews did not possess the parliamentary franchise in England, they did not possess it in New

The synagogue in New York

York, in the absence of any special enactment for that purpose.

It may have been because New York absorbed so large a part of the Jewish immigration that comparatively little was left for Pennsylvania. There were nevertheless a good many Jews in Philadelphia, and some were citizens of great influence. The name of Haym Salomon, a very wealthy Polish Jew, deserves to be coupled with that of Robert Morris for the financial aid which he extended to Congress during the War of Independence. Mr. Salomon advanced to the United States nearly $700,000, not a cent of which was ever repaid.

Jews in Philadelphia

The difference in point of liberality between William Penn's idea of toleration and Cecilius Calvert's idea was shown in the fact that Maryland's deservedly famous Toleration Act extended only to Trinitarians. By that very act disbelief in the doctrine of the Trinity was made a crime punishable with death. We need not be surprised, therefore, that Jews did not flock to Maryland. But in Georgia and South Carolina, where a more liberal policy was pursued toward them, a good many found homes and proved valuable citizens. At the time of the Revolution the principal Jewish population of North America was in Newport, New York, Philadelphia, Charleston, and Savannah.

Jews in South Carolina and Georgia

392

The French Protestants next claim our attention. During the seventeenth century, while the colonization of North America was going on, they met with their final defeats in France, and thereafter continued to exist merely on sufferance until even that privilege was withdrawn. There was something extraordinary in this tragic end of a mighty struggle, and to us who look back upon it after this interval it is one of the most impressive spectacles in history. In 1558, when Elizabeth ascended the English The throne, while Martin Luther's Refor- Huguenots mation was not yet half a century old, its prospects of success seemed at least as bright in France as in England. Within four years at least 2000 Protestant churches had sprung up in France, and with their local consistories and provincial synods, sustaining a national synod, a powerful and aggressive Calvinistic organization was rapidly coming to the front. Half the aristocracy, including a large majority of the noblemen below forty years of age, were in favour of the Reform, and of the clergy a strong party comprising one cardinal, one archbishop, six bishops, and hundreds of priests were numbered among its friends. But on the other hand, not more than one tenth of the people had become Protestants. An educated rural middle class, such as played so great a part in England and planted Virginia and New England, did not exist in France. The

393

issued decrees forbidding Protestants to leave
the kingdom under heavy penalties, and guards
were stationed on the frontiers to intercept
them, while cruisers patrolled the coasts. But
these measures were ineffective, for popular
sentiment was very far from keeping pace with
the tyrant's besotted zeal, and many fugitives
were helped on their way by compassionate
Catholics. Drink-money, too, played exactly
the same part as now and always. Guards for
a small tip, instead of detaining refugees, would
pass them on or even furnish them with guides;
and captains of ships were equally obliging.
Where such methods were unavailable, people
travelled on foot by night or disguised as peasants, driving a cow, or carrying a hod, or trun-
dling a wheelbarrow; wealthy men and women,
clothed in rags, begged from door to door; and
so in one way or another the exodus was accomplished.

Concerning the damage which this wholesale
emigration inflicted upon France, little need be
said, for the tale has often been told. It cannot
be expressed in statistics. This seven per cent.
of the total French population included a far
higher proportion of skilled craftsmen, prosper-
Terrible loss ous merchants, professional men and
to France scholars. So largely was the marine
represented that the French navy has never recovered from the loss. And then there was the

weeding out of a certain earnest Puritan type of character which no nation can afford to weaken. Altogether this emigration was in many respects a skimming of cream.

The Huguenots were largely represented in the maritime provinces of Normandy, Brittany, Saintonge, and Languedoc, and sometimes they made the voyàge directly to America. But more often the first flight was to England or Holland, where parties were formed for crossing the ocean. There was no part of English or Dutch America where they were not welcome. They maintained friendly relations with the Church of England as well as with the Independents in Boston. Numbers came to Massachusetts and Virginia, but much greater numbers to New York and South Carolina. In Boston the marks of them are plentiful. Opposite the hotel named for Paul Revere, in the square named for James Bowdoin, comes the street named for Pierre Chardon, of Touraine, whence it is but a short walk to the public hall built by the grandson of Pierre Faneuil, of Rochelle. The family of Governor Bowdoin, or Baudouin, was a cultured and respectable one in southwestern France. The French look of the name is not always so well preserved as in those cases ; sometimes it is quite anglicized. Thus the name of the Salem family of Brownes, eminent in the

eighteenth century, is simply the translation of
Le Brun, from the island of Jersey; and the
name of Philip English, which is remembered in
connection with the witchcraft panic, was L'An-
glois, from the same island. So Olney repre-
sents Aulnoy, and Dabney, of Massachusetts
and Virginia, is curtailed from D'Aubigné; and
not only such names as Gillet and Lambert, but
now and then a Collins, or a Lewis, or a Bas-
set, or a Lawrence, may indicate French origin.
Louis XIV., who had a capacity for details,
liked to gather information concerning these
refugees. Reports from Canada assure him that
there are many of the "vile miscreants" on the
Hudson River, and on a map of Boston, drawn
for the king in 1693, the situation of the Huguenot meeting-house, on the south side of
School Street, is shown by the words "renegats
françois," French renegades. But not all settled in Boston. There were the Le Barons at
Plymouth, and the Sigourneys, Bernons, Bon-
dets, Germaines, and Martins at the village of
Oxford, up in the Nipmuck country, until an
Indian massacre dispersed them in 1696.

Nowhere, however, did Huguenots fill a larger
place than in New York. There came Jacques
Desbrosses from Poitou, whose grandson was
President of the Chamber of Commerce, the first
organized mercantile society in America, and
whose family name is left upon a well-known

street and ferry. There came Étienne de Lancey, from Caen, whose son James was chief justice and lieutenant-governor of New York, and from the neighbouring city of Rouen came Guillaume Le Conte, among whose de- Huguenots in scendants in these latter days are num- New York bered two of the most eminent men of science that our country has produced. In 1689 a party of these Frenchmen obtained from acting-governor Jacob Leisler a grant of land on Long Island Sound, where they founded the pretty town of New Rochelle. In 1693 they built a New church there, but before this was ac- Rochelle complished the settlers used to walk every Sunday morning to New York, a distance of twenty miles, to attend the regular service at the Église du Saint Esprit, in Pine Street, and then they would walk back in the evening. Four times a year — at Christmas, Easter, Whitsuntide, and Michaelmas — the sacrament of the Lord's Supper was administered at New Rochelle, but at all other times it was necessary to go to the city. First the young children were carefully gathered together and left in charge of faithful friends. Then the procession started, with measured tread keeping time to music as men's and women's voices joined with fervour in some grand old psalm of Clement Marot. At a half-way place where a huge rock was shaded by cedars and fragrant pines they rested and took lunch, and then went on their way. We are assured that it was no unusual thing for men and women to do the forty miles.[1] For more than half a century they retained their native speech.

In the ancient city of Rochelle, whence most of these devoted worshippers came, one of the most important families was that of the Jays, apparently a branch of the Jays who were lords of Montonneau in Poitou. From that province, as early as 1565, the first Jean Jay whom we know, already converted to Protestantism, had come to live in Rochelle. His descendant, Pierre

The Jay family Jay, who was living there in 1685, was a wealthy merchant. One day in October a corps of seven thousand fusileers from Béarn marched into Rochelle and began plundering as if in an enemy's country. The house of Pierre Jay was one of those that had been especially marked out for pillage. He succeeded in getting his wife and children out of the house, and, although the shore was closely patrolled on land by troops of cavalry and watched from the sea by warships, he contrived to elude this guard and put them safely on board a vessel that was just starting for Plymouth in England. After they had sailed out of harm's way they were missed, and Jay was forthwith thrown into

[1] Bolton's *History of the County of Westchester*, 1848, i. 400. A slight pinch of salt seems to be needed, which I will leave it for the reader to supply at discretion.

prison for assisting them to escape. Some Catholic friends procured his release, but there was manifestly no hope of saving his property. He was expecting, however, one of his own ships from Spain, with a rich cargo of which he was sole owner. Taking into his confidence a bold and faithful pilot, he bade him watch out at sea for the ship and not let her come ashore but bring her to anchor off the island of Rhé. This was punctually done, and Jay, after lying hidden for some hours in the bottom of the pilot-boat, so near to a royal cruiser that he could hear the sailors talk, at length boarded his own ship and sailed away to Plymouth. Shortly afterward his eldest son, Auguste, returning from a voyage to Africa, found the homestead deserted and dismantled, and all the property of the family confiscated. He contrived to slip on board a ship bound for the West Indies, and after a while the family were all united in the hospitable city of New York.

One of Pierre Jay's friends and neighbours in Rochelle was the ancestor of Henry Laurens, of South Carolina, and in the next town, only eleven miles away, dwelt the ancestor of Elias Boudinot, of New Jersey, — three presidents of our Continental Congress from one little corner of the coast of France! In Benjamin West's well-known picture of the American Commissioners at Paris, in

Three presidents of Congress

405

1783, John Jay and Henry Laurens are standing while the others sit, and Laurens's face is turned with a satisfied expression toward Jay, who had detected and defeated the insidious scheme of France which would fain have made the independent United States stop short at the Alleghany Mountains. When all the past circumstances crowd in upon our memory, there is something deeply impressive in the picture.

The Huguenots, as we have observed, were free to come to any of the American colonies, but showed a marked preference for New York and South Carolina. The choice of the Quakers, and of various German sects akin to them, was much more limited, and after the founding of Pennsylvania offered them such strong inducements, they were sure to go there. For the Quakers the state which Penn founded ensured them a much greater and more useful future than they could have had in England, where they have dwindled in numbers to less than 15,000. In America there are probably not less than 150,000. From Pennsylvania they have been to some extent distributed in the west and southwest, and the civilizing work which they have done, especially perhaps in the eighteenth century in North Carolina, has been of inestimable value. It was the coming of the Quakers to Pennsylvania in

Dimensions of the Quaker exodus from England

1681 that brought also the first Germans. They came and made their first home in Germantown, hard by Philadelphia, and the reasons for their coming were closely connected with the sympathy between their views and those of the Quakers. We have seen how William Penn, who was himself half a Dutchman, made visits occasionally to Holland, and extended them into preaching tours through portions of Germany. He thus discovered many kindred spirits and held out inducements for them to come to his new colony. The first to come were the Mennonites, who were spiritual descendants of the mediæval Quietists, and may probably have contained in their ranks a few Waldenses and Anabaptists. Their differences from the Quakers were so slight that they often held meetings together, and it was not uncommon to hear the Mennonites called German Quakers. In Germany and Switzerland they were savagely persecuted by Protestant and Catholic alike; so they gladly followed Penn to the New World. Their leader, Francis Daniel Pastorius, was an enthusiastic scholar, studying science, philosophy, jurisprudence, or whatever came to hand, and reading eight or ten languages. The Mennonites were followed by the Dunkers, a sect of German Baptists who came to Pennsylvania between 1719 and 1729, leaving none of their number behind. There are

The Mennonites and Dunkers

said to be more than 200,000 in the United States to-day. About 1732, under the preaching of a singular mystic, Conrad Beissel, a portion of this sect broke off as Seventh Day Baptists, and founded a community at Ephrata, in some respects analogous to those of the Shakers. An interesting feature of these German sects is their learning and their devotion to literature. The Ephrata Community printed religious books in handsome type upon very fine paper; and they also knew good music. Besides these sects were the Labadists and Moravians, whom I must for the present dismiss with this mere mention.[1]

Another migration from Germany, of a different kind and far more numerous, was that which came from the Rhenish Palatinate. The nearness of that province to Alsace, Lorraine, and Franche-Comté, upon which Louis XIV. waged a war of conquest, often brought serious The trouble upon it. The first devastation Palatines of the Palatinate in 1674 is the one dark spot upon the honourable career of Turenne, but it had a strategic excuse. The second devastation, in 1688, partly intended as a chastisement for harbouring Huguenots, was far more barbarously performed. Sad havoc was

[1] See in this connection the admirable work of Sachse, *The German Pietists of Provincial Pennsylvania*, Philadelphia, 1895.

wrought at Heidelberg and Mannheim, and that beautiful country did not recover itself for more than two generations. Thousands of peasantry were reduced to a state of abject misery. This attracted the attention of British statesmen in the reign of Queen Anne, and a systematic effort was made to induce them to come to England in order to be shipped to America.[1] Thus in the years 1708 and 1709 more than 30,000 Germans crossed the Channel, and were soon afterward brought in English ships to New York and the Carolinas, but above all to Pennsylvania. This was but the beginning of a vast stream of migration in which Palatine peasants were taken down the Rhine to Rotterdam and there shipped to Philadelphia. Some, indeed, came to New York and settled in the Mohawk valley, where they gave us Nicholas Herkimer in the Revolutionary War; but most went into the valley of the Susquehanna in such large numbers, and remained so long without much intermixture, that their language still survives in the dialect which we call Pennsylvania Dutch, but which is really

[1] A competent scholar assigns the travels of Penn in Germany in 1671 and 1677 as the chief cause of the direction of this wave of migration to Pennsylvania. See Diffenderffer, *The German Exodus to England in* 1709, Lancaster, 1897, p. 30. See also Sachse, *The Fatherland*, Philadelphia, 1897, pp. 142–144.

intelligence and training than the native peasantry of Ireland. At the beginning of the
eighteenth century the percentage of illiteracy
in Ulster was probably smaller than anywhere
else in the world. There were then more than
a million of these Presbyterians in Ulster.
About 1720, when they began coming in great
numbers to America, those families that had
been longest in Ireland had dwelt there but
three generations, so that there is surely some
laxity of speech in calling them Irish without
some qualifying adjective.

The English experiment of thus scotticising
Ireland was defeated by a crass policy of protectionism combined with petty religious persecution. Flourishing linen and woollen industries had sprung up in Ulster, and sundry
legislative handicaps were laid upon them for
the "protection" of native industries in England. Thus did government treat its own pioneers as "foreigners" whom it was meritorious
to plunder. At the same time divers civil dis-
abilities were enacted for Presbyterians. The
result of this twofold tyranny was the largest
exodus from Europe to America that ever took
place before the nineteenth century.
Between 1730 and 1770 more than
half of the Presbyterian population of
Ulster came over to America, where it formed
more than one sixth part of our entire popu-

Exodus
from Ulster
to America

412

lation at the time of the Declaration of Independence.[1]

A few of these Presbyterians came to New England, where they have left their mark. But the great majority came to Pennsylvania and occupied the mountain country west of the Susquehanna. Thence a steady migration was kept up southwesterly along the Appalachian axis into the southern colonies. Now there was one very important respect in which these Presbyterians of Ulster had come to differ from their Presbyterian brethren in Scotland. In the " land of cakes " the kirk ruled things pretty much at its own sweet will, and was therefore in favour of keeping civil and spiritual affairs united. But in Ulster, whether in relation to their Catholic neighbours or more especially to the English Parliament, Presbyterians were in a harassed minority, and therefore became convinced of the desirableness of divorcing church from state. Accordingly, in spite of a very rigid theology, they stood for a liberal principle, and other Protestant sects, such as Lutherans, Mennonites, and Dunkers, found it possible to harmonize with them, especially in the free atmosphere of

Presbyterians in Pennsylvania

Union of the Palatinate and Ulster streams of migration

---

[1] Much detailed information may be found in the *Proceedings of the Scotch-Irish Congress,* published annually since 1889, first at Cincinnati, afterwards at Nashville.

APPENDIX I

SOME LEISLER DOCUMENTS

A

AFFIDAVITS AGAINST NICHOLSON

THE deposition of Nicholas Brown Aged Twenty three Years, the said Deponent declares that he being in the Service of ye late King Anno One thousand six hundred Eighty Six some time in July & August, did see Frances Nicholson Ye late lieu^t Governor of Ye fort at New York Several times in Ye Masse, but especially two times in Ye Kings tent at Hunsloheath in old ingland, being there to Exercise his devotions, & did Ye the same upon his Knees before the Alter in the papist Chappel, where the Mass was said, that himself, this deponent is ready to Confirm and declare upon Oath in testimony of the truth & have hereunto Set my hand, In New York this 12th day of Septem^r Anno 1689.

   Signed   NICHOLAS BROWN.
1689 the 13th 7^{ber} in New York

  Then appeared before me Nich^{ls} Brown & Sworn before me the aforesaid to be the truth.

   Signed   G. BEEKMAN Justice.

APPENDIX I

B

COMMISSION FROM THE COMMITTEE OF SAFETY

APPOINTING JACOB LEISLER TO BE CAPTAIN OF
THE FORT

There being a Present necessity that a Capt. of Ye fort at New Yorke should be appointed to be constantly there attending and to Command & order ye Soldiers appointed by this Committee of Safety to Serve ye fort in behalfe of their Majesties till orders Shall come and to order all matters of ye fortifications of said fort necessary at present this Committee therefore doe think fitt that Cap^{tn} Jacob Leisler shall be Captain of said fort as abovesaid Till orders shall come from their Majesties, & that the said Captn Jacob Leisler, shall have all aid and assistance, if need be & demanded by him from City and Country to suppress any foren Enemy & prevent all disorders which Evidently may appear

dated this 8th of June 1689, Signed Sealed

RICHARD DANTON	(L. S.)	SAM^{L} EDSALL	(L. S.)
THEUNIS ROELOFSE	(L. S.)	P DELA NOY	(L. S.)
JEAN DE MAREST	(L. S.)	MATHIAS HARVEY	(L. S.)
DANIEL DE KLERCKE	(L. S.)	THO^{S} WILLIAMS	(L. S.)
JOHANNES VERMILLYE	(L. S.)	WM LAURENCE	(L. S.)

C

COMMISSION TO CAPT. LEISLER TO BE COMMANDER IN CHIEF

Forasmuch the Committee of Safety do apprehend the difficulty & inconveniency by reason of their remote habitants and ye insuing season of ye year to commence & abide in ye City of New York to advise recommend order, & appoint ye present affairs in hand for the Interest of their most Excelent Majesties King William & Queen Mary and due preservation of ye inhabitants in ye province of New York & some others near adjacent towns, it is thought convenient and Concluded by ye Committee for ye most Safety of ye province by reason of Sundry intervals & accidental motions which may arise & for the orderly way to direct all necessary matters touching ye ruling & ordering of ye inhabitants in the Province, it being uncertain whether ye orders shall Come from their Majesties, that Captain Jacob Leisler is hereby appointed to Exercise & use the Power & Authority of a Commander in Chief of the said Province to administer such Oaths to the people, to issue out such Warrants, and to order such Matters as shall be necessary & requisite to be done for the preservation and protection of the peace, of the inhabitants taking all ways, seasonable advice with Militia and Civil Authority as Occasion require Dated ye 16th day Augt 1689 —

419

APPENDIX I

Copy was Signed Sealed as followeth,

William Laurence	(L. S.)	Sam^L Edsall	(L. S.)
D^L De Klercke	(L. S.)	Jean Demarest	(L. S.)
Johannes Vermillye	(L. S.)	P. De La Noy	(L. S.)
Richard Danton	(L. S.)	Mathias Harvey	(L. S.)
Theunis Roelofse	(L. S.)	Thos Williams	(L. S.)

D

SCHUYLER'S PROTEST AGAINST MILBORNE

Fort albany ye 15th day of novemb^r 1689

Whereas one Jacob Milborne hath with a Comp^e of armed men, come up to there Maj^{e}s fort in a hostile manner with full arms and Demanded Possession thereof from ye May^r of ye Citty who has ye Command of ye same, who Declared to keep said fort for there Maj^{es} William & Mary untill there orders comes but ye said Jacob Milborne as a Tumultuous & Mutinous Person doth Proceed to occasion great Disturbance to there Maj^{es} Liege People, by again faceing to ye fort with Loaden arms, Especially so many heathens to witt Maquase being ye Spectators thereof who seems to be upon ye Point to undertake some Dangerous Design, The Convention of ye Civil & Military officers of ye Citty & County of albany now p'sent in ye fort doe therefore Protest hereby in their Maj^{es} King William & Queen Maryes name before god and ye world against ye s^d Milborne and his Seditious Troops, for all Dammages, Murthers Bloodsheds Plunderings and oy^r mischieffs which may Ensue by

420

his Rebellious actions and charge him & them forthwith to withdraw themselves from there s^d May^{es} fort.
P^R SCHUYLER May^r
and Commander of there Maj^{es} fort

The Protest being Read hille akus Sister told y^t y^e
Indians were ^{very} much Dissatisfyed & if Milborne did
not withdraw with his Comp^e they would fyre upon
him, whereupon ye May^r Desyred Doctor Dellius &
ye Recorder to goe to ye Indians to Pacify and quiet
them for ye Bussinesse was y^t a Person without Power
or authority would be Master over ye gent^n here which
they would nott admitt; the Indians answered goe and
tell him that if he come out of ye gates we will fyre
upon him, which Doctor Dellius forthwith Communi-
cated to ye s^d Milborne at ye head of his Comp^e in y^e
Presence of a great many Burghers who made no fur-
ther attempt to goe to ye fort, but Marched doune y^e
towne and Dismissed his men

E

LEISLER TO THE OFFICERS OF WEST–
CHESTER

FORT WILLIAM February 15, 1689 [90].

GENTLEMEN, — Whereas ye ffrench have surprized
Schanegtade, & killed & taken Prisonners the most of
their Maties Subjects burning & destroying ye s^d Place:
and fearing too great a Correspondency hath bean
maintained between ye s^d ffrensch & disaffected P'sons
amongst us.

421

APPENDIX I

These are in his Maties Name to will & require you to secure all Such Persons who are resputed Papists or Do any wise despise or reflect against this Governm^t or hold or maintaine any Commissions from the Late Govern^{rs} Col^o Thomas Dongan or Sr Edmund Andros by virtue of their Authority derived from King James the second & ye same Safely to Convey to mee forthwth Given under My hand & seale this 15th ffeb^y 1689 and in ye first yeare of their Maties Reigne.

Jacob Leisler

To the Officers Military & Civill &
ye Sheriffe of the County of Westchester
Ye same to Richmond County
Ye same to ye County of Suffolk
Ye same to Kings County
Ye same to ye Country of East Jersey
Ye same to Queens County

F

LEISLER TO HIS COMMISSIONERS AT ALBANY

A 1690 1st July In Fort William

. Gentlemen — Yesterday was my last to which I Referr you, You have Referred us to ye Messengers who brought our letter but we cane understand nothing of them, my opinion Is they came here to consult with there parties. If they may safely Receive a Commission of mee what alteration in your place, there Coming here may cause us, the time will learne, beshure they are not well Tutered & keept from us I have writt you our meaning which we hoop you may be able to observe touching the major, Inclosed is a copy of a Letter Received of Governour Treat which I perceive was lifft upon the table wherein the major is absolutely Refused If Boston & Connecticut sends not their Compliment Ingaged In ye Result & approved by ye government they Brook ye Covenant & we are not obliged to any article therein the Barers are made sensible y^t what we propose about ye Council of Warr y^t the Cap^n by Turnes Every week should bee president In said Councel and so in gods name go one without a major — Except Cap^n Browne accepts of ye place but no other whatsoever — Except Mausachusetts, Plymouth & Connecticutt Colonyes Comply fully with there promise ye ffrench Knight begins to be moved of (our) march and desires to prevent ye cruelties of our Indians against ye ffrench wimens and children which Indied would bee generous if possible It could be prevented we have sent Mest^r Stole who has a speciall maxim to gaine the people & is able to assist you much in forwarding ye Business and if he should go he most be commissionated he is true, full mettall able and politique the news of Colonell Slayter is quitt vanised It would not hould — we have gott yesterday the Inclosed nues from neu England En send It for the Everi direcktet als the copie, to day the 25 I gott the Inclosed from Southampton I wish Ensign Stole was heer En Iff possible also Major Milborn we expeckt the franch ships heer the messenger raports the ar all ships, pray God to grand

& give vs courage to resist them after min respects
I remain

Sr^s

Your reall frind to serve your

JACOB LEISLER

Addressed, To the Hono^{ble} The Commission^{rs} Capⁿ
John De Bruyn, Mr Johannes Provoost
and Major Jacob Milborne Esq^{rs}   In
Albany

G

LEISLER TO GOV. SLOUGHTER

FORT WILLIAM March the 20. 1690–1

May it Please Your Excellency — This his Majesty's fort being besieged by Major Ingoldsby so farre
that not a boat could depart, nor Persons conveyed
out of the same without to be in danger of their Lives
which hath occasioned that I could not be so happy
as to send a messinger to give me the certainty of
Your excellency's Safe arrival & an account of what
was published, of which I am ignorant still but the
Joy I had by a full assurance from Ensign Stoll of
your Excellency's arrival has been something troubled
by the detencon of Ye two my Messengers, I see very
well the stroke of my enemies who are wishing to
cause me some mistakes at the End of the Loyalty I
owe to my gracious King & Queen & by such ways
to Blatt out all my faithfull service till now but I
hope have care to commit such an error, having by
my duty & faithfulnesse being vigerous to them, Please
only to Signify & order the Major in releasing me

424

from his Majesties fort delivering him only his Majesties Armes with all the Stores & that he may act as he ought with a person who shall give Your excellency an exact account of all his actions & conduct, who is with all the request, Your Excellency's Most Humble Servt

JACOB LEISLER

H

DYING SPEECHES OF LEISLER AND MILBORNE

Colleccons made on the Dying Speeches of Captain Jacob Leisler & Jacob Milborne, his son in Law, who both Suffered in New York City on the 16th of May being Saturday in the Year of our Lord 1691.

— The great wise & omnipotent creator of all things visible & invisible who from the time of our first coming a Shore in the Vale of tears, misery & affliction, hath to this present moment protected us be magnified. Praysed & Glorified for ever, Amen,

Gentlemen And Fellow Brethren all I hope in the grace & fear of the Lord Jesus, we are not at present unsensible of our dying State & Condition, as to this world a State which all the Sons & Daughters of Adam in this globe must now one after another run through ere they can be satisfied with that eternity of which so often by Divines is treated of — In consideration of which for death we may be better prepared, like penitent Mortals here on earth, we Submit our lives. & all that unto us appertaineth into the

that on both Side, that discord & dessention (which
by the devil in the beginning was created) might with
our dying sides be buried in oblivion, never more to
raise up to the inflamation of future posterity, the
Lord grant that the offering up of our blood might be
a full satisfaction for all disorders to this present day
committed, & that forever after the Spiritt of unity
might remaine among our felow brethren continuing
upon earth, knowing that in a Strange land it is the
divine providence of heaven not our desarts that have
so well protected our unhappy province this day all
that for our dying comfort we can say, as concerning
the point for which we were condemn'd, is to declare as
our last words. before that God whom we hope before long to see that our maine end, totall Intent &
endeavors to the fullness of that understanding with
which we were endowed — who had no other than to
maintaine against popery or any Schism or heresy
whatever the interest of our Sovereign Lord & Lady
that now is & the reformed protestant Churches in
those parts, who ever things otherwise Since have
hapined or being miscontructed & Scandalous reports
(we at present must confess by divers are thrown upon
us) as tho we intended to Support the dying, intrest
of the late King James & the Contradiction of which
we need not trouble many arguments, being persuaded
that every good protestant of this Country who have
been for any time acquainted with our transactions
can from his conscience averre the falsehoods & mali-
ciousness of such aspersions, as concerning Major
Ingoldesby's coming to demand the Garrison after his
arrival, he but in the least produced any Satisfaction
of his power to receive the same and discharge us, we

would as readily have delivered the fort, as he could demand the same, all of which seeing past & gone is Scarce worthy nothing —

The Lord of his infinite Mercy preserve the King & Queen from all their traytors and deceitfull Enemies, God be merciful unto & bless with peace & unity these their Kingdoms unto which we belong, God preserve this province from greedy outrageous Enemies abroad and Spite full inveterate wretches at home God bless the Governor of this place, God bless the council Assembly & Government now Established that they all may be united to propagate their Majesties interest, the Country's good & the Establishment of Piety, the Lord of Heaven of his infinite mercy bless all that wish well to Zion & Convert those that are out of the way, let his mercies likewise administer true Comfort to all that are desolute, grieved & oppressed in misery & necessity or any other affliction, Especially the deplored Souls of that poor family unto which we did formerly belong, our only comfort, in this case, is that God has promised to take care for the Widows and fatherless, recommending them all this dying moment into the hands of one that is able and willing, to save these that seek him desiring them to put their perpetuall confidence in the mercies of one that never faileth, & not to weep for us that are departing to our God but rather to weep for themselves that are here behind us to remain in a State of Misery and Vexation

Gentlemen you will, I hope all Christian like be Charitable to our poor distressed family that are to remain among you (as long as God please) that you will Join with us in prayer for the preservation of our

APPENDIX II

CHARLES the Second, by the Grace of God,
King of *England*, *Scotland*, *France*, and *Ireland*, De-
fender of the Faith, etc. To all whom these presents
shall come, *Greeting*. WHEREAS Our Trustie and
well-beloved Subject William Penn, Esquire, Sonne
and heire of Sir William Penn deceased, out of a commendable Desire to enlarge our *English* Empire, and
promote such usefull comodities as may bee of Benefit to us and Our Dominions, as also to reduce the
Savage Natives by gentle and just manners to the
Love of Civil Societie and Christian Religion, hath
humbley besought Leave of Us to transport an ample
Colonie unto a certaine Countrey hereinafter described, in the Partes of *America* not yet cultivated and
planted ; And hath likewise humbley besought Our
Royall Majestie to Give, Grant, and Confirme all the
said Countrey, with certaine Privileges and Jurisdic-
tions, requisite for the good Government and Safetie
of the said Countrey and Colonie, to him and his
Heires forever : KNOW YE THEREFORE, That
Wee, favouring the Petition and good Purpose of the
said *William Penn*, and haveing Regard to the Mem-
orie and Meritts of his late Father in divers Services,
and perticulerly to his Conduct, Courage, and Discretion under our Dearest Brother JAMES Duke of

York, in that Signall Battell and Victorie fought and obteyned against the *Dutch* Fleete, command by the Heer *Van Opdam*, in the yeare One thousand six hundred and sixty-five : In consideration thereof, of Our Speciall grace, certaine Knowledge, and meere Motion have Given and Granted, and by this Our present Charter, for Us, Our Heires and Successors, Doe give and Grant unto the said *William Penn*, his Heires and Assignes, all that Tract or Parte of Land in *America*, with all the Islands therein conteyned, as the same is bounded on the East by *Delaware* River, from twelve miles distance Northwards of *New Castle* Towne unto the three and fortieth degree of Northerne Latitude, if the said River doeth extende so farre Northwards ; But if the said River shall not extend soe farre Northward, then by the said River soe farr as it doth extend ; and from the head of the said River, the Easterne Bounds are to bee determined by a Meridian Line, to bee drawne from the head of the said River, unto the said three and fortieth Degree. The said Lands to extend westwards five degrees in longitude, to bee computed from the said Easterne Bounds ; and the said Lands to bee bounded on the North by the beginning of the three and fortieth degree of Northern Latitude, and on the South by a Circle drawne at twelve miles distance from *New Castle* Northward and Westward unto the beginning of the fortieth degree of Northern Latitude, and then by a streight Line Westward to the Limitt of Longitude above-mentioned. WEE do also give and grant unto the said *William Penn*, his heires and assignes, the free and undisturbed use and continuance in, and passage into and out of all and singular Ports, Harbours, Bays,

433

Waters, Rivers, Isles, and Inletts, belonging unto, or leading to and from the Countrey or Islands aforesaid, And all the Soyle, lands, fields, woods, underwoods, mountaines, hills, fenns, Isles, Lakes, Rivers, waters, Rivuletts, Bays, and Inletts, scituate or being within, or belonging unto the Limitts and Bounds aforesaid, togeather with the fishing of all sortes of fish, whales, Sturgeons, and all Royall and other Fishes, in the Sea, Bayes, Inletts, waters, or Rivers within the premisses, and the Fish therein taken; And also all Veines, Mines, and Quarries, as well discovered as not discovered, of Gold, Silver, Gemms, and Pretious Stones, and all other whatsoever, be it Stones, Mettals, or of any other thing or matter whatsoever, found or to bee found within the Countrey, Isles, or Limitts aforesaid; AND him, the said *William Penn*, his heirs and assignes, Wee doe by this Our Royall Charter, for Us, Our heires and Successors, make, create, and constitute the true and absolute Proprietarie of the Countrey aforesaid, and of all other the premisses, Saving alwayes to Us, Our heires and Successors, the Faith and Allegiance of the said *William Penn*, his heires and assignes, and of all other Proprietaries, Tenants, and Inhabitants that are or shall be within the Territories and Precincts aforesaid; and Saving also, unto Us, Our heires and Successors, the Sovereignty of the aforesaid Countrey; TO HAVE, hold, possess, and enjoy the said Tract of Land, Countrey, Isles, Inletts, and other the premisses unto the said *William Penn*, his heires and assignes, to the only proper use and behoofe of the said *William Penn*, his heires and assignes for ever, to bee holden of Us, Our heires and Successors, Kings of *England*, as of

Our Castle of *Windsor* in our County of *Berks*, in free and comon Socage, by fealty only for all Services, and not in *Capite* or by Knights Service : Yielding and paying therefore to Us, Our heires and Successors, Two Beaver Skins, to bee delivered at Our said Castle of *Windsor* on the First Day of *January* in every Year ; and also the Fifth Part of all Gold and Silver Oare, which shall from Time to Time happen to bee found within the Limitts aforesaid, cleare of all Charges. And of Our further Grace, certaine Knowledge, and meer motion, We have thought fitt to erect, and We doe hereby erect the aforesaid Countrey and Islands into a Province and Seigniorie, and do call itt PENNSILVANIA, and soe from henceforth we will have itt called.

AND forasmuch as wee have hereby made and ordained the aforesaid *William Penn*, his heires and assignes, the true and absolute Proprietaries of all the Lands and Dominions aforesaid, KNOW YE THEREFORE, That We reposing speciall trust and Confidence in the fidelite, wisedom, Justice, and provident circumspection of the said *William Penn* for us, our heires and Successors, Doe grant free, full, and absolute power by vertue of these presents to him and his heires, and to his and their Deputies, and Lieutenants, for the good and happy government of the said countrey, to ordeyne, make, and enact, and under his and their Seales to publish any Lawes whatsoever, for the raising of money for the publick use of the said Province, or for any other End, apperteyning either unto the publick state, peace, or safety of the said Countrey, or unto the private utility of perticular persons, according unto their best discretions, by and with the advice, assent, and approbation of the Freemen of the said Countrey, or the greater parte of them, or of their Delegates or Deputies, whom for the enacting of the said Lawes, when, and as often as need shall require, Wee will that the said *William Penn* and his heires, shall assemble in such sort and forme, as to him and them shall seeme best, and the same Lawes duly to execute, unto and upon all People within the said Countrey and the Limitts thereof.

AND wee doe likewise give and grant unto the said *William Penn*, and his heires, and to his and their Deputies and Lieutenants, such power and authoritie to appoint and establish any Judges and Justices, Magistrates and Officers whatsoever, for what causes soever, for the probates of wills, and for the granting of Administrations within the precincts aforesaid and with what Power soever, and in such forme as to the said *William Penn* or his heires shall seeme most convenient : Also to remitt, release, pardon, and abolish whether before Judgement or after all Crimes and Offences whatsoever comitted within the said Countrey against the said Lawes, Treason and wilful and malitious Murder onely excepted, and in those Cases to grant Reprieves, until Our pleasure may bee known therein and to doe all and every other thing and things, which unto the compleate Establishment of Justice, unto Courts and Tribunalls, formes of Judicature, and manner of Proceedings doe belong, altho in these presents expresse mention bee not made thereof; And by Judges by them delegated, to award Processe, hold Pleas, and determine in all the said Courts and Tribunalls all Actions, Suits, and Causes whatsoever, as well Criminall as Civill, Personall, reall and mixt; which Lawes, soe as aforesaid to bee published, Our Pleasure is, and soe Wee enjoyne, require, and command, shall bee most absolute and avaylable in law; and that all the Liege People and subjects of Us, Our heires and Successors, doe observe and keepe the same inviolabl in those partes, soe farr as they concerne them, under the paine therein expressed, or to bee expressed. PROVIDED nevertheless, that the said Lawes be consonant to reason, and bee not repugnant or contrarie, but as neare as conveniently may bee agreeable to the Lawes and Statutes, and rights of this Our Kingdome of *England* ; And Saving and reserving to Us, Our heires and Successors, the receiving, heareing, and determining of the appeale and appeales of all or any Person or Persons, of, in, or belonging to the Territories aforesaid, or touching any Judgement to bee there made or given.

AND forasmuch as in the Government of soe great a Countrey, sudden Accidents doe often happen, whereunto it will bee necessarie to apply remedie before the Freeholders of the said Province, or their Delegates or Deputies, can bee assembled to the making of Lawes; neither will itt bee convenient that instantly upon every such emergent occasion, soe greate a multitude should be called together : Therefore for the better Government of the said Countrey Wee will, and ordaine, and by these presents, for us, our Heires and successors, Doe Grant unto the said *William Penn* and his heires, by themselves or by their Magistrates and Officers, in that behalfe duely to bee ordeyned as aforesaid, to make and constitute fitt and wholesome Ordinances, from time to time, within the said Countrey to bee kept and observed, as well for

Penn, his heires and assignes shall pay the same within one yeare after such taxation, and demand thereof from such Attorney : or in case there shall be noe such Attorney by the space of one yeare, or such Attorney shall not make payment of such damages within the space of one yeare, and answer such other forfeitures and penalties within the said time, as by the Acts of Parliament in *England* are or shall be provided according to the true intent and meaneing of these presents ; then it shall be lawfull for us, our heires and Successors, to seize and Resume the government of the said Province or Countrey, and the same to retaine untill payment shall be made thereof : But notwithstanding any such Seizure or resumption of the government, nothing concerneing the propriety or ownership of any Lands, tenements, or other hereditaments, or goods or chattels of any of the Adventurers, Planters, or owners, other then the respective Offenders there, shall anyway be affected or molested thereby.

PROVIDED alwayes, and our will and pleasure is, that neither the said *William Penn*, nor his heires, or any other the inhabitants of the said Province, shall at any time hereafter have or maintain any Correspondence with any other king, prince, or State, or with any of theire subjects, who shall then be in Warr against us, our heires or Successors ; Nor shall the said *William Penn*, or his heires, or any other the Inhabitants of the said Province, make Warre or doe any act of Hostility against any other king, prince, or State, or any of theire Subjects, who shall then be in league or amity with us, our heires or successors.

AND, because in soe remote a Countrey, and scituate neare many Barbarous Nations, the incursions as well of the Savages themselves, as of other enemies, pirates and robbers, may probably be feared; Therefore Wee have given, and for us, our heires and Successors, Doe give power by these presents unto the said *William Penn*, his heires and assignes, by themselves or theire Captaines or other their Officers, to levy, muster and traine all sorts of men, of what condition soever or wheresoever borne, in the said Province of *Pensilvania*, for the time being, and to make Warre, and to pursue the enemies and Robbers aforesaid, as well by Sea as by Land, even without the Limitts of the said Province, and by God's assistance to vanquish and take them, and being taken to put them to death by the Lawe of Warre, or to save them, att theire pleasure, and to doe all and every other Art and Thing which to the Charge and Office of a Captaine-Generall of an Army belongeth or hath accustomed to belong, as fully and ffreely as any Captaine-Generall of an Army hath ever had the same.

AND FURTHERMORE, of Our especiall grace and of our certaine knowledge and meere motion, wee have given and granted, and by these presents, for us, our heires and Successors, do Give and Grant unto the said *William Penn*, his Heires and Assignes, full and absolute power, licence and authoritie, that he, the said *William Penn*, his Heires and Assignes, from time to time hereafter forever, att his or theire own Will and pleasure may assigne, alien, Grant, demise, or enfeoffe of the Premises soe many and such partes and parcells to him or them that shall be willing to purchase the same, as they shall thinke fitt, To have and to hold to them the said person and persons will-

Proprietary, or chiefe governor, and assembly, or by act of Parliament in *England*.

AND Our Pleasure is, and for us, our heires and Successors, Wee charge and comand, that this our Declaration shall from henceforth be received and allowed from time to time in all our courts, and before all the Judges of us, our heires and Successors, for a sufficient and lawfull discharge, payment and acquittance; commanding all and singular the officers and ministers of us, our heires and Successors, and enjoyneing them upon pain of our high displeasure, that they doe not presume att any time to attempt anything to the contrary of the premisses, or that doe in any sort withstand the same, but that they be att all times aiding and assisting, as is fitting unto the said *William Penn* and his heires, and to the inhabitants and merchants of the Province aforesaid, their Servants, Ministers, ffactors and Assignes, in the full use and fruition of the benefitt of this our Charter.

AND Our further pleasure is, and wee doe hereby, for us, our heires and Successors, charge and require, that if any of the inhabitants of the said Province, to the number of Twenty, shall at any time hereafter be desirous, and shall by any writeing, or by any person deputed for them, signify such their desire to the Bishop of *London* that any preacher or preachers, to be approved of by the said Bishop, may be sent unto them for their instruction, that then such preacher or preachers shall and may be and reside within the said Province, without any deniall or molestation whatsoever.

AND if perchance it should happen hereafter any doubts or questions should arise, concerneing the true

Sense and meaning of any word, clause, or Sentence conteyned in this our present Charter, Wee will ordaine, and comand, that att all times and in all things, such interpretation be made thereof, and allowed in any of our Courts whatsoever, as shall be adjudged most advantageous and favourable unto the said *William Penn*, his heires and assignes : Provided always that no interpretation be admitted thereof by which the allegiance due unto us, our heires and Successors, may suffer any prejudice or diminution; Although express mention be not made in these presents of the true yearly value, or certainty of the premisses, or of any parte thereof, or of other gifts and grants made by us and our progenitors or predecessors unto the said *William Penn :* Any Statute, Act, ordinance, provision, proclamation, or restraint heretofore had, made, published, ordained or provided, or any other thing, cause, or matter whatsoever, to the contrary thereof in any wise notwithstanding.

IN WITNESS whereof wee have caused these our Letters to be made patents : Witness OUR SELFE, at *Westminster*, the *Fourth* day of *March*, in the *Three and Thirtieth* Yeare of Our Reign.

By Writt of Privy Seale,
PIGOTT.

INDEX

451

INDEX

Bartram, John, botanist, ii. 376.

Bartram, William, botanist, ii. 376.

Batavia, Java, founded, i. 58.

Batavians, alliance with the Romans, i. 5 ; attempted independent confederacy, 6 ; and the Frisians, 6.

Baxter, George, Stuyvesant's English secretary, supports the autocracy, i. 297 ; negotiates Hartford treaty, 299 ; disaffected, 310 ; remonstrance, 311 ; is arrested, 313,

Bayard, Nicholas, ancestry, i. 231 ; and the oath of allegiance, ii. 47 ; supports Nicholson, 210 ; and Leisler, 216, 219, 220 ; imprisoned by Leisler, 231, 237 ; accused of complicity with pirates, 267, 268 ; conviction for treason, 276 ; release, 277.

Beekman, William, and the oath of allegiance, ii. 47.

Belgians, Cæsar's victory over, i. 5.

Belgium, erection of the kingdom, i. 51. *See also* Netherlands.

Bellomont, Lord, and Kidd, ii. 264, 268, 269, 373 ; character, 265 ; governor of New York, Massachusetts, and New Hampshire, 266 ; favours the Leislerians, 266–268 ; in Boston, 274 ; death, 274.

Berkeley, Lord, grant of New Jersey, ii. 12 ; sells, 19.

Bible, Erasmus's edition, i. 21 ; dissemination in Netherlands, 21.

Block, Adrian, on coast of New England, i. 120.

Block Island discovered, i. 75.

Blommaert, Samuel, patroonship, i. 159.

Bœotians as the Dutch of Greece, i. 185.

Bogardus, Everardus, second clergyman in New Netherland, arrives, i. 168 ; character, 189 ; and Kieft, 228 ; drowned, 237.

Bohemia, claim of influence on America, i. 38.

Bois, Louis du, leads Walloon emigration, ii. 397.

Boston, establishment of a post with New York, ii. 21–25 ; Huguenot settlers, 401. *See also* Massachusetts.

Boudinot, Elias, Huguenot ancestry, ii. 405.

Boundaries, New Netherland, i. 122 ; settlement of Connecticut and New York, ii. 5–7 ; line between East and West Jersey, 163 ; Pennsylvania, 172–174.

Bowdoin, James, Huguenot ancestry, ii. 401.

Bradford, Andrew, son of William, printer in Philadelphia, ii. 376 ; *American Magazine*, 376.

Bradford, William, of Plymouth, on the Dutch language, i. 98 n. ; discussion with Minuit, 143.

Bradford, William, New York newspaper, ii. 290 ; first printer in Philadelphia, 375.

Bradford, William, nephew of Andrew, printer in Philadelphia, ii. 376.

Brazil, Dutch in, i. 62.

Brockholls, Anthony, lieutenant-governor of New York, ii. 45 ; and the custom duties, 195.

Brodhead, J. R., *New York*, ii. 170 n.

Brooke, Lord, grant in Connecticut, i. 176.

Brooklyn, N. Y., beginnings, i. 135, 201 ; in 1679, ii. 89.

Brooks, Elbridge, *In Leisler's Times*, ii. 232 n.

Bruges, Belgium, prosperity, i. 23 ; decline, 54.

Brugh, Johannes van, and the oath of allegiance, ii. 47.

Bull, Thomas, and Andros at Saybrook, ii. 56.

Burgundy, origin of the duchy, i. 28 ; absorption of the Netherlands, 28 ; reversion to the French crown, 30.

INDEX

Burlington, N. J., founded, ii. 166.

Burnet, William, governor of New York, character, ii. 286; fur-trade reforms, 286–289.

Burton, Mary, and the negro plot, ii. 339–341.

Byllinge, Edward, buys Berkeley's interest in New Jersey, ii. 19; quarrel with Fenwick, 162; insolvent, 163.

Bynner, E. L., *The Begum's Daughter*, ii. 232.

Cabo de Arenas, identification, i. 85–87.

Cabot, John, voyage not followed up, i. 67; extent of discovery, 78.

Cabot, Sebastian, governor of the Muscovy Company, i. 93.

Cæsar, victory over the Belgians, i. 5.

Calvinism and public schools, i. 37.

Cambridge University, liberalism, i. 44.

Campbell, Douglas, *Puritan in England, Holland, and America*, i. 35.

Canada, Iroquois raid in 1689, ii. 204; attack on Schenectady, 224–227; unsuccessful English expeditions against, 229, 281, 283.

Canals in Netherlands, i. 16.

Cape of Good Hope, Dutch colony, i. 60.

Cape Henlopen, Del., and Cabo de Arenas, i. 85–87; named, 121.

Cape Horn discovered, i. 65.

Cape May, N. J., named, i. 121.

Carleton, Sir Dudley, ambassador, presents English claim to New Netherland, i. 133.

Carr, John, son of Sir Robert, commands on the Delaware, ii. 8.

Carr, Sir Robert, royal commissioner, i. 331; on the Delaware, ii. 4; in Boston, 9; death, 11.

Carteret, Sir George, grant of New Jersey, ii. 12; regrant, 42, 108.

Carteret, James, son of Sir George, in New Jersey, ii. 18; character, 97.

Carteret, Philip, governor of New Jersey, ii. 13; and Nicolls's grant, 14; power, 14; popular troubles, 18; relationship to Sir George, 97 n.; resists New York's claim to New Jersey, 108, 109; personal relations with Andros, 109, 110; deposed by Andros, 110; arrest and acquittal in New York, 111.

Cartwright, George, royal commissioner, i. 331; in Boston, ii. 8; captured by the Dutch, 8.

Catharism. *See* Albigenses.

Caughnawaga, Canada, settlement of Christianized Iroquois, ii. 286; danger to New York, 287; Burnet's measures against, 288.

Charlemagne, ancestry, i. 8; and the Frisians, 9; division of his empire, 10.

Charles the Bald, share in Charlemagne's empire, i. 10.

Charles the Bold of Burgundy, rule in the Netherlands, i. 29; death, 30.

Charles II. of England, and the Connecticut charter, i. 321; and Louis XIV., ii. 27, 40; and the naming of Pennsylvania, 175.

Charles V., lord of the Netherlands, i. 32.

Charters, Dutch West India Company, i. 129; of Privileges and Exemptions in New Netherland, 154; Connecticut, 320; Pennsylvania, ii. 176–178, 432–449.

Chesapeake Bay and Verrazano Sea, i. 71–74.

Chester, Penn., named, ii. 182.

Christiansen, Hendrick, at Manhattan, i. 118, 120.

Church and State, primitive union, ii. 116–119; fall of theocratic ideals in Massachusetts, 131.

Civil liberty, development in England,

INDEX

Flanders, autonomy of ruler, i. 13. *See also* Netherlands.

Flemish language, i. 7.

Flatbush, L. I., type of colonial Dutch houses in, ii. 320–326.

Flatlands, L. I., settled, i. 201.

Fletcher, Benjamin, governor of New York, character, ii. 247 ; and the assembly, 250 ; as governor of Pennsylvania, 253 ; and the Connecticut militia, 253–255 ; accusations against and recall, 265.

Flushing, L. I., refuses to enforce religious persecution, i. 272, 273.

Food, New York colonial, ii. 323, 324 n.

Ford, Philip, Penn's steward, ii. 368 ; widow's suit against Penn, 368.

Forrester, Andrew, Stirling's agent, and Stuyvesant, i. 291.

Fort Amsterdam, N. Y., built, i. 140. *See also* New Amsterdam, New York city.

Fort Beaver Road on the Schuylkill, Dutch build, i. 171.

Fort Christina, Del., built, i. 277.

Fort Frontenac (Kingston), Canada, built, ii. 61.

Fort Good Hope on the Connecticut, Dutch build, i. 135, 172, 173 ; isolated, 177 ; confiscated by Underhill, 307.

Fort Nassau on the Hudson, i. 123 ; rebuilt, 135 ; on the Delaware, 135 ; occupied by Virginians, 187 ; recaptured, 188.

Fort Orange, N. Y., built, i. 135 ; threatened trouble with the Mohawks, 141 ; named Albany, ii. 1. *See also* Albany.

Fox, George, founder of Quakerism, birth, ii. 126 ; teachings, 127 ; character, 128.

France, overlordship in the Netherlands, i. 27 ; Albigenses in, 44, ii. 394 ; temporary cessation of maritime activity, i. 92 ; failure in colonization, 149, 150 ; plan

to conquer New York, ii. 202 ; rise of Huguenots, 393 ; treatment and migration of the Huguenots, 398–401.

Franklin, Benjamin, in Philadelphia, ii. 372, 376.

Franks, origin, i. 7 ; empire, 8, 10.

Frederick of Orange, Prince, stadholder, i. 138.

Friends of God, influence on religious toleration, ii. 126.

Frisians, and the Batavians, i. 6 ; and the Frankish empire, 8–10 ; conversion, 9 ; land system, 9.

Frontenac, Louis de Buade, Count of, governor of Canada, designs on New York, ii. 202 ; designs frustrated, 204 ; character, 229 ; invasion of the Iroquois country, 230 ; defeated by Schuyler, 250.

Frontier, Palatine and Scotch-Irish settlers, ii. 409, 413.

Fur-trade, French, on the Hudson, i. 79, 92 ; early Dutch, 118 ; Dutch monopolies, 119, 121, 157 ; illicit Dutch, 162, 194 ; Kieft's reforms, 195 ; made free in New Netherland, 197 ; coveted by England, 325 ; Caughnawaga middlemen, ii. 286 ; Burnet's measures, 288 ; controlling interest in New York, 304.

Gardiner, Lyon, builds and commands Fort Saybrook, i. 177.

Gastaldi, Jacopo, map, i. 87.

Geography, Verrazano's map and sea, i. 72 ; Maiollo's map, 73–75 ; character of old maps, 83 ; early cartography of east coast of North America, 84–87 ; Ribeiro's map, 86 ; map by Santa Cruz, 86 ; Gastaldi's map, 87 ; cartography of Norumbega, 87–91.

Georgia, Jews in, ii. 392.

Germany, Penn's missionary tour, ii. 152–162 ; emigration of sects to Pennsylvania, 406–410.

INDEX

462

INDEX

boundaries, 122 ; treaty with the Iroquois, 123 ; control of the Dutch West India Company, 129 ; English claims, 131–134, 137, 144, 163–166, 170, 320–324 ; government organized, 134 ; first settlers, 134–137 ; Minuit director - general, 139 ; a threatened breach with the Iroquois, 141–143 ; intercourse with Plymouth, 143 ; government, 152 ; growth, 154, 188, 266–268, 318 ; establishment of manors, 154–159 ; early manors, 159–162 ; disputes with the patroons, 162, 240–249 ; Twiller director - general, 166 ; attempt to forestall the English, 170–173 ; controversy over Connecticut, 173–181, 291–301 ; Virginians at Fort Nassau, 187 ; trade with New England, 187 ; removal of Twiller, 191 ; Kieft director-general, 192 ; his autocratic methods and reforms, 193–196 ; character of the population in Kieft's time, 196 ; monopoly abolished, 197 ; encouragement of settlers, 198 ; English settlers, 199, 211 ; contact with New Haven, 201 ; control of Long Island, 201, 204, 291, 310, 313, 326, 328 ; wars with the Delaware Indians, 205–218, 226, 314–318 ; Kieft and the popular demands, 209–211, 219 ; financial needs, 220, 302 ; excise, 221, 222, 233, 302 ; protest against Kieft, 223–225 ; Stuyvesant director-general, 225 ; his autocracy, 230, 233–237, 296 ; step toward representation, 238 ; difficulties in the government, 240 ; Stuyvesant and the popular demands, 250–253, 264, 296, 302, 310–313, 328 ; memorial to the States General, 252, 263 ; genesis of the government, 259, 262 ; phases of development, 266 ; cosmopolitanism, 267 ; religious persecution,

267–275 ; English settlements in New Jersey broken up, 278 ; relations with New Sweden, 278, 281 ; during the first English-Dutch war, 301–310 ; internal weakness, 319 ; validity of Dutch claim, 322 ; essential to English control in America, 324, 338, ii. 1; portents of disaster, i. 325 ; Connecticut's claim, 326 ; granted to the Duke of York, 329 ; secret expedition against, 330 ; fall, 332–338 ; peaceful submission to the English, ii. 4. *See also* Hudson River, New Amsterdam, New York.

New Paltz, N. Y., Walloons settle, ii. 397.

New Rochelle, N. Y., Huguenot settlement, ii. 403.

New Sweden, origin, i. 275–277 ; warned by English and Dutch, 277 ; progress, 278–280 ; overthrow, 281.

New York, granted to the Duke of York, i. 330 ; captured from the Dutch, 332–338 ; importance to English control in America, ii. 1 ; Nicolls governor, 2 ; Duke's Laws, 3 ; autocratic government, 3, 25 ; settlement of the Connecticut boundary, 5–7 ; claims in New England, 7 ; ceded by the Dutch, 19 ; departure of Nicolls, 19 ; Lovelace governor, 20, 28 ; demand for representative government, 26, 49–51, 197 ; captured by the Dutch, 28 ; Dutch government, 28–39 ; restored to England, 41 ; York's second grant, 41 ; Andros governor, 43 ; reestablishment of English rule, 45 ; allegiance of Long Island towns, 46 ; oath of allegiance to England, 46–48 ; economic and moral conditions under Andros, 52 ; revival of claim to Connecticut, 53–58 ; importance of Iroquois friendship, 61 ; conditions around Manhat-

INDEX

Treaties, Verdun, i. 10 ; Southampton, 138, 144 ; Münster, 283, 286 ; Hartford, 299 ; Breda, ii. 19 ; Westminster, 41.

Trinity Church, New York, founded, ii. 302 ; lawsuits, 302.

Tuscarora Indians, join the Iroquois confederacy, ii. 288 n.

Twelve Men, Board of, in New Netherland, i. 209–211.

Twiller, Wouter van, director-general of New Netherland, character, i. 166–168, 182, 189–191 ; and Eelkens, 168–170 ; and the English in Connecticut valley, 173–181 ; land purchases, 188 ; charges against, 189, 191 ; recalled, 192.

Underhill, John, in New Netherland, i. 217 ; destroys an Algonquin stronghold, 218 ; manifesto against Stuyvesant, 305 ; confiscates Fort Good Hope, 307 ; later life, 307.

Union, first American Congress, ii. 228 ; William III.'s plan, 253 ; necessity of a colonial, 255, 257 ; Penn's plan, 256.

United New Netherland Company, monopoly, i. 121 ; continued prosperity without monopoly, 124 ; desires to colonize, 125.

Ury, John, and the negro plot, ii. 341.

Usselincx, William, urges Dutch colonization, i. 116 ; and New Sweden, 275.

Vane, Sir Henry, religious toleration, ii. 124.

Verhulst, William, director-general of New Netherland, i. 139.

Verrazano, Giovanni da, early life, i. 69 ; voyage on coast of North America, 70–77 ; landfall, 70 ; purpose, 71 ; Verrazano Sea, 71–74 ; in New York harbour, 74 ; in Narragansett Bay, 75 ; on coast of New England, 76 ; return, 76 ; actuality of voyage, 77 ; importance of voyage, 78 ; death, 78.

Verrazano, Girolamo, map, i. 72.

Verrazano Sea, origin, 71, 73 ; on maps, 72 ; belief in, 100.

Vickers, Robert, *Bohemia*, i. 38.

Virginia and Fort Nassau on the Delaware, i. 187.

Voltaire on Pennsylvania, ii. 115, 186 n.

Voyages, Arctic, i. 63, 96, 100 ; Antarctic, 65 ; Aubert's alleged, 68 ; Verrazano's, 70–77 ; Gomez's, 79 ; Allefonsce's, 79 ; Hudson's, 96–109.

Vriesendael patroonship, established, i. 208 ; Indian attack, 215.

Wadsworth, Joseph, and Fletcher, ii. 254.

Waldenses, persecution, ii. 397 ; emigration to America, 397.

Walker, Sir Hovenden, fruitless attempt against Canada, ii. 283.

Wall Street, New York city, origin, i. 301.

Walloons, meaning of the word, i. 136 ; in New Netherland, 136, ii. 397.

Wampum, as currency, i. 202 ; Long Island the chief source, 203.

Weise, A. J., on Norumbega, i. 82.

West Jersey. *See* New Jersey.

Whale fishery, Hudson's voyage gives impulse to, i. 101.

William II. of Orange, stadholder, marriage, i. 285 ; dissatisfaction with treaty of Münster, 285 ; death, 287.

William III. of the Netherlands and England, birth, i. 287 ; stadholder, 290 ; landing in England, ii. 208 ; letter to the colonies, 208, 219 ; proclaimed in New York, 219 ; plan of colonial union, 253 ; and Penn, 354, 363.

INDEX

THE END

The Riverside Press

Electrotyped and printed by H. O. Houghton & Co.

Cambridge, Mass., U. S. A.